UNDER SACRED GROUND

UNDER SACRED GROUND
A History of Navajo Oil, 1922–1982

Kathleen P. Chamberlain

UNIVERSITY OF NEW MEXICO PRESS
Albuquerque

LIBRARY OF CONGRESS CATALOGING-IN-PUBLICATION DATA

Chamberlain, Kathleen (Kathleen P.)
    Under sacred ground : a history of Navajo oil, 1922–
1982 /Kathleen P. Chamberlain. — 1st ed.
    p.   cm.
    Includes bibliographical references and index.
    ISBN 0-8263-2043-0 (cloth : alk. paper)
    1. Navajo Indians—Economic conditions.   2. Navajo
Indians—Politics and government.   3. Petroleum
industry and trade—Navajo Indian Reservations—
History.   I. Title.
    E99. N3C45   2000
    338.2'7282'097898—dc21
                                        00-008608

CONTENTS

Maps and illustrations following page 50

ACKNOWLEDGMENTS

Completion of this project brings a huge sense of accomplishment and relief, but also obligation. Because this book was originally written as a dissertation, my most heartfelt thanks go to Margaret Connell Szasz, friend and academic advisor at the University of New Mexico (UNM). She not only guided me through the dissertation labyrinth, but introduced me to Native American history, for which I shall forever be grateful. Other members of my dissertation committee provided invaluable support. Richard W. Etulain, Ferenc M. Szasz, Linda B. Hall, and Peter Iverson all unselfishly shared knowledge and gave encouragement.

I also thank Roseanne Willink and Leroy Morgan, who patiently tutored me through two years of the Navajo language. Al Regensberg and Robert Torres, State Records Center and Archives, Santa Fe; Mary Alice Tsosie, Nancy Brown, and Kathleen Ferris, Center for Southwest Research; and Richard Fosdick, National Archives and Records Administration, Washington, D.C., were generous with their time, as were staff in the Government Publications and Microforms sections of Zimmerman Library, the Aztec and Farmington museums, and Navajo Nation library. Special thanks go to Emery C. Arnold, Thomas Dugan, Robert W. Young, Carl Yost, Sally Noe, Bill Richardson, and several Navajo men and women, who were interviewed but wished to remain unidentified. My dear friend Sam Shepard was always close at hand to help me find elusive references.

Financial support came from the UNM History Department's L. Dudley Phillips Memorial Fellowship, Graduate and Professional Student Association's Research Allocations Committee grant, and the Office of Graduate Studies Research, Project and Travel grant. The Phillips Fund for Native American Research (American Philosophical Society) provided funds for research and travel. A grant from Charles Redd Center for Western Studies, Brigham Young University, permitted additional travel. Moreover, I thank UNM's History Department for nominating my dissertation for the Tom Popejoy Dissertation Award and the University as a whole for selecting it.

My love and appreciation go to my parents—James and Ada Mae Egan—who have been so supportive over the years; my son, David Chamberlain, who as a child got dragged to so many historical places that he actually began to like them; my cousin Lucy Egan, who has always offered encouragement; my aunt Louise Egan Breznen and late uncle Stephen Breznen; my sister Linda Egan; and Lynda Cargile. I also want to thank my late grandmother, Elvira Swanson Egan, whose kind and generous bequest gave me the initial funding to begin graduate school.

Finally, it is my hope that this research project will in some way benefit the Navajo Nation and its people.

INTRODUCTION

About a mile south of Shiprock, an unpaved road cuts east from Route 666 across the Navajo reservation. If a sudden rainstorm has not turned the wash-boards to mud, one can drive to the Hogback field, site of the first commercial oil strike in New Mexico. The original campsite no longer exists, of course. Gone are the old cable tool drills that pulverized rock by repeatedly raising the metal drill bit into the air, then smashing it onto the surface, a process dubbed the "drill in and stand back" method. Navajos living nearby must have found the noise deafening. Those herding sheep some distance away probably perceived the sound as a series of haunting thuds.

Gone, too, are the heavy oil trucks and the derricks that once towered over the windswept plateau. Hogback baseball players no longer circle bases or conspire to beat other teams. No workers lounge around the doghouse cussing and smoking hand-rolled cigarettes. Only the sheep remain, and occasionally one can spot a solitary pickup truck.

In some ways, the story of oil on Navajo land resembles so many others involving Navajos and their *bilagáana* or Anglo neighbors. Relations between these two peoples have too often been characterized by a flurry of activity as whites searched for grazing land, oil, coal, timber, uranium, or whatever the market demanded at the time, then departed. In fact, William Shakespeare's phrase from *MacBeth*, "full of sound and fury," seems particularly appropriate. In 1922, for example, convinced that oil lay beneath the reservation, corporations vied for exploratory leases, and in response, the federal government revised regulations and persuaded a new Navajo tribal council to accommodate industry wishes.

A bustle of activity followed as companies filed lease applications, sent geologists to examine land structures, and teamed with local businessmen, traders, and missionaries to extol the advantages of oil development to reluctant Navajos. A public auction ensued. Then successful bidders dragged machinery, trucks, and crews onto Navajo land, built camps, and began drilling. Suddenly, in 1929, oil prices plummeted, and activity halted. A few wells continued to operate, but most crews and machinery vanished until after World War II, when they slowly reappeared.

Yet oil brought significant changes to every aspect of Navajo life. Although in 1929 most Navajos lived as they always had, a tribal council now debated issues like land extensions, education, and health care that affected everyone and actively sought to control how oil revenues would be spent. A tug-of-war between council and Bureau of Indian Affairs (BIA) established a pattern in the relationship between Navajos and the federal government. But the tribal council did more than bring Navajos together to debate issues. It accelerated a shift within the leadership structure from traditional to agent-chosen spokesmen, which had begun in 1901 when the federal government divided the Navajo reservation into six administrative districts. In addition, the new council gave voice to an increasing number of boarding-school-educated Navajos, who had previously found themselves excluded from the decision-making process. Such changes frequently caused factions that disagreed on exactly how oil revenues might best serve Navajos. Even so, all believed the income must benefit Navajos, not the government; they merely disagreed on what those benefits were.

It is significant that factions on the Navajo reservation were not between full and mixed bloods as in most Oklahoma oil tribes. Few Navajos in the 1920s had married Anglos. Mixed bloods had Pueblo or Hispanic lineage and were often extended clan kinship. Instead, factions resulted from level of education, religious affiliation, wealth, degree of assimilation, even attitudes toward alcohol and peyote — in essence, disputes over Navajo identity. Sometimes Indian agents assigned to the six districts and allowed to operate independently created competition and rivalries between jurisdictions. Thus, oil did not cause factions, but intensified them.

Oil also expedited a shift from subsistence and barter to a wage economy. Petroleum generated income for those lucky enough to land jobs or hold allotments. It made water wells, irrigation, health care, and schools obtainable in exchange for tribal lease approval. In 1923, for example, Navajos agreed to exchange their underground wealth for more land. After stock reduction, oil wages became one alternative to direct government welfare. By 1957, Navajos financed tribal scholarships with oil revenues, and in 1976, natural resource development was the most lucrative source of tribal income, with oil bonuses and royalties surpassing those handed out by coal or uranium corporations. Oil generated jobs for Navajo men, although nowhere near the promised number, and encouraged the federal government to pave some roads across the reservation.

Despite these advantages, Navajos supplied oil for a fraction of its value. Outsiders controlled production, refining, sales, and hence profits. The tribe was too often forced to spend its revenues on immediate social needs like clean drinking water, clothing, food, and housing, which precluded making investments. In 1978 the majority of Navajos in Aneth, Utah — site of a massive 1956 oil strike — still lacked running water and electricity.

Meanwhile, Navajos also struggled with the federal government for some control over their natural resources and for a financial accounting. Oil funds were deposited with the U.S. Treasury on behalf of Navajos, and tribal leaders were required to obtain Interior Department approval for their use. From the start, Congress designated Navajo funds for pet projects — often in secret — and there is some evidence that Indian Office personnel bought cars, office equipment, and home furnishings with Indian (including Navajo) money.

Despite repeated requests for vocational training, the BIA neither prepared Navajos for the highest-paying oil jobs nor helped ease the tribe into the new capitalist economy imposed upon them. It is, therefore, an almost inescapable conclusion that although the BIA absolutely believed Navajos must learn white ways and assimilate, its agents prepared them to occupy only the bottom rung of mainstream society. The opportunities that oil offered gave the government nearly seventy years to prove otherwise, and it failed. At the same time, Navajos grew alienated from their newly implemented tribal government and angry at corporate irresponsibility. Eventually, frustrated Navajos in Utah staged a sit-in, shut down Texaco oil operations, and intimidated company officials and tribal council leaders alike.

Oil brought environmental change as well, both positive and detrimental. From the start, Anglos misunderstood the depth of Navajo concerns regarding their land and the impact of oil development. Whites frequently assumed that Indians as a whole were too unsophisticated to comprehend the complexities of commodity economics, whereas in fact it was they who could not fathom the intricacies of Navajo culture. While government paved roads and companies built air strips, Navajos grew fearful of outsider intrusion onto their land, into their homes, and even in their sacred ceremonies. Similarly, although test drilling often unearthed artesian water — ironically called dry wells — and leases stipulated that Navajos receive these wells for their stock, oil crews used precious drinking water for themselves and their machinery. Oil workers also frightened or killed livestock, inadvertently trampled sacred sites, and left leaking pipelines in disrepair. In places, too, the acrid smell of oil hung heavily over mining areas.

Lastly, oil contributed to social change. It was federal stock reduction beginning in 1934 that devastated the Navajo agricultural economy and significantly altered family structures. Women were traditionally responsible for sheep and goats. They owned and cared for the herds. They wove the wool rugs and blankets for trade and cash income. But the wage work oil offered involved digging trenches, laying pipe, and driving trucks. Women, of course, were not hired. Moreover, smaller flocks required fewer children to stay at home. More boys and girls could attend school and ultimately college, which oil revenues funded by the late 1950s. Oil, therefore, made profound changes to Navajo society, often in conjunction with other events or trends.

Unfortunately, this story contains some unavoidable silences. Voices of more traditional Navajos are relatively absent. These were sometimes medicine men or former headmen, who frequently spoke only Navajo and seldom ended up on tribal councils. When they did, records filtered their words through one or more translators. Similarly, women are relatively silent: their individual and collective voices are not discernible in the available documents, although they probably gave their opinions in chapter meetings and outside of the council. The greatest silence, however, is from the land itself, scarred by drills, roads, airstrips, leaking pipelines, and mine camps, its sacred sites and graves disrupted and trampled by outsiders. Sadly, greater involvement in Anglo society meant less reverence for the land. In 1923, only a few considered land a commodity to be bought and sold for profit. Today many more embrace this outlook. Thus, the price Navajos ultimately paid for oil can, perhaps, never truly be calculated.

THE NAVAJO WORLD BEFORE 1922

First Man and First Woman, Áltsé Hastiin and Áltsé Asdzáá, were created in the Black World (*Ni'hadithił dasika*), an underground place with dark mists. They ascended through a hollow reed to the Blue, then Yellow World, where they found animals and four great mountains. A flood forced Áltsé Hastiin, Áltsé Asdzáá, and the animals upward again to the Glittering World (*Hajiinei*). There they made the sun, moon, stars, and four seasons, devised sacred ceremonies and prayers, and created the sacred mountains—*Sisnaajiní* (Blanca Peak) to the East decorated with white shell; *Tsoodził* or Mount Taylor to the South, adorned with turquoise; *Dook'o'-oosłííd* (San Francisco Peak) to the West, covered with abalone shell; and *Dibé Nitsaa* (Mount Hesperus) to the North, decorated with jet.[1]

The *yé'ii* (Navajo gods) encircled the land with their bodies, beginning in the East and embracing the four sacred mountains to create a protective boundary. It is believed that only by living inside of this border can Navajos remain in harmony with nature and the plan of their gods.[2]

The discovery of oil on Navajo land imperiled the balance that the yé'ii had hoped to create and accelerated change among the *Diné* people. It would be wrong to assume, however, that Navajo society had remained static before this time. On the contrary, the Diné underwent dramatic change after their arrival in the Four Corners region. They adopted new skills like herding, agriculture, and weaving; they interacted with Hopis, Zunis, Rio Grande Pueblos, Apaches, Utes, and Comanches; and they alternately fought and traded with the Spanish and later the Anglo Americans.

Historians disagree on when Navajos first came to the region, but generally date the event to between 1400–1600.[3] *Diné Bikéyah*—Navajo land—lies on the southern third of the Colorado Plateau, bordered by the four sacred peaks described in Navajo legends—Sisnaajiní, Tsoodził, Dook'o'ooslííd, and Dibé Nitsaa. Elevations on Navajo land range from five thousand to eight thousand feet above sea level, and the area is generally classified as high-altitude desert. Stream channels or washes gash the land, but only the Colorado and San Juan rivers (*Tónits'ósíkooh* and *Tooh*) flow continuously. The remaining beds are ephemeral and fill on a seasonal basis or during heavy rainfall. These are nevertheless tremendously important to local communities and families.[4]

Geologically, Diné Bikéyah is typified by structures called monoclines, such as the Hogback near the western border of New Mexico, where oil was discovered in 1922. Monoclines are large layers of rock that fold gently downward like a carpet draping across a stair step. In addition to monoclines, the geology contains asymmetrical anticlines — rock formations that dip gradually downward in one direction then rise almost undetectably in another. The effect is a level, somewhat monotonous landscape.[5]

At intervals, volcanic necks — all that are left of once active volcanoes — loom like turrets over the land. Soil is thin and stony, except along rivers, and vegetation is primarily piñon pine, a juniper-pine mix, and sagebrush in the moister areas. Drought-resistant short grasses, like grama grass and Indian rice grass, grow where the land is drier. Between monoclines and anticlines lie large, flat basins like the San Juan Basin, where water permits the growth of corn and other crops.

Navajos and the Land

Once they arrived in the Southwest, Navajos began immediately to adapt to their new environment. Previously, they had probably survived by hunting, gathering, and some agriculture, but in the Four Corners region, they quickly learned from the sedentary Pueblos to grow corn, which became a staple in the Navajo diet and an important part of the culture. Navajos used corn pollen (*tádídíín*) in prayers and ceremonies, instructed their children in the care of corn plants, and created songs about the importance of corn. For example:

> The group of roots enter the ground
> Several kernels sprouted in one spot
> It starts out on opposite sides
> Its roots go down, the leaves come up
> It starts out from below
> One plant appears, two plants appear, three appear
> Four appear,
> Now the corn is green
> My corn extends its hand to me . . . [6]

Navajos also learned to weave from their Pueblo neighbors.

A ruggedly independent, self-sufficient people, Navajos lived in small clan-based groups, not in communities or towns like Pueblos. Their lives were self-contained, integrated with the world around them, not apart from it. As one Navajo man put it:

In the morning . . . the Navajo man, he gets up, he goes outside his hogan and turning to his right, he takes the end of a branch of the nearest juniper tree in his hand, and he says, "Good morning, Grandfather," and then he turns to his left and taking the pine needles at the end of a branch of a piñon tree in his hand, he says, "Good morning, Grandmother." In that way he reminds himself each day of his relationship to nature, of which he is part. Everything in nature is sacred.[7]

The Navajo world view was a two-edged sword, however, because their relationship with nature generated fear as well as balance. Life could be dangerous, fraught with disease or plagued by *chindi* (ghosts and evil).[8] Early Navajos discovered the ancient Anasazi cultures of Chaco Canyon, Mesa Verde, and Hovenweep, but abhorrence of chindi kept them away from these ruins. On the other hand, Navajo ceremonies — particularly the Blessingway Ritual or songs and prayers taken from it — were intended to avert misfortune and obtain blessings for a long and happy life.[9]

Navajos and their Neighbors

Europeans arrived in 1540 with the Francisco Vasquez de Coronado expedition, but saw little to interest them and moved on.[10] Coronado's accounts do not mention Navajos. Neither did later exploratory expeditions indicate Navajo encounters. Juan de Oñate, for example, made no specific mention of them in the records of his 1598 and 1605 explorations. Fray Geronimo de Zarate Salmeron's *Relaciones* of 1626 reported Navajos for the first time. He became acquainted with them during his mission at Jemez before 1623, and he called them "Apaches de Nabaju."[11]

Spanish and Pueblo settlements along the Rio Grande after 1610 profoundly impacted Navajos. Although Franciscan Alonso de Benavides's greatly exaggerated report claimed that friars had converted eighty-six thousand New Mexico Indians to Roman Catholicism, Navajos proved largely unreceptive to Christian proselytizing.[12] Beginning in 1623, the Spanish exposed several Pueblo conspiracies against them, especially among the Jemez people, many of whom fled to Dinétah to escape Spanish retaliation. More ran away after the 1680 Pueblo Revolt and the 1694 reconquest. Again a significant number came from Jemez, and consequently the Jemez Clan — also known as the Coyote Pass Clan (*Ma'ii Deeshgizhinii*) — originated at about this time. The early eighteenth century saw warfare between Navajos and Spanish, possibly as a continuation of the Pueblo Revolt and its aftermath.[13]

Comanches and Utes arrived about 1700 and allied with Spanish against Navajos and Apaches around 1710. In addition, the Spanish underwent periods of expansion. In the 1750s, for instance, Hispano farmers received numerous land grants in northwestern New Mexico, but Navajo raids forced many off their grants. In 1786 Governor Juan Bautista de Anza of New Mexico promised protection of Navajo lands in return for their not molesting farmers or stock. Under this peace, which lasted until about 1800, Navajo flocks and herds increased rapidly, and corn and wheat crops prospered.

Around 1800 Nuevo Mexicanos expanded again, and Navajos grew especially concerned about a growing settlement at Cebolleta, located near today's Cañoncito Navajo Reservation and the pueblos of Acoma and Laguna. By 1804 the Diné decided they must drive the farmers out. At first, Navajos were successful. But in 1805, possibly allied with Utes and Jicarilla Apaches, New Mexicans under Antonio Narbona defeated Navajos in Canyon del Muerto, a branch off Canyon de Chelly, and forced a peace that lasted for another twenty years. It is noteworthy that the close relationship between some Navajos and Spanish in Cebolleta led to factions and infighting among Diné. One leader, Cebolla Sandoval, and his followers became known as *Diné Ana'ii* (enemy Navajos) because of their alliance with the Spanish.[14]

During this period, too, Navajos placed increasing importance on raiding stock, crops, women, and children. An August 1819 treaty between Navajos and New Mexico officials specified the return of all captives, suggesting that the slave trade on both sides had reached crisis proportions. At the same time, a pattern of Navajo and Hispano intermarriage developed.[15]

The 1819 truce proved an uneasy one. The Spanish hold on New World colonies collapsed in 1821, when Mexico and areas north of the Rio Grande became independent. Aware of the weakness, Navajos raided regularly. In fact, throughout twenty-five years of Mexican rule, warfare continued in on-again, off-again fashion. Governor José Antonio Vizcarra invaded Navajo land in 1829, with marginal success. Next, an ill-fated expedition in February 1835, led by Captain Blas de Hinojos, resulted primarily in Hinojos's death and increased hostilities by summer 1836.

In another attempt, Governor Manuel Armijo negotiated a treaty with Navajos on July 15, 1839, but this treaty was lost and the terms are unknown. Navajos apparently disliked whatever agreement Armijo offered them because by September 1839 raids and warfare broke out again. Thus, when American troops arrived in 1846, Nuevo Mexicanos were frustrated in attempts to deal with Navajos, and Navajos appeared determined to defeat the non-Indians once and for all.[16]

The Navajo Long Walk

Following the 1846 Mexican-American War, Mexico ceded territory to the United States that included present-day New Mexico and Arizona. Navajos were at first happy to see Americans arrive, convinced that any enemy of the

Mexicans must be a friend of theirs. They quickly grew disillusioned. Americans did not form a new alliance. Moreover, Stephen Watts Kearny, the first commander, supported a strong military presence, and on September 18, 1846, one month after the arrival of American troops, he sent two detachments under Major William Gilpin and Colonel Congreve Jackson to scout Navajo territory.

Kearny's military campaign did not end in Santa Fe. His orders were to move on to California, which he did on September 25. Navajos interpreted Kearny's own hasty departure as a retreat and plagued his departing column by stealing its stock. Furious, Kearny ordered second-in-command Alexander W. Doniphan to meet Gilpin and Jackson with three hundred men. At *Shash Bitoo*, Americans met thirteen Navajo headmen, including Nataalith (Zarcillas Largo), Manuelito, and respected Navajo leader Narbona, who was over 75 years old. On November 22, the headmen and Doniphan concluded a treaty that was never ratified by the U.S. Senate. Nor was a second treaty negotiated two years later by Lieutenant Colonel Edward W. B. Newby with Narbona and others.

Between July 1847 and August 1849, there was no recorded instance of Navajos killing Anglo or Hispano settlers. Nevertheless, James Macrae Washington, military governor of New Mexico, and a large force scoured Dinétah. It is not clear whether the primary purpose of the expedition was to make war or to make peace, and perhaps even Washington did not know.[17] He sent word for Navajo leaders to meet him at Canyon de Chelly to discuss yet another treaty. However, near present-day Two Gray Hills Trading Post, Washington encountered a large band of headmen, among them Narbona, ill and suffering with rheumatoid arthritis, and José Largo, another elderly leader.

The headmen grew quickly irritated at the arrogant Washington and his unruly troops, but presented horses and mules to show friendship and sincerity. The talks over, a scuffle broke out between Indians and soldiers over an allegedly stolen horse, and the commander ordered troops to fire. Several Navajos, including Narbona, were killed. As a result, José Largo, Nataalith, and Manuelito—Narbona's son-in-law—rejected the 1849 treaty. It is noteworthy that this treaty was one of only two with the Navajos ratified by the Senate; the second was the Treaty of 1868. Also among Washington's volunteer troops was a young Missouri lawyer named Henry Linn Dodge, who would be appointed agent to the Navajos in 1853 and whose avowed son, Henry Chee Dodge, would become the first Navajo Tribal Council chairman and the single most influential leader responsible for early oil exploration and leasing.

In January 1852 and again in spring 1853, territorial Indian agent James S. Calhoun encouraged peaceful relations with Navajos. At the same time, military commander Edwin V. Sumner actively pushed for confrontation. Sumner oversaw the construction of numerous forts, most conspicuously Fort Defiance, which he planted squarely on Navajo land. It is probable that disputes between the military at Fort Defiance and Navajos caused much of the post-1860 hostilities.

In addition to military expeditions, the U.S. government sent crews to explore the region for a possible railroad route. In 1853 Amiel Weeks Whipple led a survey into the Four Corners country. In his travels, he took a detour and camped on November 14 near the tiny community of Cubero east of Grants, New Mexico, which contained about sixty Hispanic families. According to Whipple's account, "This being a frontier Mexican settlement, the people [had] suffered greatly from incursions of the Navajoes [sic]." They were driven frequently to seek refuge in neighboring cliffs. Many settlers had been taken prisoner. "It was once the boast of these Indians, that, if they desired, they could exterminate the Mexicans; and that they only spared them to save themselves the trouble of cultivating corn and raising sheep."[18]

Animosity between Anglo Americans and Navajos and Hispanics and Navajos intensified after 1860. The Civil War in New Mexico was short-lived; Union troops handily defeated Confederates by 1862. In 1861 a large Navajo war party led by Manuelito and Barboncito had nearly overrun Fort Defiance. In charge of suddenly idled troops, hardboiled military commander James H. Carleton ordered the militia under Christopher (Kit) Carson to pursue Navajos and defeat them. Carson's pursuit did not begin, however, until midsummer 1863. To accomplish his task, Carson seized at least five thousand Navajo sheep, goats, and mules and destroyed crops in a winter campaign that ended with the Navajos' surrender at Canyon de Chelly in winter 1863–64.[19]

By spring 1864, 8,474 Navajos were forced to take the "Long Walk" to the barren, wind-swept Bosque Redondo, located at Fort Sumner on the Llano Estacado of eastern New Mexico, where they were impounded with Mescalero Apaches. Carleton's plan was to teach Navajos white ways and assimilate them, or if that failed, "engulf them . . . until they become known only in history and at length are blotted out, of even that, forever."[20]

Of course, thousands of Navajos did not surrender, but instead hid from Carson's militia and managed to stay behind. For those imprisoned at the Bosque, however, starvation, severe weather, disease, and Comanche raids plagued them. Still, when special Indian agent Julius K. Graves visited the experiment in early 1866, he praised the new *Acequia Madre*, or main irrigation ditch, and lauded new orchards swaying in the breeze. Graves noted corn planted by Navajos and Mescaleros and recommended keeping the Indians in eastern New Mexico.

But interracial problems occurred from the onset. Pecos River herders hesitated to graze their sheep because of the Indians living there. Carleton awarded supply contracts to friends, which drove prices up, quality down, and often resulted in slow delivery. In addition, crops began to fail after 1865. Although Graves liked what he saw in early 1866, corn production that year dropped from 423,582 pounds in 1865 to 201,420 pounds in 1866. Wheat, oats, and sorghum, which had yielded over 50,000 pounds the year before, were not even planted in 1866. Fodder, beans, pumpkins, and other crops produced far less after 1865 because of drought. Worse, affrays broke out between Navajos and locals and between locals and the army. Measles, smallpox, and fevers were alarming.

Finally, under a joint resolution of March 3, 1865, a committee of seven peace commissioners was appointed to study conditions of Indians living west of the Mississippi. In early 1867 Secretary of War Edwin M. Stanton replaced Carleton, and also in 1867, authority was removed from the War Department to the Department of the Interior. Complaining of costs, Acting Commissioner of Indian Affairs C. E. Mix, on January 10, 1868, began drawing up plans to move the Navajos, and on May 28, peace commissioners arrived to discuss the situation with headmen. Barboncito in particular related the horrors of the Bosque, and on May 31, General William T. Sherman and Commissioner Samuel Tappan announced the decision to send the Navajos home.

The Treaty Reservation and Executive Order Land

On June 1, 1868, Navajos signed a treaty that they would later dub "*Naaltsoos Sáaní*" — the Old Paper. The same day, Sherman ordered his army to prepare for the move, and by late July, Navajos began arriving in Dinétah. They were granted only 3.5 million acres, an area that would later be called the "Treaty Reservation." Nevertheless, according to observers, "many Indians had to be restrained by their companions . . . when they caught sight of Mount Taylor [and broke into] thankful hysteria."[21] They were not the same people, however, who had gone east four years earlier.

In dire need of rations by 1869, the Indian Office purchased 35,000 sheep and goats to feed Navajos; only 14,000 arrived. Families took their stock ration and disappeared into the interior of Dinétah to live quietly isolated lives. Undoubtedly half of the stock was by necessity slaughtered that first winter, but with Navajo thrift and care herds multiplied, thereby freeing many from having to rely on government handouts.

Soon after *Naaltsoos Sáaní* was signed, Federal Peace Commissioner S. F. Tappan asked Special Agent Ward to make recommendations regarding Navajo "rehabilitation," and the August 14, 1868, reply suggested, among other things, a political reorganization of the tribe. Superintendents, the report advised, could appoint *Naat'áani* or headmen to deal directly with Indian agents on behalf of other Navajos. Naat'áani could help make tribal decisions and act as mediators in disputes.[22] Despite the Navajo admonition against wealth, many of these headmen began to amass substantial amounts of livestock and grazing lands, suggesting at least that wealth stratification was occurring this early.

By 1878 Navajos needed more grazing land. With no surveyed boundaries, some simply ventured beyond the confines of the reservation, a situation made more complex because the Enabling Act of 1866 had granted huge chunks of public land in western New Mexico to the Atlantic and Pacific Railroad for a right-of-way. The "checkerboard," as it was called, included unsurveyed land occupied or claimed by Navajos, railroad land, and land sold by the railroad to whites.

In 1878, a presidential executive order withdrew public domain for Navajo use and incorporated that land into the reservation. Additional withdrawals were made in 1880, 1882, 1884, 1900, and 1901 (subdivided into Navajo and Hopi land use areas in 1962). Such presidential extensions did not require Congressional approval. On the other hand, executive order lands granted no title to the Indians and were often vague regarding area or specific land use. Eventually these periodic withdrawals created a large executive-order reservation whose legal status was unclear and which further complicated land claims.

The Atlantic and Pacific subdivided its original grant in 1900 between the New Mexico and Arizona Land Company; the Atchison, Topeka and Santa Fe Railroad; and Aztec Land and Cattle Company, making the checkerboard a conglomeration of obscurely owned lands. Between 1907–1917, a series of executive order additions added the checkerboard to the reservation. Moreover, Navajo ancestral lands had originally incorporated everything between the four sacred peaks. So Navajos sometimes drifted from the reservation, although for them it simply meant returning to land they had previously used. With such ill-defined boundaries, the Indians were unable to determine exactly where their land ended and public domain began.

More often, whites squatted on Indian land, probably unintentionally. Discovery of high-quality artesian water in the checkerboard after 1900 attracted many Anglo and Hispano sheep and cattle growers eager to winter their herds. Despite attempts by the BIA to legally obtain the disputed area for Navajos in 1907, the situation continued.

Over time, however, Navajos grew less nomadic and more tied to specific pasture areas. Although the concept of private ownership remained foreign to Navajos, a distinct feeling of proprietorship existed, and Navajos grew protective of family grazing areas.[23] With smaller parcels of land available, families were less inclined to share than in the past. Individuals and small families could only increase land by living together and combining pasture, settling virgin regions (of which there were few), fighting for the land, or trying to inherit by herding for a family that held land-use rights. Making matters worse, whites and their livestock squeezed Navajos more and more tightly by the early years of the twentieth century. Not until the 1930s would pieces of the exterior border be filled in by congressional action, with Cañoncito, Ramah, and Alamo gaining reservation status much later.

Anglo-American Settlers Arrive

Whites were slow to call northwest New Mexico home. Mormons were among the first to arrive, establishing communities like Cedar Hill on the Animas River in 1877, Kirtland and Fruitland in 1880, and Jewett in 1884. Brigham Young, Jr., reportedly maintained a home in Fruitland during anti-polygamy raids near Salt Lake City in the 1880s.[24] In 1902, Joseph Lehi Foutz, one of nineteen Mormon families driven from Tuba City, also arrived in Fruitland with wives, sons, and daughters, and opened a trading post. Eventually the family owned and operated twenty Navajo trading posts.[25] The eldest son, Junius, or June as he was called, would play a minor role in the sale of oil leases in 1922. In 1871, John D. Lee built a ferry across the San Juan River. Called Lee's Ferry, the crossing was bordered to the north by a steep, precarious climb up from the river, which served, in part, as protection from anti-Mormon whites.

South of Cedar Hill, Frank and George Coe from Lincoln County homesteaded land in the 1880s. More settlers eventually moved into the region, and a town was planned in 1890. The town was named Aztec for the Pueblo ruins nearby, which many mistakenly believed had once belonged to a northern branch of the Aztec Indians of Mexico.[26] In 1876, whites also built at the confluence of the San Juan, La Plata, and Animas rivers, a place Navajos called *Tóta'* or "between the rivers." In 1879, the town was platted, and because local stockmen frequently purchased green vegetables and forage for animals there, it became known as Farmington.[27]

Bloomfield, originally called Porter, was settled in 1877 or 1878. Located on the San Juan River about nine miles south of Aztec, Bloomfield was at first a wild town known for rustling. In fact, the notorious Port Stockton of Lincoln County War fame was killed there in 1881. Bloomfield was also the site of a trading post called Hu-Shani built in 1880 by General Horace Porter, a Civil War veteran, from whom the place received its earliest name. The store burned in 1882, but Bloomfield prospered. Like the other towns, Bloomfield represented the start of a flourishing border-town economy that evolved along the fringes of Navajo land after 1868. Such communities depended heavily upon trade with Navajos, even though the number of trading posts on the reservation also multiplied rapidly and continued to proliferate well into the twentieth century.

Other towns included the tiny communities of Waterflow; Shiprock (*Naa'táanii Néz*), created as the seat of the Northern Navajo agency in 1903;

and Floravista, established as a farming and ranching area around 1878. On the Navajo reservation lay Toadlena ("water bubbling up"), where because of its many fresh-water springs the first tribal council met in 1923. Naschiti (*nahashch'idí* or "badger") was the site of an 1886 trading post. Sanostee or *Tsé' Alnáozt'i'í* ("rocks overlapping") also grew up around a trading post.[28] Newcomb, originally called "Nava," was a trading post founded in 1914 by Arthur and Frances Newcomb. The BIA built a day school at Newcomb during the 1920s. Day schools were also constructed at Mentmore, a Baptist mission, and Rehoboth, founded in 1903 by the Christian Reformed Church.

In 1884, the Aztec Land and Cattle Company purchased one million acres in Arizona, and Cebolla Cattle Company bought land in western New Mexico. The Hash Knife, as the Aztec Company was nicknamed because of its distinctive brand, brought in thirty-two thousand head of Texas cattle from Continental Land and Cattle — the original Hash Knife ranch — and allowed them to roam wild across Mormon and Navajo land. Hash Knife employees were typically roughshod cowboys and undesirables. "Some were good men, but many were professional gunfighters."[29] These hoodlums attacked Mormon farmers in what became known as the Pleasant Valley War, forcing many to abandon the area.[30]

On February 24, 1887, San Juan County was carved out of western Rio Arriba County, and Aztec became the county seat. Area whites primarily raised cattle and sheep, but using an irrigation method called "neighborhood ditches" along the San Juan River also began to produce apples, peaches, plums, pears, cherries, apricots, quinces, wheat, vegetables, and alfalfa. In fact, boosters claimed that the new San Juan County had the largest water supply in New Mexico for irrigation, and as a result, was "the greatest farming center of the state [*sic*]."[31]

The lawless element also arrived. There were the typical bullies, who harassed Hispanic and Mormon farmers and Navajo herders. Many rowdies also bootlegged whiskey to the Indians. The most infamous were the previously mentioned Ike and Port Stockton, who once rode with the equally disreputable Clay Allison. Court records in San Juan County soon filled with charges against the Stocktons and other criminals who found that northwest New Mexico lay beyond the reaches of the law. Farmington and Aztec, in particular, became dangerous places to live. In addition, violence on the reservation — a direct result of liquor — left twenty traders murdered between 1901 and 1934. Despite Indian Office and later tribal attempts to ban alcohol, the problem remained.[32]

South of San Juan County lay McKinley County. Anglos built Fort Fauntleroy near present-day Gallup (*Na'nízhoozhí*) in August 1860. The area, called Shash Bitoo by Navajos, had long been a watering hole for herds.[33] The fort was renamed Fort Lyons in September 1861 when Colonel Thomas T. Fauntleroy defected to the Confederate cause, then abandoned in December during the Confederate invasion of New Mexico. It was re-established in 1868, again renamed, this time "Wingate," and regarrisoned to control the new Navajo reservation. The agency was located at Fort Defiance, Arizona, at which historian Frank McNitt suggests Agent Henry L. Dodge situated his head-quarters in September 1855.[34] In 1925, the Indian Service built a school here.

Gallup grew around the construction of the Atlantic and Pacific Railroad in 1881. The railroad company had earlier sent John Stewart and Alex Bowie to find deposits of coal, which were required to power locomotives. The pair found plenty near Gallup, so the railroad pushed forward into the area.[35] Old-timers claimed railroad workers referred to payday as "going to Gallup" be-cause the auditor and paymaster was David L. Gallup. Gallup was eventually promoted to comptroller and reassigned to New York City, but when the town was incorporated on July 9, 1891, it was named for him.

Ramah, south of Gallup, was originally called "Navajo" by Mormon farmers in 1874. However, these farmers discovered that New Mexico already had a town named Navajo, so selected the name Ramah from the Book of Mor-mon.[36] Navajos called the place "Tl'ohchiní," meaning "onion" for the wild onions that proliferate there. Crownpoint, located in the New Mexico checker-board east of Gallup, grew after the BIA established its Pueblo Bonito juris-diction on April 1, 1909. In July, its superintendent, S. F. Stacher, relocated from the canyon to the present site. The Eastern Navajo Agency was abolished in 1935, but the Crownpoint Subagency was located there from 1935 to 1961. Currently, it is the Eastern Navajo Agency.

Similarly, a community developed at Fort Defiance. The fort was estab-lished officially on September 18, 1851, and by September 1855, as previously mentioned, Agent Dodge headquartered here. Government agents estab-lished themselves in 1868 and distributed sheep and other supplies to Navajos returning from the Long Walk. On August 28, 1868, Lehman Spiegelberg of Santa Fe became the first licensed trader at Fort Defiance. He did not remain active on the reservation for long, however, but opened the way to a parade of other traders.[37]

In 1901 Fort Defiance became the headquarters for the Southern Navajo Agency when the federal government created five agencies with a superin-tendent in each one. By 1936, Commissioner of Indian Affairs John Collier would centralize BIA and tribal headquarters several miles away. Unhappy with Collier's move, Navajos called the place "Nee Alneeng" and said the name meant "center of the Navajo world." Officials eventually discovered that they had been the target of Navajo humor—Nee Alneeng meant something akin to "Hell." Collier renamed it Window Rock.[38]

The First Oil and Natural Gas Discoveries

Prospectors also journeyed into the Four Corners region seeking wealth in the form of gold, silver, and copper. The Indian Office encouraged them. In 1913, for example, the BIA suggested that placer gold might lie undiscovered in the river beds.[39] Although none was ever unearthed, the reservation was later found to contain immense beds of fire clay, gypsum, iron ore, borax, and bituminous coal from one to forty-five feet in depth. Moreover, in 1898, trader John Wetherill first discovered uranium near Moab, but at the time was seeking carnotite, which contains uranium.[40]

Oil proved a nuisance to early prospectors and farmers alike. Natural gas, which almost always occurs with oil, was unwelcome as well. In 1879, prospector E. L. Goodrich discovered oil seeps along the San Juan River near what is now Mexican Hat, Utah. In 1907, he drilled a "gusher" and opened the Mexican Hat field, but the operation was not profitable at the time.[41] Homesteader Sylvester Black was even less fortunate. In 1888 he hitched his mule to a swing-pole attached to an upright beam with steel bit, figuring to locate cool artesian water for his family. Instead, he encountered a depressing black ooze, then a blast of natural gas. Afterward, the Black family had to content itself with water from a spring while, reportedly, passersby dropped lighted matches into the gas hole to amuse themselves with the mild "pouf" that resulted.[42]

A similar "gasser" was unearthed quite unexpectedly in 1923 when Producers and Refiners Company hit "the largest natural gas well in America to date." The well blew ten-ton tools right out of the hole with an explosion that could be heard for ten miles. One viewer remarked that "to one who has never seen the power of nature as seventy million feet of gas is being forced upward 2,370 feet from the bowels of the earth, it is sure a sight."[43] In 1923, as in 1888, natural gas lacked commercial value.

Oil and gas—the result of deeply buried natural decay and maturation of organic substances when subjected to elevated temperatures—are generally found in sedimentary rocks beneath the earth's surface. Oil forms in organic-rich, dark-colored shales and leaks into more porous, permeable beds made of sandstone or porous limestone. It can also seep down, or if the rocks are filled with water, rise to the top of the water strata. When its migration is halted, deposits accumulate in oil pools or tiny pores within the rocks. The simplest trapping mechanisms for oil migrations are anticlinal folds.[44] Where oil and gas are trapped, deposits form commercially viable fields.

Navajos and Oil Exploration

Thirty years before Navajos began to lease their oil lands, several tribes in Oklahoma had discovered pools of black gold. In an attempt to open these lands to exploration and drilling, Congress enacted a law on February 28, 1891, that allowed Indians to lease lands deemed unproductive for other uses if approved by the tribe or a council speaking for all. Navajos were protected also by the Treaty of 1868, specifically Article Ten that forbade "the cession of any portion or part of the reservation . . . which may be held in common," unless agreed by "at least three-fourths of all the adult male Indians occupying or interested in the same."[45] But neither the 1868 treaty nor the 1891 legislation addressed executive order lands.[46] Clearly, the land tangle that had been allowed to develop — unclear legal status, unsurveyed boundaries, and an influx of unauthorized whites on public land — would continue to plague Anglos and Navajos alike.

Furthermore, chaos characterized the oil industry overall in 1923. It is not surprising that oil companies explored the Navajo reservation in piecemeal fashion and without a comprehensive plan. Ironically, though, Navajos may have benefited by federal incompetence and corporate ignorance. Geology was an inexact science, and wildcatting was the leading method of discovery. Nevertheless, few companies could afford to hire geologists or knew how to utilize their skills. Sophisticated geophysical methods developed in Europe after 1920 were not employed in the Four Corners region until World War II.[47]

In addition, a complete lack of state and federal regulation meant the "law of capture" prevailed; companies could take as much oil as they could drill in a particular location, hence "capturing" the oil even if it was siphoned from neighboring fields. Once drillers discovered petroleum in a field, they bored holes indiscriminately to capture all they could. Waste was rampant. The industry lived in fear of monopoly, especially the dreaded Standard Oil. In 1895, for instance, New Mexico territorial coal oil inspector M. S. Hart warned that Standard Oil representatives were lurking in New Mexico and Colorado and noted "they are very foxey [sic] and will do most anything to get advantage of us."[48] The presence of Standard Oil influenced decisions of other companies, often to the detriment of the entire industry.

In 1906 the U.S. Bureau of Corporations investigated Standard Oil and on May 2 charged the company with dominating the industry through secret railroad rebates.[49] In 1911 U.S. v Standard Oil of New Jersey broke up the monopoly, but six other integrated companies — Pure Oil, Texas Oil, Gulf, Sun, Union, and Shell — had already stepped forward to challenge the Standard monopoly. As a reaction to Standard and to these other corporations, small independent oil companies shunned regulation and feared that any restrictions whatsoever might drive them, not the monopolies, out of business. The situation encouraged instability and wildly fluctuating prices.

As a matter of fact, before 1922, several independents tested the area outside the Navajo reservation. Durango Oil and Fuel Company drilled the first area oil test well east of Aztec in 1901, to a depth of 1,500 feet, but ended up with only a dry hole. In 1913 San Juan Oil drilled nearby, but lacked the money to complete a test well. In many such cases, shallow wells were left open, and locals enjoyed them as places to meet after dark and sit by the glow of their private lights.[50] On October 21, 1921, Aztec Oil Syndicate discovered natural gas at 985 feet and oil at 1,750 feet, but, like those before, went broke. However, a group of locals borrowed a drilling rig, recruited volunteer labor, and laid a pipeline from the Syndicate well two miles into the town of Aztec. By December, Aztec became the first town in New Mexico heated by natural gas. Unfortunately, the unregulated pipeline pressure resulted in fires, and a number of homes in Aztec burned to the ground.[51]

During this time, the Indian Service fielded scores of inquiries regarding oil and gas exploration on Navajo land. Interest focused primarily on the San Juan area, so Navajos there bore the brunt of pressure to lease their land after 1907.[52] Early meetings of the San Juan Navajos provide a window into the haphazard quest for oil before 1921 and into Navajo responses.

San Juan Councils Before 1921

There is no indication that Navajos met as a tribe prior to 1923. As previously noted, the Naat'áaní probably met with Indian agents periodically, deliberated local problems, and perhaps distributed annuities to the people. Their role dwindled in the final years of the nineteenth century, and the Naat'áaní were mentioned for the last time in the 1897 annual report. Father Berard Haile witnessed headman councils between 1900 and 1910.[53] In addition to meeting with Naat'áaní, the superintendent selected a head chief; for many years this was Henry Chee Dodge, whose fluent English allowed him to act as interpreter. His friendship with whites secured compliance with government programs.[54]

Nevertheless, by 1900 the Indian Office had devised a plan to administer the reservation more efficiently by dividing it into six jurisdictions, each with its own superintendent. The Tuba City Agency was established in 1901, Keams Canyon (Hopi) in 1902, San Juan (Shiprock) in 1903, Pueblo Bonito (Eastern) in 1907, and Leupp in 1908. The original and largest agency was at Fort Defiance. Haile concluded that the division of Dinétah into separate agencies "split the tribe into factions" because agents encouraged rivalries between jurisdictions. Once the six agencies were created, he claims, local headmen councils rapidly disappeared.[55]

In 1907, members of the San Juan jurisdiction met for the first time as a group, and the gathering reinforced Haile's contention that agents manipulated such forums. In fact, an Indian inspector sent from Washington used the assembly to create a smaller, more easily controlled business council, which may never have met, but was nevertheless a forerunner of the 1923 Navajo Tribal Council.[56]

On March 8, 1907, nearly two hundred Navajos converged on the San Juan Indian School to meet with U.S. Indian Inspector James McLaughlin and San Juan agent William T. Shelton.[57] At a few minutes after 1:00 P.M., McLaughlin told Navajos he was there to ascertain if they favored granting a mineral lease in the Carrizo Mountains. Through an interpreter, McLaughlin explained that under the Indian Mineral Leasing Act of 1891, Navajos could lease unproductive lands, and their mountains contained many such acres. A lease could mean royalty payments if oil were discovered. Navajos did not need to fear a permanent presence on the reservation because after ten years the lease could be discontinued or renegotiated.[58]

Farmington boosters drooled over the prospect of a $2.5 million company wanting to drill for oil, especially when that firm expressed plans to establish local offices. *Times-Hustler* editors crowed that this was only the first step in an eventual allotment of all Navajo lands, and soon the entire reservation would open to settlement.[59] Navajos, on the other hand, had mixed emotions. They remembered all too well that a 1901 council had leased the entire reservation to George Franklin Huff, a Pennsylvania capitalist. Fortunately for them, Huff failed to comply with provisions of the lease, and it was subsequently canceled. But, because the lease had been signed at Fort Defiance — the only agency in existence in 1901 — Navajos from the Carrizo district were never consulted.

Navajos also charged deception. The Fort Defiance council had refused to sign the Huff lease, insisting he receive only 640 acres, not the entire reservation. Yet, when the lease was rewritten without tribal knowledge, "640 acres" somehow became "the entire reservation." In addition, Navajos asked for time to consider the deal and met a second time in November 1901. This time Huff and Pennsylvania Congressman John Dalzell attended. During this second meeting, Navajo Agent G. W. Hayzlett told Navajos the Government favored the lease as "it would be to the best interest of the Navajoes [*sic*]."[60] The Navajos signed, but were unaware of an amendment restoring Huff's claim to the entire reservation, not the 640 acres agreed upon by the tribe.

The Secretary of the Interior never approved the amendment because technically it included executive order lands. Even so, Huff's prospectors combed the reservation. Later, Huff assigned his lease to his father-in-law, Judge J. Murray Burrell, who reassigned it to Maurice S. Wormser in 1906 without Indian approval and despite cancellation. Wormser, informed by the BIA that the Huff-Burrell lease was dead, applied to the Secretary of the Interior for permission to negotiate a new lease with the Navajos. It was this request that led to the 1907 meeting of the San Juan council.

This council turned thumbs down. Delegates expressed weariness with prospectors trekking across Diné land. "We are glad there is no gold there, for if there was, the white people would burn the whole ground to get it; all the grass on the Carriso [*sic*] Mountains would be destroyed."[61] Besides, Navajos claimed, the mountains were sacred. Despite protests, McLaughlin utilized the one strategy that would encourage compliance; he linked their approval with the will of the government. From 1868 forward government had held this trump card in any negotiation. As tribal chairman Peter MacDonald wrote in his 1993 autobiography, the Long Walk generation and its offspring feared that what the government gave, it could also take.[62] Thus, Navajos tended to go along with the will of government officials.

In 1907 McLaughlin, the BIA's most experienced field officer, played a similar hand. This former agent of the Standing Rock Sioux Agency, who in 1890 had masterminded the arrest of Sitting Bull, believed unequivocally that Indians should be set adrift to work out their own salvation. He told Navajos: "You should understand that the Government is the best friend of the Indian . . . the Government has been very good to you Navajos . . ."[63] Now, McLaughlin explained, federal officials wanted something in return. They desired to know if the Carrizos contained valuable minerals. "I would be very sorry if I had to return to Washington and say that you people did not listen to what I had to say to you, especially where you have nothing to lose and a great deal to gain." When the council balked and asked for more time, Shelton added, "I would be ashamed . . . if this man had to go back to Washington and say that you people had to wait four months to make up your minds."[64]

Navajos reluctantly agreed to make a lease with any parties properly vouched for by authorities in Washington and appointed a committee of eleven leading Navajos to enter into that lease. They pointedly voiced their feelings that land was not a commodity: "We have given up a great thing; in the first place we have let you take this mountain, which we consider the same as a human being, the same as our mother, and now you will tear through her skull and dig out her heart."[65] Whether the eleven ever met is not known. Clearly, McLaughlin and Shelton ignored Navajo objections in favor of mining interests. The Secretary of the Interior approved a lease with Wormser that covered both Carrizo and Lukachukai Mountains in Arizona. It was later canceled.

The status of executive order lands, however, continued to baffle the government. In 1913 Senator Albert B. Fall (R-NM) discovered that the 1891 law forbade the leasing of executive order lands.[66] Thus Fall, a staunch advocate of unrestricted land use, made private development of public lands—Indian reservations included—a priority.

THE QUEST FOR LEASES, 1921–1923

In early times, the Navajo world was smaller than today. Mountains marking the limits of Dinétah were closer together and when the Sun followed his path each day, he passed nearer to the earth's surface than he does today. The people prayed to the four winds to pull the mountains further apart. Accordingly, Nílch'i ha'a'aahdę́ę́'go (East Wind) pulled as did Nílch'i shádi'áahdę́ę́'go (South Wind), Nílch'i e'e'aahdę́ę́'go (West Wind), and Nílch'i náhooksdę́ę́'go (North Wind). They all pulled at the same time. By the fourth day, each had pulled his mountain further from the center of the earth. The sun traveled further away and things were cooler. Once they accomplished this task, the Navajo people never again asked to have the face of the earth changed.[1]

Between 1921 and 1923, oil exploitation came to the Navajo reservation. No oil or natural gas leases existed before January 1921, but by October 15, 1923, four promising structures—Hogback, Rattlesnake, Table Mesa, and Tocito—lay in the hands of oil companies. In 1921, San Juan area Navajos assembled for the first time in fifteen or twenty years, only to be replaced in 1923 with a reservation-wide tribal council. A small cast of Navajo and white leaders emerged who would significantly influence early oil development.

But nobody better illustrates the aggressive, pro-business perspective than Albert Bacon Fall. In fact, Fall wielded such tremendous influence that for years after the Teapot Dome scandal reduced him to *persona non grata* in Washington, newspaper editors continued to link him with laissez faire exploitation of the land and dubbed his methods "Fallism."[2] His reputation is not surprising because throughout his public life Fall eagerly boasted, "I stand for opening up every resource."[3]

This cigar-chewing New Mexico lawyer turned rancher and politician, whom Bureau of Mines director H. Foster Bain once called "forceful" and "sure of his ground," exhibited absolute disdain for government interference. Fall once compared prosperity in Texas to poverty in New Mexico and directly attributed the difference to the percentage of federally controlled land. Texas contained no public lands, while New Mexico embraced sizable chunks of forest reserves and Indian reservations.

Elected to the Senate in 1912, Fall wasted no time seeking ways to restore public lands to private ownership.[4] His disgust was obvious when, on February 11, 1914, he mockingly suggested to Congress that if government took over more lands, perhaps New Mexico could "ask to be included within an Indian reservation or a national park."[5] In 1920, Fall told a Colorado Springs audience that without natural resource exploitation, America was like a miser who "buries his gold in the ground and carries the secret of the hiding place to his grave."[6]

Fall's biographer David H. Stratton called the New Mexican "a remnant from a more extravagant age."[7] When Warren G. Harding named Fall Secretary of the Interior in 1921, conservationist Gifford Pinchot remarked, "It would have been possible to select a worse candidate, but not altogether easy."[8] Thus it surprised no one when Secretary Fall eagerly sought oil development across the West. In his first annual report as Interior Secretary, Fall wrote that Indians as a rule were "not qualified to make the most of their natural resources," and the federal government should do it for them.[9]

Reporters portrayed Fall as a man eager to hand over every shred of land to his oil friends, but his greater goal was development of public land overall. On April 29, 1921, he wrote a presidential order to transfer the U.S. Forest Service from the Department of Agriculture to the Department of the Interior. Harding, however, never signed it. In 1922, Fall urged legislation to transfer all agencies governing land in Alaska to his department, again to gain control of millions of acres of federally owned virgin forest and mining lands. Fortunately, the legislation never materialized.[10]

One of Fall's first acts as Secretary was to ask Senator Holm O. Bursum (R-NM) to draft a bill to "quiet" the claims of non-Indians upon Pueblo Indian lands. Dubbed the Bursum Bill, this notorious legislation was designed to divest Pueblos of thousands of acres of their land.[11] During his short term, Fall also tried to appropriate two thousand acres of Mescalero Apache reservation for an All-Year Southwestern National Park, with "excess" leased to ranchers, most notably his own Three Rivers Ranch, which bordered Mescalero land.[12] Sadly, Fall's views were not unusual among Westerners, just somewhat extreme. In his 1931 book *Only Yesterday*, Frederick Lewis Allen noted that during the 1920s business was so frequently associated with the Bible that "it was sometimes difficult to determine which was supposed to gain the most from the association."[13]

The United States Grows Desperate for Oil

The demand for oil in the United States reached frenzied proportions in 1921. Ten million automobiles graced American roads, and homes and businesses began converting from coal to oil.[14] Large strikes in California, Texas, and Oklahoma heralded a return to business-as-usual, pre-war waste and corruption. On November 17, 1921, for example, four oil magnates met at New York City's Hotel Vanderbilt to purchase 3.3 million barrels of oil for $1.50 per barrel. E. A. Humphreys sold the oil through a mysterious firm called Continental Trading Company, recently incorporated in Canada. Continental immediately resold the oil to the four at $1.75 per barrel, a tidy $3 million profit, which they split among themselves. Harry M. Blackmer, for one, took home $763,000 to his personal safe deposit box. Blackmer was president of Midwest Oil, the first company to strike oil on Navajo land.[15]

Ironically, as the industry battled waste and depravity, the United States feared it would run out of oil within ten years.[16] British and Dutch companies in particular kept U.S. corporations away from many of the world's most lucrative oil deposits. In 1919, Standard Oil returned to pre-war holdings in the Middle East and discovered the region was under British military occupation and closed to U.S. business. In 1920, Britain gave France a sphere of influence in Mesopotamia and handed Italy some economic concessions, but excluded Americans.[17]

In addition, powerful Dutch corporations monopolized the Pacific fields. As a result, the United States turned to its own hemisphere and conducted extensive searches in South America, Mexico, and remote regions of the United States. The Navajo reservation was one part of this effort. Tucked quietly away in northwest New Mexico with little previous outside contact, Navajos were therefore drawn into domestic and international oil affairs whether they realized it or not.[18]

Until 1920, however, the 1891 law governed only mining on treaty reservations and land purchased for tribes, but not executive order lands. This made leasing chaotic and spawned attempts to create laws more amenable to business. In 1904, for instance, Texas Congressman John Hall Stephens attached legislation to an appropriations bill that mandated allotment of Indian lands, with leftover land turned over to mining interests. The Stephens bill, which considered Indian lands to be public domain as far as minerals and mining rights were concerned, was defeated. In 1912, Arizona Senator Henry F. Ashurst attempted to obtain passage of a bill to extend the 1891 mining law to executive order lands, but that legislation never came to a vote. Carl Hayden, also of Arizona, introduced similar bills in 1916 and 1917; in 1916, no vote was taken, and opponents defeated the 1917 version. The 1917 bill fixed royalty payments to Indians at 5 percent or higher, whereas the 1916 mandate limited royalties to only 5 percent.

Congress passed the Metalliferous Mining Act in 1918 ostensibly to assist the war effort. Sponsored by senators Ashurst, A. J. Gronna of North Dakota, and Fall, the legislation allowed the Interior Secretary to lease sections of Indian reservations in nearly every western state for the purpose of mining gold, silver, copper, and other valuable metalliferous minerals. It opened nearly thirty-one million acres to prospectors and designated 5 percent royalty to Indians. The Metalliferous Mining Act did not, however, pertain to oil.[19]

The General Leasing Act of February 28, 1920, was passed in part to provide western states a source of revenue because the federal government owned so much of their land. It permitted mineral and oil leases on the public domain, with subsurface mineral rights accruing to the federal government. The act allowed 2,560-acre prospecting permits, and once oil was discovered, companies could keep one-quarter of the land; the rest would be available for competitive bidding in 640-acre lots. A maximum of 3,200 acres in any given geological structure was permitted regardless of the number of prospecting permits a firm held. Moreover, the act turned 37.5 percent of the royalties over to states. But this legislation did not specifically apply to Indian lands, and so Navajo treaty lands remained under the 1891 Indian Mineral Leasing Act.

Legally, Fall could not change the status of treaty lands. On January 14, 1922, the Commissioner of the General Land Office (GLO) rejected a prospecting permit for E. M. Harrison on Navajo executive order land, stating that the office had no jurisdiction under the 1920 legislation. Harrison appealed the GLO's decision to Fall. On March 9, Fall instructed Charles H. Burke, Commissioner of Indian Affairs, to put in writing how much treaty, Congressional grant, and executive order land lay in the hands of the Indians nationwide. Fall discovered some 22 million acres in Arizona and New Mexico alone and pressured Congress to permit oil and gas leases on executive order lands under terms similar to those of the General Leasing Act.[20]

On May 17, 1922, Homer P. Snyder introduced another bill, but before Congress could vote, an impatient Fall issued his own administrative decision on June 9, ruling that executive order land had once been public domain and could be restored to the public domain. Fall's decision removed nine million acres from Navajo control for mining purposes and many more acres from Indian control overall. On December 12, 1923, the Committee of One Hundred, a group of reform-minded educators and politicians, assembled to discuss Indian issues. They severely criticized Fall's decision and requested that U.S. Attorney General Harlan Stone consider the judgment.

On May 12, 1924, Stone declared that the General Leasing Act did not pertain to executive order lands. Only Congress could decide ownership of subsurface minerals and the status of these lands. If Navajos retained mineral ownership, executive order lands would be on essentially the same legal footing as treaty lands. Stone also ordered 425 prospecting permits—including Harrison's—canceled. The companies seeking permits filed a lawsuit. As a result, on January 25, 1925, the U.S. District Court in Salt Lake City, Utah, found in their favor and against the Stone interpretation. Thus, by 1925, a federal court had ruled in favor of Fall's 1922 decision, and the U.S. Attorney General had ruled against it. This situation generated a parade of legislation to resolve the issue. However, in 1921, oil companies were most interested in treaty land, not executive order land.

Navajos Versus the Washington Coalition

Between summer 1921 and October 1923, prospectors combed the Navajo reservation seeking promising oil structures. Beginning in 1921, Evan Estep, superintendent of the San Juan jurisdiction, called area Navajos together four times to consider oil and gas leases. Estep noted that no San Juan council had met in at least fifteen years. The superintendent had worked with Navajos for years and generally respected their views. This caused oil developers to label him "too conservative" or "anti-progress."[21] When San Juan Navajos refused to turn over their land to outsiders, both Navajos and Estep found themselves pitted against a deadly combination of Washington bureaucrats and oil companies.

Like Fall, Commissioner Burke endorsed development. It has been said that Fall's politics dominated Burke, and certainly the Secretary of the Interior, not the Bureau of Indian Affairs (BIA) Commissioner, set policy.[22] Moreover, Fall's successor in March 1923 was Hubert Work, a Colorado physician. Less extreme than Fall, Work upheld assimilation and was adamantly pro-business. Burke, a former South Dakota congressman, was also an avid assimilationist. In 1921, he even supported the suppression of Indian dances and ceremonies nationwide. Burke actively sought oil development on Indian reservations and repeatedly warned Estep to foster a positive attitude toward oil for "their own good."[23]

On January 11, 1921, Estep wrote that "the tribe as a whole" greatly opposed prospectors on their land.[24] Four companies—Midwest Refining Company, Western States Oil and Gas, E. T. Williams, and Kinney Oil and Gas—conducted preliminary surveys at their own expense and drew up maps of the Hogback structure in anticipation of obtaining leases there. Midwest already leased acreage on the Ute reservation in northern New Mexico near the Colorado border. The company petitioned the Interior Department to waive regulations limiting the amount of land that could be leased within a state, calling its explorations in New Mexico "strictly wildcat" and "not encouraging."[25]

Most important, the companies needed Navajo approval and asked for a meeting. To apply for a prospecting lease, company officials had to first petition the Indian Office. If the BIA agreed, companies were required to present their credentials to the local agent, and a regional council would in turn approve or disapprove the lease. Because the tribe was divided into six agencies, each was viewed as an independent entity with its own interests.[26]

So, on March 3, 1921, over Estep's vehement objections, Assistant Commissioner E. B. Meritt directed him to call a council of San Juan Navajos to approve the four applications.[27] Navajos gathered in Shiprock on May 7, debated, and refused all petitions. Estep said that Navajos had been considering the lease matter for some time and "came in knowing what they wanted to do." He claimed, "I [had] no idea that the vote would be unanimous either way."[28] Estep noted that elders remained suspicious of the oil men. The younger men, especially former boarding-school students, tended to embrace "progress," but when they voted deferred to the elders.

The oil companies refused to accept the Navajo decision. They argued that Estep had dominated the council, introduced only the Midwest representative, and denied the others an opportunity to speak. Hence, Navajos had not rejected the leases; the Indians had never heard all of the proposals.[29] Proceedings reveal that Estep introduced M. O. Danford, who represented all four companies, but the council did not choose to listen. Estep accepted the council's decision and sent the oil companies packing.[30]

Danford immediately refiled the four applications. Three months later Burke ordered Estep to call a second council. On August 13, nearly two hundred Navajos jammed into the hot, dusty San Juan agency athletic field. As always, Navajos selected a few leaders to speak for them. The agent chose several translators—one of them was Chee Dodge from Fort Defiance—and a recording secretary. As government employees sliced mutton and stoked coals for lunch and dinner barbecues, Navajo men squatted and women sat with skirts flared around them under makeshift shelters from the blazing summer sun. They waited patiently for Estep to begin the meeting, no doubt wondering what he might say that differed from the previous gathering.[31]

Since May, a few changes had occurred. Midwest was lobbying hard in Washington. On the reservation, men from all four companies disrupted agency life and besieged Navajos with presents. They appealed to traders and missionaries for support. Furthermore, a letter from Burke so strongly stressed Indian Office support of oil leases that Estep thought it necessary to highlight the "considerable importance of deliberation" to Navajos in attendance. Estep presented George B. Jenkinson of Midwest, who sweetened the pot by promising to hire Navajos for all unskilled work in exchange for a lease.[32]

Navajos hesitated. Elders recounted stories of years past, when *bilagáana* prospectors had traipsed indiscriminately across Diné land, digging here and there to find gold, silver, and other minerals. Now, maybe whites would take the land altogether or fence off Navajo livestock. Would whites build houses on Navajo soil? How many outsiders would come to live among them? How large were derricks and towers, and what kind of wages would Navajo workers receive? Two dollars per day was not enough, they argued, and through interpreter Robert Martin, Navajos negotiated $2.50 per day.[33] Moreover, hadn't the council already denied leases on exactly the same tracts of land? Under pressure, Navajo leaders debated and asked for time to talk with the others. After a private, late-night session, spokesmen returned to the meeting and reluctantly approved one 4,800-acre lease to Midwest. They wanted no more arguments from the other oil companies. Having consented to a single lease, Navajos gathered their families, horses, and wagons and departed.[34]

The three rejected companies objected again. This time Estep emphatically blamed elders: "The young men who speak English and who have some business experience" desired leases, he told Burke. But the old men dominated the councils, and when a vote was taken "all the young men who had talked in favor of the lease voted against it."[35] Besides, Navajos preferred a conservative approach. If Midwest struck oil — and a large, established corporation was more likely to be successful than a smaller, less experienced one — Navajo land would increase in value, and leases might be sold more profitably.[36]

The Midwest lease was a compromise. Its Ute Dome operation had struck a massive deposit of natural gas earlier that summer, and people in the area believed an oil strike could not be far behind. Midwest seemed successful, a good omen for Navajos. The decision did not please Fall, Burke, or the rejected oil companies, however, and they increased the pressure on Estep and the San Juan Navajos. Estep signed the Midwest lease on August 15, 1921, and the Interior Department approved it on November 4. Navajos received 15 cents per acre for the first year's rental, 40 cents for the second, and 75 cents afterward, plus 12½ percent royalty on the gross percentage of oil produced and $100 for gas in each well.[37] Midwest's lease specified neither length of time nor number of test wells to be drilled. Of course, terms of non-Indian leases also varied, and no-term leases were fairly common, although after 1900 courts usually upheld an implied agreement to develop within ten years.[38]

Applications soon flooded the San Juan agency. Kinney Oil and Gas, E. T. Williams, and Western States Oil and Gas refiled. A local company named San Juan Oil Syndicate and owned by James Wade — a licensed trader on the reservation — and R. C. Gillis of the Southern Pacific Railroad got the endorsement of New Mexico Senator Bursum.[39] Furthermore, Midwest wanted land adjacent to its Hogback lease awarded to friendly companies that would benefit from Midwest's refining capability. Corporate officials went so far as to hint that Midwest might build its refinery near Gallup or Farmington and lay a 100-mile pipeline at an expense of about $20,000 per mile if the company got what it desired. Without concessions, however, officials could not promise either the refinery or the pipeline. So, on November 3, Burke ordered a third council, and despite Estep's misgivings that a new council might reject all applications out-of-hand, the superintendent on March 6, 1922, announced a March 25 meeting.[40]

Again, Navajos assembled. Estep introduced the same applicants. After an hour debate, Navajos unanimously said "nay" to more leases.[41] The rejected applicants refiled, this time suggesting to Burke that Estep had "been with the Department for a long time" and seemed out of accord with a "progressive policy for . . . the Reservation."[42] Estep had shown his true colors when he wrote "the tendency of the oil companies is to crowd the Indians pretty hard . . . and if we try to hold them back to give them time to consider it, they [oil companies] think we are trying to block their game."[43] Officials complained that Estep had given them only a five-day notice of the meeting, and since few Navajos had attended, maybe he had neglected to notify them as well.

Burke forwarded the complaint to Estep with a brusque reminder that the BIA wanted the leases approved. He recommended that Estep ask Navajos to delegate him authority to sign leases. Failing that, they might prefer to select a "representative Indian" to make decisions for them.[44] Estep resisted. No white man, even him, could influence that council. Estep reminded Washington that oil companies had hired an educated Navajo man, June Foutz, but "the Indians refused to listen to him or anyone else . . ." Navajos disdained the $45,000 bonus offered them; their main concern was not money, but fear of whites on their reservation.[45]

Still, applications continued to arrive, and newspaper editor and businessman F. G. Bonfils of Denver suggested that Navajos were really just "up in the air" regarding leases. If pressured, they might acquiesce.[46] Similarly, on August 18, Kinney Oil and Gas claimed Navajo views had softened. Exactly why Bonfils and Kinney thought this is unclear, but maybe it had something to do with a so-called business council in Fort Defiance, which had recently hinted it might approve a lease that San Juan Navajos had turned down only days earlier.

Kinney and E. T. Williams reminded Burke that they had spent $400,000 thus far. Besides, Midwest wanted them to have adjoining lands. Predictably, Burke told Estep to try one more time and reiterated the representative Indian approach. A federal employee nearing retirement, Estep obeyed, but asked for help.[47] He felt overwhelmed; he needed help controlling speculators, bootleggers, and criminals, who overran the reservation with liquor and bribes. Agents from Producers and Refiners Company had even barged into a Navajo sing to present their case.[48]

Herbert J. Hagerman, who would in 1923 take over as special agent, verified Estep's claim in a 1924 report. Applicants had indeed taken "hours and days" of Estep's time and bribed Navajos with presents. Among whites, "ninety-eight percent of the people in that vicinity [had] gone crazy. . . . Lands [had] leaped up in value" in anticipation of a boom.[49] Farmington, Gallup, and Aztec wanted oil money and wanted it badly. But Burke failed to send the assistance that Estep needed.

By September 1922, rumors began to circulate that Midwest had struck oil but shut down operations until the situation was more to the company's liking. On September 29, San Juan Navajos met one final time. They granted a single lease to Producers and Refiners Company for Tocito, about twenty-five miles south of the Hogback, but refused all others. Paradoxically, the Interior Department never approved the Tocito lease. Meanwhile, Midwest insisted that its new well lacked commercial value, and after four councils the Indian Office elected not to call a fifth. "They [the Navajos] are suspicious of putting too much power in the hands of a few," Estep warned.[50] He pleaded with Washington to let Navajos proceed at their own pace. Burke dismissed Estep on June 28, 1923, and later reassigned him to the Yakama reservation in Toppenish, Washington.[51] Six months after that, Estep wrote to Hagerman that the Yakama suffered from easy money, drink, and drugs, and he hoped money would not have the same effect on Navajos. If it did, "the oil will be a curse instead of a help to them," he added.[52]

The Fort Defiance Business Council Challenges

Unlike San Juan Navajos, those in Fort Defiance and their agent Peter Paquette favored oil leases. In 1922 Chee Dodge, Charlie Mitchell, and Dugal Chee Bekiss, all closely allied with Gallup businessmen and traders, established a business council. Dodge, for example, owned stock in the Gallup State Bank and sported an active interest in mineral resources.[53]

As previously noted, Henry Chee Dodge was a mixed-blood Navajo born about 1857. His mother disappeared during Kit Carson's Canyon de Chelly siege, and an aunt raised young Dodge. After four years at the Bosque Redondo, Dodge and his aunt returned to Fort Defiance. Dodge was a member of the *Ma'ii Deeshgizhnii* clan, suggesting that his mother was at least part Jemez. Dodge's father was never absolutely verified, but most likely was Henry L. Dodge, Indian agent to the Navajos from 1853 until his death in 1856. Dodge swore in an 1888 affidavit that his father was a white army officer; Henry Dodge's brother, Augustus C. Dodge, admitted he had a half-Navajo nephew.[54] Moreover, the army apparently believed Chee was the agent's son and encouraged the boy to attend school. Dodge learned to read and write; he spoke fluent English, Navajo, and Spanish, and in 1881 was hired as interpreter for the Fort Defiance agency. At age 24, he was appointed head chief of the Navajo tribe, reportedly by aging Navajo headman Manuelito. Indian agent D. M. Riordan paid Dodge an annual salary of $600 to represent the Navajo people.[55]

Besides affiliation with whites, other traits set Dodge apart from most Navajos. Not baptized Roman Catholic until the 1930s, Dodge was nevertheless a longtime acquaintance of Franciscan friars at the St. Michaels Mission.[56] This connection removed him from the influence of medicine men, even though he remained in touch with Navajo traditions. Dodge owned sheep and property worth over $200,000 and, like whites, considered grass, water, and stock commodities. He held interests in several Gallup businesses.[57]

Although rich Navajos were often regarded with suspicion in a society where most believed that a person could not accumulate wealth if he helped relatives as he should, Dodge lived in a white-man-style home designed by a German architect and drove a Buick.[58] Dodge has been described as arrogant with young Navajos, but paradoxically subservient in public with government officials.[59] Despite this, Navajos sought his assistance in handling disputes and respected his knowledge of white ways, suggesting that wealth alone did not always invoke Navajo hostility. Thus, oil companies clearly targeted Dodge for his assistance. He believed all Navajos should share royalties, and everyone — not just San Juan Navajos — should approve leases. Conversely, pro-oil Navajos in the San Juan area claimed that consent and revenues belonged solely to them.[60]

Oil representatives also made friends with traders who lived among the Navajos and with missionaries of various denominations. Traders, for example, possessed tremendous influence over Navajos. The economic core of the reservation, the relationship between Indian and trader was symbiotic.[61] In fact, after Midwest obtained its lease, corporate officials designated one trader as paymaster; Navajo workers were obliged to go to a single trading post to receive their paychecks. Since Navajos were often paid in scrip rather than real money, they naturally spent most of their income at that trading post as well. Traders who felt left out allied with other oil companies hoping to establish themselves on the reservation. A. B. Bouton, Producers and Refiners agent, for one, had no trouble procuring the aid of traders angry at Midwest in his quest for the Tocito land in 1922.

Missionaries played an instrumental role, too. Friars at St. Michaels, Lukachukai, and Immaculate Conception Mission at Tohatchi, strongly supported petroleum. In early 1923, they accused Protestant missionaries in San Juan of opposing oil development, although in reality Protestant Navajos were generally pro-development as well.[62] Haile criticized Estep and the Protestants for trying to "control the opinions of those Indians."[63] But it was the traditional elders who spoke most vehemently against oil leases. Furthermore, Haile and Dodge were said to have ties to Standard Oil, generating tremendous suspicion among San Juan residents.[64] The Fort Defiance interest in the oil situation created tremendous animosity between the two jurisdictions and may have encouraged Fall to rewrite regulations and establish a reservation-wide tribal council.

Fall Appoints Herbert J. Hagerman

When Navajos witnessed the "curious gyrations of white men" regarding oil and gas leases, they were said to have watched "in a polite and amused tolerance."[65] Had Navajos witnessed the machinations in Washington, they might have been less entertained. Fall grew impatient with the obstinate San Juan Navajos, especially once rumors about a Midwest oil strike began to circulate.[66] Midwest suppressed the news, however, hoping to obtain leases at discount prices for favored companies that might also utilize its refining capabilities. But local real estate men quivered in anticipation as applications flooded Estep's desk every week.[67] The pace became so hectic by late 1922 that the Bureau of Mines director suggested requiring competitive bids.[68]

Fall wired former New Mexico territorial governor Herbert J. Hagerman on his Roswell ranch in late December 1922 and offered him the position of special commissioner to negotiate with Navajo Indians. The younger of developer James J. Hagerman's two sons, Herbert was educated at Cornell University and served in the diplomatic corps in Russia in 1901–1902. As territorial governor in 1906, Hagerman's progressive ideals had alienated the Republican Old Guard like Bursum and Fall, and on March 4, 1907, the machine got him charged with land fraud. The investigative committee was comprised entirely of Hagerman foes, and President Theodore Roosevelt removed him from office.

In 1918, Hagerman became president of the New Mexico Taxpayers Association, a group devoted to tax reform, and served in that capacity until his death in 1935. At some point, Hagerman patched up differences with fellow Republicans. Why Fall selected him as special commissioner is not altogether clear, although Hagerman's account of his years in the foreign service indicates at least some interest in overseas oil development.[69] Whatever the reason, Hagerman boarded the train at Lamy, New Mexico, after New Year's Day 1923 to discuss the proposition with his former adversary.

Sequestered together in the stark Interior Department office in mid-January, Fall told Hagerman he preferred to lease the entire Navajo reservation to one responsible lessee for leisurely and well considered exploration and development under a businesslike technical program. As he puffed on a cigar, Fall paced and let Hagerman know that Midwest might be the best choice. Its president Harry Blackmer was an old friend. "Whether the idea was his or the company's, I never knew," Hagerman remarked. But he disagreed with the single lease concept, and Fall backed down with a shrug.[70]

Hagerman concurred, however, that executive order lands were indeed public domain because theoretically the president could cancel Indian tenure at any time. Fall's interpretation was the only possible one. "They [Indians] can have no other rights except the right of occupancy," both concluded.[71] Hagerman also asked Fall to draft a resolution granting some of the many leases pending on the executive order lands to "vastly facilitate my negotiation with the Indians." He added, "I could point out to them that the Government in its keeness [sic] to protect and help them had secured the passage of the resolution . . . "[72] Before he left Washington, Hagerman accepted the position.

Fall promulgated regulations on January 27, 1923, which authorized Hagerman's position and instituted a Navajo tribal council with one delegate and one alternate representing each of the six jurisdictions. Jurisdictions were to hold elections, and if they failed to do so, the secretary would appoint delegates. He could also remove or replace delegates. Council meetings were forbidden without Hagerman's express permission or outside of his presence. Hagerman was responsible for recording council actions and resolutions and sending proceedings to Washington.[73] Not surprisingly, San Juan Navajos protested Fall's scheme through Estep, who asked the Indian Office why seven thousand Navajos in the San Juan jurisdiction would get equal representation with smaller districts. Besides, the threat of removal made delegates subservient to Washington, and constant supervision discouraged debate. Estep's protest fell upon deaf ears.[74]

In March 1923, Fall resigned under the shadow of the Teapot Dome investigation. His successor, Hubert Work, reaffirmed Hagerman's appointment and revised Fall's regulations on April 24, expanding Hagerman's authority over tribal affairs, but also basing council representation on population. San Juan got three delegates, Tuba City two; Pueblo Bonito, Leupp, and Keams (Hopi) each received one; Fort Defiance acquired four. Each jurisdiction secured an equal number of non-voting alternates.[75]

Hagerman and the Navajo Tribal Council

Hagerman spent his first months on the job conducting land surveys and putting Work's regulations into motion. He encountered two major problems. First was the unrelenting assault of large oil interests, including Midwest, whose agents reportedly followed him, "snooping around hotel lobbies and elsewhere."[76] On the other hand, the independents complained bitterly about Standard Oil muscling them out of Navajo fields. As Aztec attorney George F. Bruington put it, Standard Oil intended to "buy, borrow, beg or steal all the good oil lands in this part of the country, especially on the reservations." He predicted that if Standard were allowed to "walk off with everything in sight" the resulting scandal would be "another teapot."[77]

Bruington accused Midwest of spreading misinformation about its Hogback lease. "They have two producing wells at present (if allowed to produce)," and a third that it erroneously called a dry hole because it contained water. A Standard subsidiary, its strategy was to force independents to lose interest and fool the BIA into thinking the area contained no oil. To counter such tactics, Bruington suggested that future leases be sold at public auction. Standard would refuse to pay large cash bonuses on unproven land, and even if proven, "they won't pay what its [sic] worth because the independents haven't the inside information and the money to make them do it."[78]

The Indian Office itself created problems as well. According to Hagerman, Estep's dismissal undermined his own ability to perform his duties. Navajos had liked and trusted Estep. Moreover, Hagerman seemed to think "influences in the Indian Office are after my scalp" and "throwing obstacles in the way of my accomplishing the very things you want accomplished." He further complained, "they are stacking cards so that council called by me at Toadlena July seventh can be controlled by certain large oil interests. . . . I don't know where I stand with the Indian Bureau. That Bureau [is] skating on mighty thin ice."[79] Still, Hagerman thought that many Navajos, "especially the older men are very appreciative of having someone sent to them from Washington charged with the duty of looking after their tribal affairs."[80]

The first Navajo tribal council met July 7, 1923, in Toadlena, centrally located and blessed with an abundance of spring water. The twelve delegates included three future tribal chairmen — Chee Dodge, Jacob C. (Jake) Morgan, and Deshna Clah Cheschilligi. The meeting heralded a major political change for Navajos. Never again would they be without a council. In its infancy, however, the group was associated almost exclusively with oil development, even though they discussed many other issues. Hundreds of Navajos attended council meetings, but the crowd tended to represent those who lived near the host agency. Most "ordinary" Navajos knew little, if anything, about the council, and while delegates were supposedly selected by popular vote, it is almost certain that agents chose them.[81] This is perhaps why so many boarding-school-educated men like J. C. Morgan — not the elders — represented San Juan Navajos. Cheschilligi was also educated and pro-oil.

Once assembled, Hagerman told Navajos that the government wanted them to consider oil and gas applications favorably. The reservation, he reminded them, was much larger than in 1868, but could barely support the growing population. The government, he explained, was trying hard to solve the problem, but balked at land extensions. Nevertheless, "there is a good chance to find something for you if you will cooperate with the government," Hagerman hinted. Because oil was not a sure thing, the Indian Office proposed granting several exploratory wells. Then, if companies found oil, Navajos could approve drilling leases later. Hagerman warned that if Navajos disagreed with the government, they would "suffer . . . more than any one else."[82]

Not all Navajos liked the idea. One feared drilling might prove dangerous to them and harmful to Earth. Others reminded the elders that drilling also produced water, and therefore could prove beneficial.[83] Some Navajos apparently sat quietly and allowed those who spoke English to lead the way. Chee Dodge, selected tribal chairman over the protest of San Juan Navajos, assured Hagerman, "we want to do what the government says [since] we have been under the government for years and years."[84]

Led by Dodge, Fort Defiance Navajos persuaded the new council to vote power of attorney to Hagerman, which allowed him to negotiate and sign leases on behalf of the tribe and, in essence, gave the council only "yea" or "nay" authority. Delegates directed the Secretary of the Interior to grant one lease not exceeding 4,800 acres on each oil dome or structure where there was no approved lease. Although San Juan Navajos had opposed the measure for two years, the new council approved leasing alternate 640-tracts on the Hogback adjacent to Midwest's claim.[85] Following these actions, Hagerman praised Dodge and the council: "I am delighted with the harmony and co-operation that you have shown. It rather disproves that there was anything unpleasant on this reservation."[86]

Nevertheless, hostility between San Juan and Fort Defiance bristled. Morgan protested Estep's dismissal; he eventually backed down, but Navajos remember him as perhaps the first councilman to challenge the government. Then the council tried to move on to other topics. Hagerman reported that Navajos never seemed "dazzled" by oil development on their reservation, even though they liked the idea of revenue and employment. They were, however, "very much interested in some other matters" like land purchases and "theft" of their children to attend boarding schools. Hagerman told Work, they are "looking to me to do a number of things for them which may be hard to do."[87] But, the oil business concluded, Hagerman left these issues for future councils.

Leases Sold at Public Auction

With exploratory leases approved, Work still faced an administrative nightmare — how to actually grant the leases. Midwest's Hogback strike and dissolution of the San Juan council had led to a free-for-all. Oil companies large and small continued to vie for land, and the *Dallas News* noted derisively, "this is how government disposes of mineral rights of the Osage."[88] Companies no longer besieged tribal delegates, however; most petitioned Hagerman, while others went to higher authorities. All demanded priority consideration. Kinney Oil and Gas, for example, met with Work and claimed that Navajos had never formally denied its application. A public auction, the company argued, would destroy its rights, cautioning that there were "too many opportunities to drill on proven structures to waste time and money on a wildcat structure."[89] Moreover, it had shared the expense of geological work and mapping with Midwest and deserved priority consideration.

On July 30, 1923, H. C. Bretschneider, formerly with Midwest Oil and now operating as an independent, visited Fall in retirement at his Three Rivers Ranch near Tularosa to request the Rattlesnake structure.[90] Bretschneider reasoned that although he had filed applications on behalf of Midwest, now that company no longer sought leases, and he should be considered the original applicant. Bretschneider insisted that he possessed adequate personal funds to comply with lease terms and also protested distributing leases at public auction.[91]

Ohio Company, another Standard subsidiary, demanded priority on the Rattlesnake structure. Similarly, Inca Oil Company wanted special consideration on Table Mesa. Its attorneys warned that since Inca was a New Mexico-owned firm, the state pioneers might feel discriminated against if Navajo acreage went solely to out-of-state companies.[92]

Despite all of these arguments, the Interior Department eventually determined that leases would be awarded at public auction. Even Hagerman at first questioned the fairness of an auction; he also criticized the limitations that such a method imposed upon the government's ability to control who acquired leases, determine the best qualified, and prevent monopoly. Only the latecomers and those companies and individuals hoping to evade regulations would benefit, he claimed. Besides, the early applicants had offered large bonuses, a rarity in wildcat territory.

In addition, Hagerman worried that Navajos and oil companies might change their minds altogether. Ohio Company, for instance, had already threatened to leave New Mexico entirely in case of an auction, and Producers and Refiners was "very depressed" about the whole situation.[93] On September 9, Hagerman's assistant, Mark D. Radcliffe, wrote that in his opinion the various companies had joined together to discourage development and reduce bids on the different structures.[94] The Indian Office scheduled the public auction for October 15 anyway.

Compounding these problems, Hagerman possessed no surveys or maps of the structures to be leased. In fact, as late as September, nobody even knew if the Hogback consisted of one or two structures.[95] The science of geology, of course, was still in its early years, and not until the mid-1920s did European scientists devise new geophysical methods to detect underground deposits of oil and natural gas. In 1923, geologists were largely anticline hunters, and only the largest companies employed them or knew how to utilize their skills. Despite all of the excitement over oil leases, Bureau of Mines geologist K. B. Nowels had time to give Navajo territory merely a cursory examination.[96] His report released October 15—the day of the auction—covered only the Hogback.[97]

One month before the auction, Hagerman told Ralph C. Ely of Cleveland, Ohio, that no structural maps of the area existed except a blueprint of the Hogback.[98] The only available reports, Hagerman noted, were a 1913 professional paper by Herbert E. Gregory titled "Geology of the Navajo Country"—a study of local water supplies—and Bulletin 726-E by the U.S. Geological Survey.

Thomas Gorman of Delmar Oil voiced the concern of many oil men when he announced "the principal objection that we see to bidding on these tracts at this time is the fact that the bidder has no means of knowing the locations of the structure unless his own organization would go out there and make a geological survey."[99] Radcliffe made several attempts to map structures prior to the auction, but the job was largely piecemeal. Only oil firms like Midwest Company and Metropolitan (soon to be Santa Fe Company)—both of which spent large amounts of money to survey—had any inkling as to what might lie underground.[100]

Yet another problem had surfaced. During the past year, the oil industry had overcome its previous shortage problem. Now, large strikes in California created a glut of petroleum on the American market and a 50 percent decline in oil prices.[101] William M. Davis, president of Midcontinent Oil and Gas Association, wrote on the eve of the sale to warn Hagerman that the auction could plunge prices even lower. Production remained high throughout the entire country, and to make matters worse, the industry was entering its slow season with over a million gallons in storage. Davis compared the oil industry to a patient running a temperature of 105 degrees who insists "upon getting up every time there was a drop of one half a degree or even less in his temperature."[102] To open Navajo land at this time went against the welfare of the Indian owners as well.

Regardless, the auction proceeded as planned, and there is no indication that Hagerman relayed the Oil and Gas Association's concerns to anybody. Commissioner Burke arrived in Santa Fe to take charge personally; Hagerman assisted. A telegram sent to Secretary Work the day of the auction announced the sale of four exploratory leases on Rattlesnake, Tocito, and Table Mesa, and several tracts on the Hogback.[103] Pleased, Work rewarded Hagerman a week later with a new Buick Six, claiming, "It is hardly fair to pay a man a salary of $5,000 a year and ask him to wear out a $5,000 car in the service."[104]

John Collier, executive secretary of the American Indian Defense Association — organized to fight the notorious Bursum Bill on behalf of the New Mexico Pueblos — praised Hagerman so highly that Work finally quipped, "When you read it [his press release] you will think possibly that he is your 'long-lost brother.'"[105] So, although nonexistent in 1921, by October 1923 a Navajo tribal council was in place, and government had presided over the first auction of oil leases on the reservation. Oil companies had finally succeeded in imposing their will onto Navajos.

3 THE FIRST NAVAJO OIL BOOM, 1923–1927

When archaeologist Alfred Vincent Kidder climbed the tall rocks above Gobernador Wash in 1917, he found remains of Navajo hogans and Pueblo pottery mingled together. He had unearthed the hiding place of Pueblos who took refuge when the Spanish returned from exile after the 1680 Pueblo revolt. Similarly, Hopis joined Navajos during long periods of drought. Indians seemed to be able to live with each other for a while, then separate, having mixed their blood, but maintained a kind of organic integrity. The same can not be said of Europeans whose approach to life included low tolerance for difference and a belief that land was theirs to conquer.[1]

The auction over, local whites in Farmington and Aztec eagerly awaited the oil boom they felt certain would follow. Headlines predicted "Two Million Barrels of Oil" and anticipated a city reaching from the mouth of the La Plata River to the Hogback field within twenty-five years.[2] Albuquerque businessmen clamored for railroad links to the San Juan Basin before Denver or Salt Lake City procured the all-important lines.[3] The Indian Oil Leasing Act of May 1924 amended the 1891 law, made public auctions the law of the land regarding Indian leases, and extended lease periods from ten years to "so long as oil and gas are found in paying quantities."

Navajos, however, remained ambivalent. Most viewed themselves as caretakers of their land and believed that if they did not live in harmony with it, the Glittering World like those before might be destroyed.[4] To disturb the land was to hasten the loss of Navajo culture, stories, and spirituality. Unless they lived near leased structures, of course, it was unlikely that ordinary Navajos were even aware of oil. In 1923, most simply herded sheep and grew corn. Although impoverished by white standards, they survived independently of government handouts. So it can be said that when the tribal council voted in favor of development, it did not necessarily reflect the wishes of the Navajo people. Still, as intrusive as petroleum might have seemed, it had advantages.

Navajos needed land, irrigation, and improved health care; Bureau of Indian Affairs (BIA) officials insisted that oil income could buy all of these.

Yet oil markets remained distant and required a laborious mountain haul over narrow-gauge railroad to reach outlets in Alamosa or Durango, Colorado.[5] No oil pipelines existed, and the unstable nature of Navajo crude made their construction expensive. Even though companies believed the reservation contained valuable oil deposits, corporate officials had no idea if the region would, in fact, prove profitable. Thus, 1923 to 1927 was a period of experimentation for Navajos, industry, and government. Companies struggled to maximize profits, Hagerman tried to control operations, and Navajos fought for the right to utilize income as they saw fit even as they eyed the growing number of *bilagáanas* with trepidation and worried that the environment might suffer. By the time the problems began to work themselves out, the oil boom ended.

Navajos Resolve: "All Royalties to the Tribe"

Robert Young, a leading Navajo scholar and longtime BIA employee, says early council delegates were generally chosen by superintendents and usually from among Navajos living near the agencies. If agents held elections at all, these were monitored to make sure only select Navajos won.[6] This view seems to reinforce two notions. First, having found something they wanted on Indian land, whites resorted to their old tactics of identifying Indians who would approve the scheme and influence the rest to go along, always careful to couch demands in terms of what was best for Navajos.

The second conclusion is that the first tribal councils accomplished little. It is true that like many other Indians, Navajos had long since discovered it was easier to put up with what white men arranged than to fight. Navajos also disliked making quick decisions—as whites wanted them to do—without discussing issues with families and clans.[7] Nevertheless, councils in the 1920s made some tremendous gains and learned much that would later prove useful. At first, Navajos appeared to give obligatory consent to government schemes, but in other ways, Navajos clearly voiced views on a variety of topics. Although oil was the only matter of importance to Washington, the same was not true of the delegates.

Factions surfaced immediately, but served as one means of debate and compromise. Delegates elected Dodge chairman over the vehement objection of San Juan delegates, clearly a continuation of jurisdictional rivalry.[8] Dodge, however, was quick to blame disputes on "others" and asked officials not to think "we only hold meetings for the purpose of quarreling among ourselves."[9] Ironically, whites saw Indian factions as proof of childlike behavior; in Congress such altercations were symbols of sophisticated politics at work.

When San Juan delegates realized that they could not keep oil revenues to themselves, one of the Shiprock "troublemakers," Deshna Clah Cheschilligi, made an immensely important proposal: he asked that Navajos hold oil and gas rights in common rather than distribute income on a per capita basis, possibly to keep the money out of wealthy Navajo hands. As one condition of sharing tribal benefits, Cheschilligi even demanded that allottees agree, which they did unanimously.[10] This resolution — and because Navajo income was small — protected Navajos from the type of abuse heaped upon Osages of Oklahoma after 1919. There, whites purchased or leased Indian land, then joined with oil producers to seize control. Whites who were appointed guardians of native "wards" confiscated approximately $8 million of their money. Moreover, white men lay in wait to marry Osage women, leading to a plot uncovered by the FBI in which several men contracted to have their wives, children, and in-laws murdered to collect their land and oil.[11] It is noteworthy that a Gallup newspaper advised Navajos to restrict intermarriage and permit no white to "establish tribal relationship by fictitious means."[12]

The choice to relegate funds to the tribe rather than on a per capita basis to individuals served as the financial core of the future Navajo Nation government. It is interesting, but probably not surprising, that Hagerman took credit for Cheschilligi's resolution: "They realize (perhaps I helped them see it) that to divide these funds on a per capita basis amongst 30,000 Indians would be a perfectly futile thing."[13]

Cheschilligi was himself a full-blood Navajo whose name meant roughly "left-handed man with curly hair." He worked in a Shiprock trading post in the early 1920s and later purchased a filling station and garage. He served as interpreter for Albert H. Kneale, Shiprock district Indian agent from 1923 to 1929. Anthropologist and director of the Eastern Association on Indian Affairs, Oliver La Farge called Deshna a "remarkable example of an Indian breaking away from the ordinary cattle and sheep raising restrictions and going to a better industry."[14] One of fifteen children, Cheschilligi had received an education in Fort Lewis, Colorado, yet maintained his Navajo ways. He was maternal great-uncle to future chairman Peter MacDonald.[15] Fellow San Juan delegate J. C. Morgan strongly maintained that only San Juan Navajos should profit from the oil money since they alone lived on the oil-producing land and had to put up with the intrusions. This sentiment was, of course, an extension of the old Fort Defiance and San Juan animosity. Morgan also claimed that Navajos needed job opportunities as much if not more than they needed sheep. Born in 1879 near Crownpoint, New Mexico, Morgan was the son of "uneducated traditionals." He recalled that as a youth he accompanied his parents to Fort Defiance, where he met a Navajo schoolboy dressed in a shirt, trousers, boots, and wide-brim hat. Young Jake had felt ashamed of his moccasins, white muslin trousers, homemade shirt, and hatless head.[16] Taken from his family, he went to boarding schools in New Mexico and Colorado, then to Hampton Institute in Virginia. When he returned home, his family barely knew him, and he remained an outsider. Morgan joined the Christian Reformed Church, and his religious zeal reinforced the desire to shed ancestral ways for those of the white world.

It has been theorized that because Navajos placed so little intrinsic value on white schooling, the able Navajo child with an aptitude for herding—hence an economic unit in the family—was kept at home. When forced by the Indian Office to send children to school, Navajos sent what they considered the "weaker, less intelligent" ones. When these children reappeared years later, they returned almost as foreigners, profoundly alienated.[17] Many returned students owned no land or livestock and were, therefore, poor by Navajo standards. Hence, the tribal council gave these isolated, former boarding-school students a voice, and they willingly organized around Morgan.[18]

Factions and the Tribal Council

In 1925, the council appropriated funds to each of the six jurisdictions according to the formula used to determine council representation—Fort Defiance would receive four parts of the money; San Juan three; Western Navajo two; and Eastern, Leupp, and Keams Canyon one part each. Council delegates and agents from each jurisdiction would determine how to spend these funds.[19]

The unresolved status of executive order lands haunted Navajos as much as it did whites. The problem was compounded when in 1911 President Taft rescinded the executive order withdrawal made by President Roosevelt in 1907, returning the land to the public domain.[20] Thus, Navajos backed BIA efforts to pressure Congress for a ruling. Many feared the government would take more executive order lands from them altogether, prompting Dodge to ask for clear title: "Try to see if Congress will not do something about this so they won't be scared all the time that they are going to take the land away from them." Some on the council offered to divide oil money with states on a fifty-fifty basis if necessary; others preferred sending a delegation to Washington to discuss options, a request that Hagerman denied.[21] Before turning to other matters, delegates denounced Hagerman's plea to amend Midwest Company's lease from a term of ten years to "as long as oil or gas shall be found in paying quantities," in order to comply with the Indian Oil Leasing Act.[22]

The oil discussion finished, Navajos turned to livestock issues and argued over building day schools to replace off-reservation boarding facilities. Although disagreement was normal in Anglo politics, Navajos traditionally debated issues to a consensus even if that meant coming to no final decision for months — or at all. Annual councils did not provide for such a method, and it cannot be stressed enough that these meetings represented the first time in years — if ever — that Navajos had met as a tribe to resolve reservation-wide matters. An absence of factions and differences of opinion would have been surprising.

Beyond jurisdictional animosity, religious divisions and missionary involvement created factions. Ministers agreed, "If [Christian] Navajos were asked by a white person what his religion was, the reply would either be Catholic or Protestant," but the situation was far more complicated.[23] Medicine men played a major role, too, as did a growing number of peyotists.[24] Especially in Arizona and Utah, there were Mormon Navajos as well. Some Protestants were intolerant of each other. For example, Shiprock boarding-school students were divided between denominations for religious instruction. One Presbyterian minister claimed that if any assigned to the Christian Reformed Church inadvertently went to his church, Morgan "would be right at my doorstep or I'd have a letter from him." Mrs. Morgan "was even more suspicious and bitter" than her husband.[25] Complicating matters further, in 1924, Mennonites announced a new mission.[26] And in several instances, Cheschilligi protested the presence of Catholic priests in council meetings.[27]

Wealth, language, and degree of assimilation divided delegates. Some, like Dodge, owned large sheep herds and controlled hundreds of acres. Others were wage workers. George Bancroft from Western Navajo district was a truck driver with a mail contract for his region. Educated Navajos usually advocated education and business opportunities for Navajos, but did not always oppose measures to increase Navajo grazing lands. A few on the council spoke English; most spoke only Navajo. Compounding these differences were, of course, personality clashes.

Navajo Funds versus Reimbursable Debt

The year 1926 brought additional problems. Navajos discovered that $100,000 of their oil funds was earmarked to build a bridge over the San Juan River at Lee's Ferry, Arizona, a project Cheschilligi dubbed "the Grand Canyon hole" beneficial to "congressmen and a few tourists."[28] Virtually no Navajos would ever use the bridge, but the structure opened a convenient automobile route to the Grand Canyon for tourists and greatly benefited the Fred Harvey Company, which owned concessions there.

The predicament went back to 1914, when Congress had authorized irrigation projects on Indian reservations paid by the federal government with the understanding that these projects might one day be reimbursed from tribal funds.[29] Eventually, projects went beyond irrigation. On February 26, 1926, the bridge was authorized by Congress; on March 4, Congress charged

$100,000 to Navajos, with the understanding that Arizona would pay an equal amount. Secretary Work praised the bridge as an important outlet for the Navajo Indians.[30]

John Collier, however, accused the government of looting Indian funds, and when Matthew K. Sniffen, secretary of the Indian Rights Association, visited the proposed construction site, he found not a single Navajo living within twenty-five miles. Sniffen argued that Work's "important outlet" went into a region that has "never interested them and never will." Once the bridge was built, he noted, it would be necessary to construct a $300,000 road, since there was no approach to the site. Sniffen discovered, too, that the few whites in that region were notoriously hostile to Indians.[31] Collier added sarcastically that the only "civilizing" influence would be in "sitting on the banks and watching the Fords and Packards cross the bridge, if indeed, the Indians cared to go a hundred miles or so to watch the spectacle."[32]

Commissioner Burke defended the reimbursable portion of the project to Congress as he wrote to Navajos via Hagerman, promising to spend tribal moneys for tribal purposes, specifically the breeding up of native sheep, agriculture, and water development.[33] But Assistant Commissioner Meritt noted that Navajos should help pay for the bridge because Arizona "lost many thousands of dollars each year due to the nontaxable status of Navajo land."[34] Hagerman told Navajos not to worry even as Calvin Coolidge signed the bill into law. Both Dodge and Morgan made it very clear that they opposed using tribal funds for the bridge, and Morgan proposed that hereafter Navajos approve — or at least be consulted regarding — all appropriations.[35]

But the reimbursable debt continued to grow. The *Santa Fe New Mexican* noted in April 1926 that $771,000 was chalked up against Navajos and assumed more would be liquidated out of future income. Hagerman had to admit, "Congress has been in the habit for a good many years of making appropriations 'reimbursable' out of Indian funds."[36] In fact, the Navajos were charged $21,606 for several off-reservation bridges, $4,000 for bridge repair, and $91,995 for a road from Gallup to Mesa Verde.[37] Navajos protested. The government had always financed projects on the condition that they be "good Indians." They had kept their end of the bargain since 1868, and government should forgive the debt.[38]

Nevertheless, another bridge — the Bloomfield Bridge, which lay entirely off the reservation — was added, evidence to Navajos that the Indian Office was eager to loot their funds while neglecting education, health, and economic development. What Navajos did not know was that Burke already entertained the idea that if the tribe "should happen to come into great wealth, they could afford then to have taken from their funds sufficient to reimburse the government for the construction of [other] bridges," thus pretty much guaranteeing that Navajos would never become self-sufficient.[39] Reformers aimed a scathing attack at Burke's administration and accused Congress of acting as the BIA's willing partner in the scheme.[40] By 1927 the debt was nearly $900,000, and the cost was eventually apportioned to the various districts and paid out of oil funds.

In 1926, Chee Dodge asked that future oil auctions be held closer to the reservation so Navajos might attend and observe: "It is very disturbing to the Indians not to be able to see first hand the way their lands are handled at the sales." He requested that the special commissioner relocate his office to Gallup or Farmington, adding "To [Navajos], he might as well be in the far East as Santa Fe . . ."[41] Burke countered that a Santa Fe auction was convenient for oil companies. Hagerman pleaded that his work on the Pueblo Lands Board and the need to travel frequently precluded moving his headquarters.

Hagerman had the unenviable task of asking Navajos to extend the terms of five leases. He requested a resolution altering the length of time from ten years to "so long as oil and gas is produced in paying quantities" as he had done in 1925 with Midwest's lease. Oil companies pressed hard for the change, claiming there was little inducement to invest in expensive extraction and stabilization equipment or conservation measures under leases with less than $7\frac{1}{2}$ years to run.[42]

Aware that delegates were hesitant to alter leases, especially when presented as five separate leases and each one written in quadruplicate, Hagerman combined them. His goal was to obtain three signed originals and photostat them. Then he would certify all as "official."[43] Burke reminded Hagerman that under the 1924 law he could grant extensions without council approval, but added it was probably best to get Navajo consent since "it is desirable to have them feel that they are being consulted from time to time with reference to their tribal interests."[44]

Angry over the reimbursable debt, Navajos debated, then Dodge announced that leases would stand unchanged.[45] What occurred afterward is clouded. The minutes clearly reveal the Navajo refusal; Hagerman even wrote that "at the Tribal Council held on July 7, 1925, the Indians objected to the passage of such a resolution . . ." Yet, Hagerman's transmittal letter sent along with the council minutes states that a blanket stipulation for Midwest, Santa Fe Company, Continental, Gypsy Company, J. C. Bailey, and Navajo Company leases was included.[46] No doubt Hagerman followed Burke's advice and took it upon himself to approve the lease extensions.

Competing Oil Legislation

Still another controversy was brewing in 1926. Congressman Carl Hayden introduced legislation to solve the matter of executive order lands and provide a Congressional solution to the contradictory Attorney General and court decisions, especially since the 1924 Indian Oil Leasing Act did not address executive order land. The Hayden bill initiated a huge debate. It proposed that all leases fall under the jurisdiction of the Oil Leasing Act. In lieu of a production tax, 37½ percent of rents, bonuses, and royalties would go to states and be used for roads within the reservation or educating Indian children in public schools. The legislation reinstated the 425 exploratory permits granted by Fall and placed them under the 1891 Indian Leasing Act, which meant if any of these companies struck oil they would pay only 5 percent royalties.

Two competing bills emerged. One written by Senator Andrieus A. Jones, a New Mexico Democrat, placed executive order lands under the General Leasing Act and granted only 52½ percent to Indians. Sam Bratton, another Democrat from New Mexico, introduced the other bill, which put executive order leases under the 1924 law and allowed 62½ percent to the Indians, but removed the strings attached to the state's percentage. Of the three proposed pieces of legislation, the BIA supported Hayden's bill because, according to Collier, Burke feared Navajos would end up losing all royalties on executive order land otherwise.[47] Hayden's plan, he reasoned, was the best they could expect, and it solved the issue once and for all.[48]

Hagerman's testimony before the Senate Committee on Indian Affairs raised eyebrows, however. He endorsed Fall's 1923 interpretation as the correct one, and stated that the BIA should consent to the royalty split. Most controversial, Hagerman claimed he could get Navajos to agree to the bill without much trouble, and in fact, he said they would probably surrender 50 percent.[49] It is true that in 1925 Dodge had agreed to a fifty-fifty split with states or even to relinquish subsurface rights on executive order land altogether in exchange for clear title. But Hagerman did not specifically ask them about the Hayden bill or any of the others. It is noteworthy that the New Mexico Taxpayers Association supported the bill, and Hagerman was its president. The American Indian Defense Association questioned Hagerman's motives, and later the special commissioner admitted to a Senate subcommittee that he had never even read the bill.[50]

Ralph H. Cameron (R-AZ) eventually introduced a substitute bill that placed executive order lands under the Indian Oil Leasing Act of 1924, gave Indians 100 percent of the royalties, but subjected the money to a state production tax. Coolidge vetoed the bill on July 2, 1926, and on March 3, 1927, signed an amended Cameron bill called the Indian Oil Act, which additionally prohibited future alteration of executive order boundaries. The Hayden legislation and the Lee's Ferry Bridge discussions were conducted almost simultaneously; Hayden used the bridge issue as part of his election bid for the Senate.

Government agreed to consult with Navajos regarding royalties and their use, with Congress, of course, having the final word.[51] The legislation was on one hand a victory for Navajos since it acknowledged the importance of tribal input and awarded them all royalties. On the other hand, it was considered a triumph for oil interests in the San Juan Basin because the act settled the executive order question and allowed operators on government land to compete more easily with off-reservation developers.[52]

Chee Dodge Lobbies Congress

By 1927, factions continued to battle over how to spend revenues, and land was at the center of this controversy. In January, and against his better judgment, Hagerman gave Dodge permission to take a Navajo delegation to Washington to discuss purchasing new land using oil proceeds. Hagerman admitted, "personally I think it is rather foolish for them to go there at this time, but I also believe it would be unwise to advise them not to do so if they have their hearts set on it." The excluded council members grew enraged when they discovered that Hagerman had allowed Dodge to use tribal funds to pay the delegation's expenses "if [they did] not stay too long."[53]

Hagerman neither accompanied the group—professing he had already spent too much time in Washington and wanted to return to New Mexico—nor did he bother to wait for them to arrive before heading home. From the time the group boarded the train at Lamy, Hagerman heard criticism. Why were only pro-land-extension Navajos and agents asked along?[54] Navajos also learned that once in Washington, Dodge asked Congress for a $1 million loan to purchase public domain land and pledged to repay it in $50,000 annual installments taken from oil revenues. He furthermore offered to surrender all mineral rights on this land. By the July tribal council meeting, delegates were still fuming.

Incensed by what he saw as a blatant misuse of authority, Morgan confronted Dodge at the July 7–8 council meeting, with some six hundred Navajos attending.[55] "Did you forget," he snapped, "that the council passed a resolution in 1926 setting aside 50 percent of all oil and gas royalties to pay for land, but the Indian Office reduced the amount to 20 percent? How could the tribe commit more royalty money than the government allowed?" Besides, Dodge had gone behind council's back; he had sacrificed mineral rights without negotiation. "When I buy a suit of clothes, I do not buy [the] coat alone but I insist the vest and pants go with it," Morgan chided.[56]

Hagerman no doubt shifted uneasily in his seat and tried to explain that the delegation had really been a waste of time: besides, the bill was almost surely headed for defeat in Congress. Furthermore, "the income from oil to the Navajos will average around $500 a day or $15,000 a month," not enough to repay a million-dollar loan. In fact, total receipts for the previous year amounted to only $560,596. The balance after expenses was a mere $446,992, and reimbursable indebtedness, "including the cost of six bridges (Lee's Ferry among them) was $900,000."[57] Many leases were already abandoned, and drilling on Little Shiprock and Bitlabito — both auctioned in 1926 — was delayed. "If [you] have an idea that there may be several million dollars available for purchasing new lands . . . [you] are mistaken," Hagerman told the council.

Hagerman also cautioned council members to think of the tribe as a whole, not just the wishes of a few individuals.[58] Ironically, in June, Hagerman had informed Burke that $10,000 of the moneys earmarked for Western Navajo District alone and turned over to Agent Robinson had apparently been utilized, but "what he has done with it we don't know. It appears a good deal of it has been spent around Kayenta." Hagerman added that in general he believed agents frittered away much of the Indian money, making it even more difficult for Navajos to commit sums for specific projects or tribal desires.[59]

Dodge, however, stood his ground. Crownpoint Navajos were desperate for land. In fact, all Navajos needed additional pasture. Responding to accusations that he wanted the land for himself, Dodge explained to Hagerman, "It [was] not my idea that those lands should be purchased at any particular point but that the Indian Office and you would select them." Business experience, he claimed, had taught him that land was a sound investment, and tribal animosity arose purely from a misunderstanding of the purpose behind this plan.[60]

By the conclusion of the 1927 council meeting, Navajos reluctantly consented to set aside 25 percent of annual royalties to pay off the $1 million debt should Congress approve Dodge's bill; the Indian Office again reduced the amount to 20 percent. Because Morgan remained unreconciled to using such a large sum for land when Navajos needed water, reservoirs, sawmills, doctors, farm equipment, and trade schools, council members also designated a $10,000 revolving fund to build homes. In the end, Congress tabled the bill altogether.[61]

Hagerman Faces Growing Problems

In 1928, Meritt conducted the tribal council meeting in Hagerman's absence. A voting discrepancy in the Southern District resulted in two delegates, both claiming legitimacy. Navajos rejected Meritt's patronizing suggestion that each delegate get one-half vote and seated the individual they deemed most qualified. Moreover, many conservatives and elders won in the 1928 elections, so instead of education and boarding schools, these men favored land acquisition.[62] Also in 1928, Dodge's four-year term as chairman ended, and delegates elected Deshna Clah Cheschillgi to replace him.

Navajos discovered that oil prices were dropping nationwide. Companies had curtailed production, and from June 1927 to June 1928, the tribe made only $70,000. Burke had already informed Dodge that future oil funds would probably be insufficient to acquire much additional land, so Navajos should not count on obtaining new grazing areas. The council argued that there were perhaps many more promising oil tracts, but reluctantly admitted that low prices meant waning interest in oil overall. In a letter to the *Farmington Republican*, Cheschilligi admitted that of all leases auctioned in 1926, only one tract was drilled. Under these conditions, maybe "the action of the Government in refraining from offering further acreage for lease at the present time [is] wise." [63]

It is necessary to say a few words about Herbert J. Hagerman, whose role as special commissioner placed him frequently between Navajo needs and Indian Office demands. Hagerman served as liaison between Navajos, oil companies, missionaries, traders, and locals. He oversaw leasing and production and transmitted data, including royalty statements, to the Interior Department. Hagerman finalized pipeline and refinery plans with corporate officials and mediated controversies between oil companies and government. Hagerman administered BIA programs and coordinated the six agencies.

Headquartered in Santa Fe, Hagerman seemed to prefer his trips to Washington, California, and Colorado, and his stays in luxury hotels like the Hotel del Coronado in San Diego, to reservation visits. Several times, he questioned whether local agents could not do his job as well.[64] In all fairness, Hagerman appears to have received inconsistent support from the BIA. For one thing, he was repeatedly forced to rely on outdated geological information. Also, once drilling began, the government trusted the oil companies to provide accurate production and royalty data and created no monitoring mechanism. Hagerman often doubted the accuracy of company reports, but had trouble obtaining information to counter them. It is likely that Hagerman kept tribal councils ignorant because he simply had no answers. On the other hand, Hagerman was a man who liked to avoid what he called "unpleasantness."

John Collier at first praised the special commissioner and then severely censured his performance. Collier accused Hagerman of practically giving away two of the most promising oil structures—Beautiful Mountain and Rattlesnake—to Albuquerque attorney Neill B. Field and S. C. Muñoz, president of Metropolitan Oil Company (he later incorporated the Santa Fe Company to deal with the Rattlesnake lease) for minimum bids of $1,000. Hagerman, however, blamed Midwest. The low bids, he argued, came at least in part because Midwest had withheld information and neglected to conduct deep well tests as the government requested. The company's fourth well, begun just a few weeks before the sale, struck water one day before the auction, and the negative publicity, Hagerman estimated, lost the Navajos between $50,000 and $75,000 in bonuses.[65] Other tracts sold for minimum bids as well, including two 640-acre leases adjacent to the proven Hogback, which went for $500 and $600 respectively. Nobody raised questions about these, Hagerman protested.[66]

A major obstacle was that Midwest tended to slow operations whenever it wanted something. The company halted production in 1923 after Navajos denied them a blanket lease to the reservation and again when the Interior Department put tracts adjacent to its Hogback field up for bid instead of persuading Navajos to simply sign them over to friendly companies as desired.[67] Midwest continually tried to circumvent regulations. To obtain more than two 4,800-acre leases on Indian land in one state — against government rules — Midwest argued that its Ute Dome site in New Mexico only produced natural gas, and therefore was not specifically oil property. Again in 1925, officials held up deep well tests to pressure for an extension of lease terms.

Hagerman worried that Midwest's antics might discourage other companies — especially independent drillers — from deep testing, the only way to determine the extent of Navajo oil deposits. Smaller and less financially secure operators could decide that deep tests were too expensive or even abandon leases altogether.[68] Hagerman took steps after the auction to make sure everyone possessed adequate revenues. He even rejected several, including the tract awarded to his controversial friend Neill B. Field, with whom Hagerman had participated in the Santa Fe social whirl during his days as governor.[69]

In general, independent companies needed to strike oil quickly and lacked the financial capability to endure long dry periods. Nearly all the oil drilled on Navajo land in the 1920s was found in very shallow sands, sometimes less than 500 feet. Small operators were likely to take what they could and leave the rest untested. Companies like Midwest resented the rapid drilling schedules imposed on them by federal leases, but could afford to deep test. So, Hagerman sometimes faced a dilemma.

Another challenge was transportation. One narrow-gauge railroad served the entire Four Corners region. Roads were insufficient. Markets were distant. Companies at first hired independent contractors to truck oil from sites. Hal Nabors, who in 1924 at the age of twelve helped his father haul oil from Rattlesnake's first well, claimed that roads were passable only in good weather. "It was largely build your own road with a pick and shovel many, many times . . . [with] mud all the way up to the axle."[70]

One option was, of course, a Gallup-to-Shiprock road, but that took time and money. Another was the extension of railroad lines to the region. For the first few years, this was a primary goal. Muñoz, whose Santa Fe Company obtained the Rattlesnake lease, accused New Mexicans of being asleep regarding potential oil wealth and told businessmen that they were far too slow when it came to authorizing railroad lines.[71] Albuquerque, not Denver or Salt Lake City, should become the oil capital of the region, he claimed.[72]

Finally, in 1926, rumors predicted a new Bernalillo-to-Farmington railroad line, but the plan never came to fruition.[73] The New Mexico Oil Men's Association complained that existing rates made shipping oil out of state to be refined cheaper than processing the crude in New Mexico. Such a situation had similarly retarded development of the lumber, wool, and beef industries for years.[74] Because of transportation problems, Standard Oil distributed gasoline to filling stations along the narrow gauge or sold the product for four cents per gallon to Farmington-area residents, who claimed it had more pep than the thirty-cents-per-gallon petroleum.[75] Bumper stickers boasted "This car burns Hogback crude." When the companies stopped selling oil "straight from the well," Farmington's Civic Club protested the move as "unfair to Navajos and the residents of the Basin."[76] In 1923, daily airline service began operating from Aztec to Albuquerque, financed by W. R. DeHart of Aztec, who had an interest in oil land on the reservation. This service transported only oil representatives, not oil, and oil companies needed another alternative. Pipelines seemed to provide the solution.

Pipelines and Refineries

Oil companies were eager to build pipelines. Midwest completed its first pipeline from the Hogback to Farmington on August 15, 1924. From pipelines, oil was loaded onto railroad cars and shipped via narrow gauge to Salt Lake City for refining. On December 5, Midwest announced that it had purchased fifteen acres in Farmington for a small refinery, but in the months that followed, the company experienced lengthy delays in obtaining the materials to build its plant.

On October 10, 1924, Muñoz announced five producing wells on Rattlesnake and revealed that Mutual Oil—a Standard Oil subsidiary (later Continental Oil) and the largest distributor of gasoline in the Rocky Mountain area—had purchased one-half interest in the two hundred producing acres of his lease. This purchase gave rise to speculation that Santa Fe Company had merely served as the "dummy" for Standard Oil and that accusations against Hagerman regarding the $1,000 bid were true.[77] The purchase price was $300,000. As part of the deal, Mutual agreed to build a refinery in Farmington and construct a pipeline to connect Rattlesnake with the new refining operations.[78] This line was completed March 15, 1925, and began operations on April 1. In 1926, Mutual erected a crude on-site stabilizing plant and refinery as well.

The two companies also split responsibilities and expenses; Mutual Oil handled drilling operations and kept production and financial accounts on the two hundred acres involved, while Santa Fe Company tested the remaining property. The arrangement created a corporate structure similar to Midwest's, whereby oil sales were internal and closed to outside scrutiny. By June 1926, Muñoz sold one-half of the entire 4,800-acre lease to Continental (previously Mutual) for more than $3 million. Thereafter, Continental managed production on the structure and completed a pipeline between the Rattlesnake and Hogback sites.[79]

Local businesses lauded pipelines and refineries as signs of progress. But these were hardly built on the grand scale that Secretary Fall had anticipated back in December 1922, when he told the El Paso Chamber of Commerce that pipelines and railroad extensions would cost "a tremendous sum" and entice "big men," not the "little fellow," to New Mexico.[80]

Meanwhile, Hagerman struggled to get Midwest and the others to deep test, warning Midwest in 1924, "the extent of the pool within your leasehold is . . . still a matter of doubt."[81] The refinery, he said, might prove a mistake since there were only eight wells sunk and these located in shallow sands. Hagerman repeatedly cautioned that the Hogback might contain fewer than two million barrels, scarcely enough for a line, let alone a refinery.[82]

Nevertheless, others in the San Juan Basin viewed pipeline construction as confirmation that oil was about to boom. Of course, elsewhere in the United States, pipelines denoted monopoly. Standard Oil had once used its extensive pipeline network to negotiate secret railroad rate agreements and to strengthen its domination of the industry by denying access to inexpensive transportation. Consequently, the Hepburn Act of January 4, 1906, stipulated that "all pipelines be made common carriers subject to Interstate Commerce Commission (ICC) regulation," and thereby reduced Standard's advantage.[83]

But pipelines in northwest New Mexico did not span more than seventy miles and were limited in size to three or four inches, hardly the massive lines built in Texas, Oklahoma, and Kansas and targeted by the ICC.[84] Even so, the reservation pipelines had their own peculiarities. As Hagerman noted in September 1926, Santa Fe Company and Continental owned a pipeline from their Rattlesnake site to Midwest's Hogback operation. Part of the crude was shipped to Hogback, then combined with Hogback crude and sent to Farmington, where the companies owned a small refinery. Another pipeline, also jointly owned, went from Rattlesnake to Gallup ninety-four miles away, where it was shipped via railroad to refineries in Texas and elsewhere. Thus, although small, these pipelines provided important alternatives to narrow-gauge railroad transportation and trucks.[85]

Whether carried in pipelines, railroad cars, or trucks, Rattlesnake and Hogback crude presented significant problems. Rattlesnake crude was seventy-four degrees gravity (average was thirty-two to thirty-six degrees) and had to be stabilized before being placed into railroad cars or pipelines. Light amber in color, resembling apple-cider vinegar as it came from the well—not the dark, thick mixture that gave oil its name "black gold"—Rattlesnake crude boiled at a temperature of 32 degrees Fahrenheit. Despite specially-devised aluminum-painted, vapor-proof receiving tanks, frost and moisture always covered flow lines, separators, and tanks. During summer months, a tank of fresh oil was in constant turmoil as atmospheric temperature throughout a twenty-four-hour period was above the initial boiling point of the fresh oil. The oil created pipeline gas-locks and prevented drainage from tanks by gravity unless it was first cooled.[86] Hagerman suggested that companies combine the high-gravity crude with lower grades, which they eventually did, but even then, movement through pipelines remained difficult.

Oil Wage Work for Navajos

As early as December 1922, the *Aztec Independent* remarked that "despite the winter weather, people are rushing into Midwest City and making their plans to start building as soon as the weather permits." Located near the Hog-back site, Midwest was "the fastest growing town in the southwest," boasting a short-order cafe and bedrooms for fifty people.[87] A rival town, Navajo City, was erected across the river. After Continental Oil sank its first drill in 1924, the town of Rattlesnake also began to grow, complete with electricity, hot and cold running water, houses, and dining hall.[88] Although no population figures are available, the towns were large enough to support baseball and football teams, which played each other and those from nearby towns. It seems that these communities prospered along with the wells. Evidence regarding how Navajos felt about the intrusion is lacking.

Leases, however, stipulated the use of Navajo labor, especially in the building of pipelines. At first, Muñoz used machinery to dig trenches, but when Mutual took over operations, its foreman ordered trenches dug by hand. In some cases, Navajos hauled supplies in and out of camps by pony and wagon. But Navajos repeatedly accused companies of using machinery in lieu of hiring them, and council members asked that companies teach Indian workers to operate drilling machinery even though agents informed them "it was not quite so simple as it looked."[89]

Collier later advocated that Navajos be taught to operate drills and technical jobs in stabilization plants and laboratory procedures, but as late as 1960, this was rarely done. If companies took the time to notice, Navajos were keen observers who learned by watching. Hagerman noted, "those who treated the Navajos like children never really got anywhere with them. They may think they did, but in the end find that the Indians have simply been making use of them and laughing in their sleeves while doing so."[90]

White men living in the oil camps reported few problems and little animosity between Navajo and Anglo workers. Sometimes, according to one early oil worker, "we'd go over [to a hogan] and shout these people out and borrow some water from them."[91] But, workers were outsiders, and they used precious resources, no doubt causing some Navajos to wonder if the few jobs awarded Navajo men were worth the intrusion. A language barrier existed, but did not interfere with work. One day, it was reported, sixty-three Navajos showed up for work on the Continental pipeline. None spoke English, and only one Anglo spoke Navajo, but a minimal grasp of the Navajo language did not cover the special terms needed to direct a crew. Therefore, the foreman of the project "picked out one and gave all of the instructions to him." Jackrabbit, as he was called, "threw down his pick and shovel and never would dig again . . . but always ran with orders to the others." Navajos, the foreman claimed, worked long hours and hand-dug trenches four- to five-feet deep in all but the rockiest areas.[92]

Navajos also showed up for work carrying camping equipment. While whites wasted time traveling back and forth to the main Rattlesnake camp — and when the line was too far to return to camp, they stayed at trading posts — Navajos slept where they worked. One white worker noted, "Indians' salary must have been damned near nothing," whereas whites got $4 per day plus room and board. Continental Oil sometimes hired Indian workers through trading posts, forcing Navajos to purchase products there or accept their pay in merchandise instead of cash.[93] Oil companies preferred to work with traders, and there is no indication that Hagerman complained about the arrangement or salaries. But Navajos did; in 1928 when Navajos laying gas pipeline on Ute land received about three cents per foot of pipe laid, they quit.[94] Navajos voiced displeasure over the use of scrip instead of real money, too.

A few Navajos expressed dissatisfaction with pipelines crossing their land or claimed that their families had not been properly compensated for the loss of water. In addition, the unstable crude combined with inadequate construction and testing of pipes resulted in leaks. Oil sometimes seeped into the ground and water.[95] Navajos themselves tapped lines for gasoline, causing large leaks and occasionally fires.[96] But few whites worried about environment during this period even though destruction was at times significant.

Meanwhile, Collier and other Indian rights spokesmen, including the Committee of One Hundred, the American Indian Defense Association, the National Popular Government League, and the Women's Federation, scrutinized operations on the Navajo reservation. Unhappy with the way Navajos were treated, they held forums, penned letters, and wrote editorials. Collier, for instance, composed monthly articles for *Sunset Magazine* bitterly denouncing the Indian Office. Judson King of the National Popular Government League circulated a memo titled "Scheme Before Congress to Loot Rich Indian Lands" and predicted that legislation would leave a stain upon Coolidge's administration that would make Teapot Dome look insignificant.[97]

Demands for deep well tests, requests for more wage work, the need for better legislation, and attempted reforms, however, were impeded by falling prices and glutted oil markets. Corporations even began to request federal production control in 1928, and by 1929 both the American Petroleum Institute and Federal Oil Conservation Board proposed limiting the yield nationwide to 1928 levels. The move was unsuccessful because government lacked authority to enforce the plan, and President Herbert Hoover refused to support coercion.[98]

Instead, the president convened a meeting of governors from oil-producing states on June 10, 1929, in Colorado Springs. Hagerman attended, but otherwise New Mexico was poorly represented.[99] Overall, two hundred delegates from large and small oil companies alike attended the convention. In the end, little came of the event, but independent interests used it to protest against a March 1929 presidential order closing the public domain to oil prospecting. The meeting also revealed animosity between western states containing public, untaxed land and states like Texas with none, and between small firms and large corporations that favored government conservation.[100]

The first Navajo oil boom ended in 1927. With overproduction and chaos, most corporations were unwilling to cope with remote markets and transportation problems on top of everything else. Nor did they intend to invest in deep testing as Interior Department leases stipulated. So, too, did Hagerman's enthusiasm wane. Most important, the crash left the Navajo tribal council uneasy. Would oil revenues continue to offer hope for land purchases, education, and livestock? Moreover, since as far as the BIA was concerned oil was the sole reason for the council's existence, what was its future role?

✦ TRANSITION AND TURMOIL, 4 1927–1932

Hózhó or beauty is the core of the Navajo world view. There is no apt English word for it. It bespeaks the righteousness of creation. To fall out of congruence for whatever reason is to create disharmony and invite physical illness.[1]

Oil prices dropped nationwide after 1929 as the exploitation of the massive East Texas and California fields resulted in vast overproduction. Exploration halted in the Four Corners region, although drilling continued on proven structures like Rattlesnake, Hogback, and Table Mesa. Boosters in Farmington and Aztec watched with dismay as a promising enterprise slipped away. Even though most Navajos remained unaware, council members realized that lower prices and a lack of new exploration would jeopardize future spending and land purchases.

During this period, John Collier and a number of progressive reformers forced a Senate subcommittee hearing designed in large part to force Hagerman from office and heap blame upon the Indian Office for an assortment of ills, including missing oil revenues. These years were also characterized by increasing factions, the best known of which was the Returned Students Organization established by J. C. Morgan and Howard Gorman of Ganado. This group opposed land purchases and wanted to wean Navajos from their herding and agricultural lifestyle. The Returned Students also demanded that grazing fees be imposed on large stock owners in order to reduce the number of sheep on the reservation.

This period was one of transition for the Indian Office as well. In 1929 the Institute for Government Research — Brookings Institute — had published *The Problem of Indian Administration*, dubbed the Meriam Report for Lewis Meriam, who headed the investigative team. The Meriam Report captured the attention of government officials with graphic descriptions of poverty, disease, inadequate diet, and substandard housing.

President Hoover replaced Charles Burke with Charles J. Rhoads, president of the Indian Rights Association, and directed him to implement the

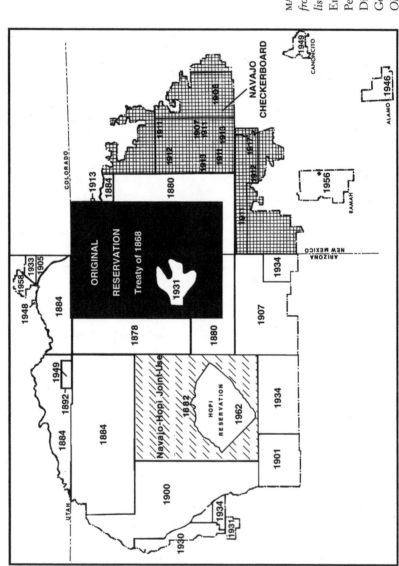

MAP 1. *Navajo Land. Derived from a map originally published in* The Navajo Atlas: Environments, Resources, People, and History of the Diné Bikéyah *by James M. Goodman, University of Oklahoma Press.*

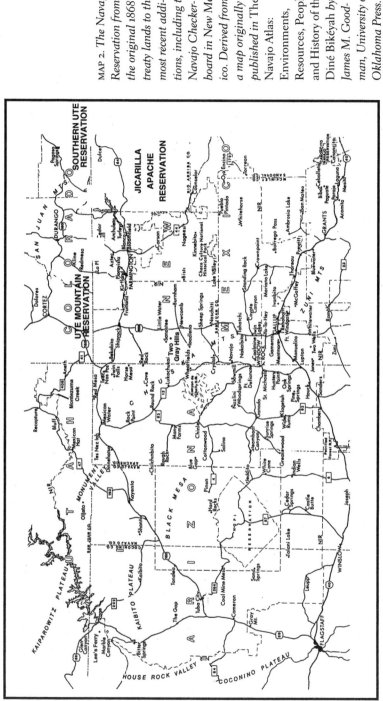

MAP 2. The Navajo Reservation from the original 1868 treaty lands to the most recent additions, including the Navajo Checkerboard in New Mexico. Derived from a map originally published in The Navajo Atlas: Environments, Resources, People, and History of the Diné Bikéyah by James M. Goodman, University of Oklahoma Press.

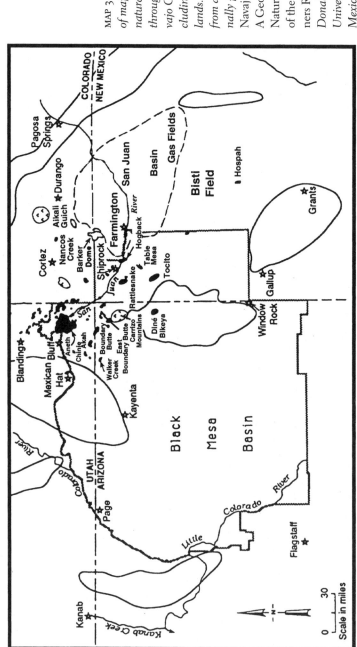

MAP 3. Locations of major oil and natural gas fields throughout Navajo Country; including adjacent lands. Derived from a map originally published in Navajo Country: A Geology and Natural History of the Four Corners Region by Donald L. Baars, University of New Mexico Press.

COLORADO
NEW MEXICO

Pagosa Springs ☆

Aikali Guich ★Durango

San Juan

Basin   Gas Fields

Nancos Creek

Cortez

Barker Dome

Shiprock

Farmington ☆

Hogback

River

Bisti Field

● Hospah

Rattlesnake

Table Mesa

Tocito

Grants ☆

San Juan

Boundary Butte

Chinle   Akah

East Boundary Butte

Carrizo Mountains

Diné Bikeya ●

Window Rock ★

Gallup ☆

Walker Creek

Blanding★

Mexican Hat ☆

Aneth

Kayenta ☆

Black   Mesa   Basin

UTAH
ARIZONA

River

Colorado

Page

Little

Colorado   River

Flagstaff ☆

Kanab ☆

Kanab Creek

N

0   30

Scale in miles

1. Henry Chee Dodge, first Navajo tribal chairman. Photo courtesy Museum of New Mexico.

2. Herbert J. Hagerman, former territorial governor of New Mexcio and special commissioner to the Navajos. Courtesy Museum of New Mexico.

3. Navajo tribal council (James Stewart and Sam Ahkeah, vice chairman, seated on platform, Henry Chee Dodge at extreme left behind the flag, and Paul Jones interpreting). Photo by Milton Snow, courtesy Museum of New Mexico.

4. S. C. Muñoz ca. 1920. As president of the Metropolitan Oil Company he helped open oil fields on
Navajo lands. Courtesy Farmington Museum from
the Tom Dugan Collection (1991.23.14).

5. Pipeline crew working on line from the Hogback, ca. 1923.
Courtesy Farmington Museum from the Tom Dugan Collection (1991.23.6).

Midwest Refining Company field camp at the Hogback field in 1925.
Courtesy Aztec (New Mexico) Museum and Historical Village.

7. Hogback baseball team, ca. 1925. Courtesy Aztec Museum and Historical Village.

8. *Early oil truck in the 1920s.*
Courtesy Aztec Museum and Historical Village.

9. *Rattlesnake oil refinery, ca. 1926.*
Courtesy Farmington Museum from the Bessie Gibson Collection (1989.38.11).

10. *Semi-trailer hauling a tower, 1930s.*
Courtesy Farmington Museum from the Tom Dugan Collection (1991.23.25).

11. *Rig at the Rattlesnake oil and helium site with Shiprock in the background, 1950s.*
Courtesy of Tom Dugan.

needed reforms. Joseph H. Scattergood was named assistant commissioner. Like Rhoads, Scattergood was a banker, philanthropist, and Quaker, and under their dual leadership, the BIA began a series of reforms nationwide, including replacement of incompetent field service workers with qualified ones and reversal of the government boarding-school policy. Under distinguished educator Dr. W. Carson Ryan, the Indian Office began to replace boarding schools with reservation day schools wherever possible.

As part of this reform spirit, the Senate Committee on Indian Affairs in 1929 began on-site studies of reservation conditions. Historian Angie Debo contends that this was the first sincere attempt in thirty-seven years to discover anything at all about the Five Tribes of Oklahoma, and it was easily the first such investigation of Navajos. Subcommittee members assigned to conduct the survey arrived in New Mexico and Arizona in spring 1931. By that time, however, oil issues were virtually absent because so little was being produced.

The Production and Royalty Debacle

When production slowed on Navajo land after 1927, exploration and drilling on off-reservation land also halted, leaving area boosters in dismay. As early as 1927 a Farmington newspaper had lamented that insufficient funds and poor equipment severely hampered the ability of oil men to explore and drill, but the reservation still held economic promise.[2] Now, that future was in doubt. True, Farmington and Aztec had grown in the past ten years, just not as dramatically as envisioned. Moreover, the federal government had constructed 110 miles of surfaced road across the Navajo reservation at a cost of about $1 million, which according to the *Farmington Republican* served as an important link to existing roads in San Juan and adjacent counties. In turn, federally constructed roads opened the way for company-built tributary roads to oil fields.[3] Nevertheless, non-Navajo residents had hoped for more.

Fortunately, just as Navajos avoided the excesses of the Oklahoma, Texas, and California oil booms so did they escape the worst problems associated with prolonged oversupply and price collapse.[4] Continental Oil drilled its Rattlesnake well number twenty-four in September 1930 and operated the Farmington refinery at full capacity. Trainloads of Rattlesnake petroleum went regularly to Durango.[5] Similarly, the Hogback produced at a steady pace, even as oil declined overall as a factor in Navajo economic development.[6]

Yet, when Navajos after 1929 asked the special commissioner for royalty figures, they faced the same two formidable obstacles they had always encountered. First, government failed to monitor production or obtain accurate royalty figures. For one thing, oil records were kept by separate agencies: production and royalty reports were housed with the San Juan area superintendent while operations registers were held at the Bureau of Mines office in

Shiprock. Verification, therefore, required cross-checking at two government offices.[7]

The second problem lay specifically with the way the large drillers conducted business. As previously noted, Midwest and Santa Fe/Continental (Mutual) Oil began almost immediately to refine their own oil. Continental built a pipeline to the Hogback site, where Rattlesnake and Hogback crudes were mixed and shipped to Farmington, and erected a small on-site stabilizing plant and refinery at Rattlesnake. Although Hagerman apparently never quite figured out how this joint or three-way partnership worked, he realized it set up a sophisticated internal operation allowing the companies to essentially buy and sell crude oil to themselves and hence to juggle figures at will.[8] Moreover, these arrangements, and the government's inability to manage production and royalties, figured prominently in Collier's attempt to remove Hagerman and eliminate BIA control.

Government leases stipulated that royalties be paid on the amount drilled, not the amount sold after refining. But Hagerman discovered that prior to completing its refining operations, Midwest paid royalties of $2 or higher per barrel, whereas afterward prices dropped significantly. Hagerman challenged the figures, but the inability to monitor production made verification almost impossible.[9]

At one point Hagerman had suggested that it might be best if Navajos took their royalties in oil and marketed it locally.[10] He pointed out that drillers sold crude right from the wells for 10 cents a gallon (about $4.50 per barrel), and locals purchased it in Farmington for around 25 cents per gallon.[11] "Ridiculous," Burke chided. If Midwest claimed that $1.50 per barrel was accurate, "we assume [it] is that at which the company sold the oil." Furthermore, Burke reminded Hagerman, companies on the reservation had trouble transporting oil because of the remote location. Certainly the Indian Office did not wish to be accused of interfering.[12]

On November 20, 1924, Hagerman contested the low royalties on the basis of the high quality of Navajo crude. In addition to its high gravity, Navajo crude was relatively free of impurities. It also contained an extremely high percentage of gasoline. Yet Continental and Midwest both denied quality made any difference at all, and in fact said the gasoline content—three times more than the average Oklahoma crude—made Navajo oil more expensive to handle. Its explosive nature caused several wells to ignite, and sometimes workers were seriously injured. One such fire occurred March 22, 1925, and according to John C. Nicklos, who was in charge of Rattlesnake operations, a driller required hospitalization in Farmington. The previous December a Midwest worker had been so badly burned that he was still in the hospital when the March fire occurred.[13]

In addition, Midwest asked to deduct transportation charges, hence lowering the price-per-barrel even more.[14] Midwest's November 1924 $2,789.35 payment amounted to $1.25 per barrel, although Hagerman thought $2.72 a fair minimum price.[15] Then, soon after, Hagerman noted that the Muñoz partnership with Continental Oil was creating a similar "inside" situation.

Companies Reject the Wyant Solution

The solution was an independent Bureau of Mines study, and L. D. Wyant, Bureau associate refinery engineer, conducted the investigation.[16] His report verified that Hogback and Rattlesnake crudes were free of impurities. For every gallon of oil taken from the well, closer to a full gallon was produced for sale. Navajo crude should, therefore, command higher than average prices. Because New Mexico wells were classified with mid-continent fields for pricing purposes, Wyant suggested the cost of Navajo oil be established at 60 cents per barrel above the average price paid for mid-continent crude of 36 to 38.9 gravity. Companies operating on the Navajo reservation could also deduct 15 cents per barrel for travel charges. If, for example, the current price in Oklahoma or Kansas was $2, Rattlesnake and Hogback oil should command $2.45 or 45 cents more.[17]

Midwest, Continental, and Santa Fe Company called the report "seriously flawed." Fifteen cents per barrel for transportation did not take into account that oil companies were at the mercy of a single railroad. Muñoz offered a straight $2 per barrel, adding that the deal represented a tremendous sacrifice on his part.[18] Moreover, the high quality was a curse, not a blessing, he claimed. The high gas content made the petroleum more volatile and in need of additional treatment, not less.[19]

Midwest ignored the Wyant report altogether and argued "our own self-interest should be ample assurance to you that we will use every endeavor to get the best possible price."[20] Its officials appealed. On April 19, 1927, the Interior Department granted a hearing. Midwest demanded a rate of 20 cents above the highest mid-continent posted price for 17-degree gravity crude. The government turned down Midwest's proposal, but on January 3, 1928, modified its decision and allowed royalties to be paid based upon actual sale prices if companies submitted detailed records. In other words, payments were again at company discretion. Nevertheless, on the basis of the 1928 ruling, Santa Fe and Continental immediately demanded a $58,000 refund for overpayment.[21]

Hagerman endorsed the Wyant report as just and equitable, fearing further challenges would result in less income for Indians.[22] But, by 1928 most of the leases auctioned in 1923 and 1926 were abandoned, and when in 1931 Midwest announced royalties of a mere $1.08 per barrel, nobody representing the

Navajos argued.[23] However, Hagerman's inability to control the royalty problem simply contributed to the perception that he was corrupt or utterly inept.

Indeed, by 1931, the royalty rates paid to Navajos were generally higher than the national average. Fortunately, Navajo crude never dropped to 10 cents per barrel as oil did elsewhere, and at times it climbed to $2, perhaps because of local sales.[24] Newspapers bragged that no bootlegging, price slashing, or competition wars occurred in the San Juan fields.[25] But, unhappy with royalty amounts — and probably more significantly, unhappy with the BIA — some members of the 1931 tribal council voted against renewal of the Rattlesnake lease. Under pressure from the BIA, delegates eventually renewed it for ten years, but only after chairman Deshna Clah Cheschilligi voted to break the tie.[26]

Senator William H. King, progressive Utah Republican, later issued a scathing indictment of the BIA; he accused officials of failing to repay capital and allotment funds and using Indian money for personal items like furniture, rugs, draperies, quarters, wallpaper and paint, houses, and automobiles.[27] Although his attack was aimed at the Indian Service nationwide, Hagerman had earlier admitted that agents on the Navajo reservation occasionally frittered away Navajo income.

After 1929, labor practices also came under attack, especially as companies laid off more Navajos than whites. Commissioner Rhoads claimed, "If they [oil companies] pay their royalty lease money, that is all they have to do." But Navajos correctly insisted that leases guaranteed them jobs, jobs that were becoming increasingly elusive.[28] Furthermore, companies neglected to protect the land as they were supposed to, especially from pipeline leaks. Still, Chairman Cheschilligi praised government improvements, namely a Shiprock-to-Gallup road, and claimed Navajos were so pleased that men living nearby volunteered to donate two days of labor per year free of charge to maintain the highway.[29]

The Land Extension Controversy

After 1929, the land extension debacle intensified as well, and Navajos were caught in the middle. As special commissioner, one of the first things Hagerman had discovered was the importance of land for Navajos living on and outside of the reservation. Indians especially wanted to acquire approximately one million acres around Crownpoint, which included railroad grant land, private holdings — mostly homesteads — public domain, and national forest. Although certainly Hagerman could not be considered particularly effective, it must in all fairness be noted that solutions to the land extension controversy remained elusive long after his departure.

In September 1923—before the first oil auction—Hagerman had met with Chee Dodge concerning land extensions around Crownpoint and asked Agent S. F. Stacher to gather all data connected to the matter.[30] On October 16, 1923, when Commissioner Burke was in Santa Fe for the auction, Hagerman took the opportunity to call a meeting that brought together Dodge; Howell Jones, New Mexico Land Commissioner; New Mexico's Lieutenant Governor; E. J. Engle, vice president of the Santa Fe Railroad, and Senator Holm O. Bursum. As a group, all agreed something must be done, and that something was legislation appropriating $200,000 to purchase private homesteads and authorizing the exchange of railroad land for lieu lands elsewhere in New Mexico.[31]

Immediately after the auction, Hagerman drew up a bill, but soon discovered that the proposed legislation elicited violent opposition from New Mexicans left out of the agreement. Senator A. A. Jones had previously told Hagerman, "generally speaking, I am opposed to any more Indian reservations," adding that if Indians paid taxes perhaps he would think differently.[32] In early November, Jones made it quite clear that he did not support the legislation. Similarly, Governor James Hinkle resisted, contending that instead of giving federal land to Navajos, the BIA should consider turning responsibility for Indians over to states along with Indian trust funds.[33]

Local stockmen, many of whom leased railroad land for winter pasture, spoke out so loudly against the plan that by early 1924 it became obvious the bill would fail. Ranchers asserted that if it passed, the loss of land would put "75 per cent of the residents of Sandoval, Valencia, and Rio Arriba counties out of business." Thus, by March, Hagerman told Dodge not to expect passage and suggested—perhaps inadvertently—that Navajos think about sending a delegation to Washington to gain support.[34]

The Tribal Council continued to stand behind BIA efforts. By 1927, however, much of the land was no longer available, and what was still on the market cost far more than the 1923 price of $200,000. The New Mexico Cattle and Horse Growers Association and Wool Growers Association drew up strong resolutions against extensions, Governor Hinkle asked the railroad to block exchanges, and Jones lobbied the opposition in Washington. Hagerman expressed his frustration in late 1927, when he noted that although practically all arrangements had been made, the plan was failing.[35]

Nevertheless, Ashurst wrote Senate bill 3159 in 1927, which authorized Navajos to spend 25 percent (up to $100,000 annually) of their oil royalty income for land. The Interior Department would hold the title in trust, and the lands were subject to taxation to be paid from trust funds. It was this bill that Dodge and his Navajo delegation traveled to Washington to support in January 1927.

Their testimony resulted in a proposed amendment to allow the Navajos to also take a $1 million loan, which they agreed to repay from oil royalties.

Still, Anglo and Hispano stock owners, especially in McKinley County, were so vocal that New Mexico senator and owner of the *Santa Fe New Mexican* Bronson Cutting amended the bill to pertain only to Arizona. The Arizona boundary bill passed Congress on June 14, 1934, and added land especially along the southern border of the reservation. At the same time, Stacher complained that at the rate of $100,000 per year purchases would be painfully slow; every delay compounded the situation and increased the expense. Was it not possible, he asked, to speed the $1 million loan and make purchases?[36] The bill was never brought to a vote.

Hagerman presented his third and final proposal on January 1, 1932. His plan added three million acres reservation-wide including the Paiute Strip in Utah—originally sought in 1930—plus approximately 100,000 acres near Crownpoint.[37] Hagerman was removed from office on July 1, 1932, however, and was unable to steer the proposal forward.

Two other problems hampered the land extensions. In the first place, the oil excitement made some homesteaders who had been eager to sell in October 1923 less willing in 1924. They had long known that oil in small quantities lay underneath their land, but had no money to thoroughly test for commercial quantities or to develop wells. Until companies like Midwest moved into the area, most farmers and ranchers considered the black ooze that seeped into water and soil from time to time a nuisance.[38] By the time Congress considered the bills in 1924 and 1927, many of these same men hoped to strike it rich.

The second problem was, as usual, a general lack of knowledge regarding boundaries. The government still had not funded surveys on or around the reservation, so determining exactly what land should be purchased or exchanged was difficult even though the plan to consolidate Navajo borders was not new. Friar Anselm Weber had proposed consolidation in 1914—maybe even earlier—and Stacher had pushed the plan in 1921, but to no avail.[39] Oddly, John Collier's American Indian Defense Association censured Hagerman's continuing inability to complete the Navajo land purchases. The reformers accused him of acting too slowly and of favoring New Mexico ranchers. Despite the criticism, however, Collier's efforts after 1933 would prove equally frustrating and in the case of New Mexico every bit as ineffective.

Hagerman and the Senate Subcommittee

The failure to obtain adequate royalties and production data and the inability to solve land extension problems were only two reasons why in 1931 John Collier and a handful of progressive Senate leaders sought to remove

Hagerman from office. But, there were other reasons as well. In late January 1931 Indian Office doctors, nurses, and educators, anthropologists, and assorted bureaucrats, including Indian reformers representing organizations like the American Indian Defense Association (AIDA) and Eastern Association on Indian Affairs, assembled in a U.S. Senate hearing room. Collier, executive secretary of AIDA and looking as gaunt as ever in his rumpled suit, shivered slightly from having braved one of Washington's typically bleak, biting winter mornings. He spread out volumes of crumpled files across the table reserved for those testifying before the subcommittee of the Senate Committee on Indian Affairs.

Behind Collier, engulfed in a haze of cigarette and cigar smoke, sat Hagerman, holding no documents, nervous perhaps, but looking confident and collected. Off to one side perched Rhoads, quite probably irritated at having to leave his warm office to listen to wholesale censure of his Bureau. A table dominated the room, and seated there were the senators who would listen to four days of testimony.[40] Around nine o'clock they filed in. Fiery Lynn J. Frazier of North Dakota raised the gavel and called the hearing to order. Nearby sat Robert M. LaFollette, Jr., son of the formidable Wisconsin progressive; W. B. Pine of Oklahoma; Burton K. Wheeler, whom Hagerman described as one of the crudest men he ever met; and Elmer Thomas, also representing Oklahoma. A clerk prepared to record proceedings.[41]

Secretary of the Interior Wilbur did not attend, but former commissioner Charles Burke and Assistant Commissioner Joseph Scattergood were there. Since 1928, neither Charles Rhoads nor Scattergood had successfully reversed Secretary of the Interior Ray Lyman Wilbur's pro-allotment mentality or his domination of Indian policy. At first, Rhoads had shown a willingness to work with Collier, but broke with him when Wilbur and Hoover voiced displeasure. Collier called the pair "timid" and belittled their lack of effort.[42] However, both Rhoads and Scattergood stood rigidly behind Hagerman.

Collier, who had compiled hundreds of damaging documents regarding the special commissioner's tenure with Navajos, was also determined to damn Hagerman's performance on the Pueblo Lands Board, which the American Indian Defense Association had flogged since its inception in 1925. Collier maintained a special relationship to and fondness for the Pueblo peoples of New Mexico, and it is likely that if Hagerman had not served on the Lands Board, Collier would have ignored his work with Navajos. Indeed, as Secretary Work's appointed representative to the Lands Board, Hagerman had allegedly attempted to reorganize the Pueblo Council along the lines of the Navajo Tribal council, according to Collier, in order to create a compliant group and circumvent traditional leaders. Hagerman had also concurred with board members to deny San Juan Pueblos compensation for two-thirds of their lost land and in making other adverse decisions.[43] Thus, as the hearing got under-way, it became quite apparent that Collier was prepared to attack Hagerman on many fronts.

The two most severe accusations against Hagerman in his role with Nava-jos were fraud in the sale of oil leases and misrepresentation of the Indians dur-ing the Hayden bill hearing. In a letter to the subcommittee, Frear suggested that Hagerman's actions were "a heritage from the Fall regime."[44] In testimony before the Senate Indian Affairs Committee on March 9, 1926, the special commissioner had suggested that Navajos endorsed the bill that turned royal-ties over to states, when, in fact, he had never sought Navajo views at all. In-deed, in 1924 Chee Dodge had volunteered to surrender royalties in exchange for clear title to executive order land; he also offered to give up mineral rights to obtain land title in 1927. Strangely, Hagerman never used either of these in his defense.

Although Collier maintained that Hagerman dominated Navajos and that his rule constituted a sort of permanent martial law, Hagerman's real sin was disillusionment caused by six years of government red tape, incompetence, and boredom. Hagerman hardly dominated Navajos as Collier suggested; after 1926, he barely seems to have visited the reservation at all.[45] Neverthe-less, without asking for the council or anyone's else's advice Hagerman did tell Congress that Navajos knew about and supported the Hayden bill, which Collier called a "well-engineered" coup d'etat.[46] More than likely, during the Hayden bill hearings Hagerman spoke on behalf of New Mexico taxpayers rather than Navajos. It was this lack of commitment to Indians that angered Collier and ultimately made Hagerman a failure as special commissioner.

Gertrude Bonnin of the National Council of American Indians testified that she wrote to Chairman Dodge in March 1926 to verify Hagerman's claim that Navajos endorsed the legislation. She told the subcommittee that her let-ter had been intercepted — she assumed by Hagerman — and forwarded not to Chee Dodge, but to Burke, whose scathing reply she found inappropriate.[47] Nevertheless, in a letter to the *New York Times*, Oliver La Farge called the charge ridiculous and the entire hearing a personal attack on Hagerman ini-tiated by Frazier "at a time when public interest is diverted to other matters."[48]

Additional complaints surfaced. Clara D. True, one-time BIA teacher at Santa Clara Pueblo, contributor to the *New Mexico State Tribune*, and avidly anti-Hagerman, claimed that as a rule Navajo Tribal Council meetings were poorly publicized and attended only by select Navajos. True had this to say: "I couldn't find any but a few hand picked Navajos who knew anything about [the meetings]." True believed Hagerman manipulated the council. She thought it "amusing at night to see the activity of Mr. Hagerman's handy man . . . with the delegates," where his tactics resembled those of a steam roller.[49] In reality, councils attracted five hundred or more Navajos. While it is possible that publicity fell short, council meetings were certainly not closed-door affairs, and attendance was normally large.

Dr. Herbert Spinden, president of the Eastern Association, crisply accused Collier of using the hearings to turn New Mexico Indians against everyone except his own AIDA. Hagerman, Spinden argued, had to consider state welfare "in a state where many see Navajos as a non asset." Spinden assured senators, however, that Hagerman had always devoted "heart and soul for the Indian."[50] "Really?" Collier challenged. Weren't Hagerman's roles as special commissioner and Lands Board member to represent Indians, not New Mexico? If he did not represent Navajos and Pueblos, who did? The state, he reminded senators, had enough advocates.

Collier presented yet another charge against Hagerman when he inquired why the special commissioner had allowed the auction of Navajo oil properties in October 1923, when he knew prices were low. Hagerman countered that he had been unaware of the situation at the time, but as Collier pointed out, industry journals had been rife with reports of low oil prices and nearly all had predicted improvement by spring 1924. Furthermore, William M. Davis, president of the Mid-continent Oil and Gas Association, had notified Hagerman just days before the sale of the problem and requested that he use his influence to delay the auction.[51]

Perhaps Hagerman had had insufficient time following receipt of the letter to call a halt, but leasing Rattlesnake and Beautiful Mountain for minimum bids of $1,000 at such a time amounted to gross negligence, Collier argued. Hagerman had later claimed that he believed oil values might continue to drop. But at the hearing, he never mentioned that. It is doubtful that when Hagerman leased Rattlesnake and Beautiful Mountain he had anything so diabolical in mind. He was merely eager to initiate test wells on these structures, and in the end, failed to endorse Field's lease. Still, Collier claimed that when neither Rattlesnake nor Beautiful Mountain sold on the morning of the auction, Muñoz invited Hagerman, Field, and Burke to lunch. They "left in a body," returned together, and with few people present, Field leased Beautiful Mountain and Muñoz, Rattlesnake.[52]

Of course, at the time, Hagerman and oil officials possessed only the September 28, 1923, Kenneth B. Nowels report, and even that was not officially released until the day of the auction. It suggested that Tocito, Table Mesa, and Rattlesnake were potentially as productive as the Hogback—Beautiful Mountain was less likely to be a large producer—but Nowels freely admitted that he had not yet examined the structure.[53] Thus, Nowels's conclusions had come too late to encourage higher bids, although one might argue that Hagerman probably should have withdrawn these structures until a later date.[54] Still, the BIA was eager to deep test the reservation, and thus threw caution aside.

Collier, on the other hand, was overly zealous in equating the situation with the Teapot Dome scandal and connecting the Fall appointee with scandal.[55] Muñoz no doubt suspected the Rattlesnake was worth more than $1,000; he had hired three geologists to examine the Hogback and Rattlesnake independently of the Bureau of Mines and knew Rattlesnake in particular was a good location.[56] But that is hardly evidence of fraud. Moreover, Clara True testified that:

> Lem Towers, private Secretary and cousin to Commissioner Burke, told me in the old Federal Building in Santa Fe the day before the auction of the Rattlesnake lease that it was going for a thousand dollars and that it would make somebody a millionaire. . . . Mr. Hagerman was conducting all Indian Service affairs. Somebody must have known the [Rattlesnake] lease was valuable. Mr. Towers knew it, at least.[57]

There appears to be no further corroborating evidence regarding what Mr. Towers "knew" or what Clara True saw.

Scattergood challenged Collier, claiming that Hagerman had not been responsible for the auction results. For one thing, it was the BIA's duty to get an immediate return for the Indians. Senator Wheeler reminded the assistant commissioner that "on the Crow Reservation, Mr. Scattergood, you were actually not interested in seeing the Indians get immediate development." There, the Indian Office let big oil companies "block up their wells over the Indians' protest" time and time again. Why was the story so different with the Navajos?[58] But Rhoads and Scattergood had not been with the BIA in 1923.

Collier finally asked the subcommittee, "If Mr. Hagerman is not responsible for these matters, does not know about them, has nothing to do with them, what is his job?"[59] Collier's question was a good one and not easily answered. In 1928 Work had actually removed Hagerman from office, but Rhoads reinstated him and even expanded his responsibilities to include the administration of Indian reservations in four states—New Mexico, Arizona, Colorado, and Utah.[60] Collier pointed out that Hagerman had failed to so much as submit an allotment bill, and at the time of the hearing was promoting Senate Resolution (S.R.) 5577 to cancel further Navajo allotments on public domain. This legislation was never submitted to the tribal council. Moreover, although delegates had on March 4, 1930, designated all remaining tribal funds—a total of $1.2 million—for land purchases, Hagerman never carried out the extensions.[61]

Collier added that, when a 1930 blizzard buried the Navajo reservation under five- to six-foot snowdrifts, killing two hundred thousand sheep, Hagerman's response to the crisis was "one trip by rail to the city of Gallup . . . one letter . . . and thereafter Mr. Hagerman has read the newspapers at Santa Fe and in the Mayflower Hotel in Washington. . . ."[62]

A number of employees claimed that under Hagerman's administration or lack thereof, "extreme and sensational abuses" occurred, but Hagerman did nothing to stop them. BIA doctors and nurses testified that when diseases raged through one of the three government boarding schools, Hagerman ignored pleas for help. One doctor went behind his back and wrote to Burke, then was fired from his job. Several school matrons complained to Hagerman about bad food and dangerous overcrowding and like the doctor tried to circumvent the special commissioner when they got no satisfaction. The matrons were also terminated.[63] Furthermore, "espionage of the most extreme character" was encouraged among employees on the Navajo reservation, some claimed.[64]

Mrs. Joseph Linden Smith of the New Mexico Indian Affairs Committee testified to the contrary. She said that Hagerman had acted quickly and with concern when almost 40 per cent of the children in the three boarding schools were found to have trachoma. The affected students were all quarantined into one of the schools so that doctors could contain and treat the problem. "They [doctors and teachers] would not have acted if it had not been on a memorandum of H. J. Hagerman," she protested.[65]

The *New Mexico Tribune* suggested, accurately it seems, that Hagerman had simply lost interest. Indeed, his career reveals just such a pattern. Hagerman called his Colorado law practice from 1897–1898 drudgery. After two years as second secretary in the American Embassy in St. Petersburg, Hagerman wrote that the position was "more or less a waste of time."[66] As New Mexico territorial governor, he was most interested in the social whirl of Santa Fe and Albuquerque.[67] After 1905, Hagerman seems to have dabbled in politics. W. C. Reid, Albuquerque attorney and friend of the Hagerman family, also observed:

> It had appeared to me . . . that Herbert Hagerman lacked fighting spirit; that he had too often shied away from combat when he should have taken a decisive stand and fought back. It had seemed to me, also, that Herbert Hagerman had always thought he was battling alone, while in truth . . . he had many good people on his side, although apparently he did not know it.[68]

Fall repeatedly said he had called Hagerman "out of retirement" in 1923, but the former governor was only 51 years old and does not seem to have been participating in a profession from which he had to retire. In a telling comment, Hagerman wrote this in 1926:

What I really need is to take two or three months vacation and get rested up before doing much of anything further, and I may, after the tribal council is over, just simply make up my mind to give up the whole business and quit. . . . There is really no use killing one's self for the government or the Indians either.[69]

Collier asked that the Senate recommend dismissal. Admitting that he had supported Hagerman in 1923, Collier added, "after the 1926 episodes, particularly the attempted 37½ per cent betrayal of the Navajos, I ceased to be taken in . . . Hagerman had misled me as he had misled others."[70] But the hearings concluded without recommendation, and the Indian Office made no move to relieve the special commissioner of his duties. Afterward, crowds met Hagerman at the Lamy depot upon his return and visually expressed opposition to "outside interference" by hanging Collier in effigy. According to Hagerman, even Navajos called Collier "the drowned rat."[71]

Senators Conduct On-Site Hearings

In April 1931, the Senate subcommittee went to the reservation as part of the nationwide survey of conditions. The Farmington Chamber of Commerce wined and dined the senators, then delivered pleas for new hospitals, water projects, and schools on behalf of Navajos. Morgan and several missionaries requested an Indian boarding school in Farmington.[72] The survey continued well into May. Amid other topics, a parade of Navajos criticized and praised the special commissioner, who claimed illness during the entire period and attended none of the on-site hearings. Council member Howard Gorman stated that Hagerman seldom visited the reservation. He had discussed neither the Lee's Ferry nor Bloomfield Bridge with the council, and he had failed to explain provisions of the Indian Oil Act. Actually, tribal meeting records clearly indicate that these bridges were the subject of numerous council debates, and Hagerman had been outspoken against them. Gorman accurately recalled that Hagerman had provided few answers regarding royalty amounts, concluding that "The United States Government ought to look after its wards a little closer."[73]

In his address to senators, Morgan concurred that Hagerman often ignored council resolutions and spent money without tribal consent. John Curley (Leupp) added, "I do not know of anyone who recommends Hagerman," and remembered only one or two visits to Leupp between 1923 and 1930: he got out of his car only long enough to fill the vehicle with gasoline.[74] Marcus Kanuho maintained that his district (Leupp), although 150 to 175 miles from Lee's Ferry, still had "to stand their proportionate cost" for the bridge. And elections under Hagerman were unfair: only two or three hundred were ever called to vote, and that in a district with eighteen hundred or more eligible.[75] Yet Cheschilligi insisted that Hagerman had worked hard to obtain adequate oil leases and improve conditions on the reservation.

By May, support for Hagerman was eroding even in New Mexico. Collier noted that some newspapers there began attacking the special commissioner. Several superintendents during questioning admitted that Hagerman had proven "inactive, ineffective." Fellow members of the Pueblo Board were hard at work "in an effort to rectify the faults," and in fact, Hagerman's only supporters were Rhoads, Scattergood, and little circles within the Eastern and New Mexico Indian Affairs Associations. Wheeler declared that he would exhaust his efforts in the next session, forcing Hagerman off the government payroll once and for all.[76] Congress formally removed Hagerman in March 1932 effective July 1, 1932, on the grounds of incompetence, "superfluity," and because "several superintendents would at any time in the past have handled this job better than Mr. Hagerman has handled it."[77]

The Indian Office Blamed for Fiscal Mismanagement

Although many charges against Hagerman appear true, he seems to have shouldered much of the blame rightfully directed at BIA ineptitude. When Wheeler concluded, "it is impossible to read his testimony and say that Mr. Hagerman knew what he was talking about when he first came before the committee or at any subsequent time," at least some of this can be blamed on Washington.[78]

Ironically, Rhoads and Scattergood, even before the May investigation, wrote a letter to the subcommittee declaring him "unequivocally innocent" of all "present and future" allegations, prompting one Collier confederate to label Hagerman Rhoads's "injured darling."[79] Collier responded: "I should suppose that even a minimal intelligence would have led [Rhoads] to realize . . . that it was essential that he preserve his objectivity."[80]

Over and above the charges against Hagerman, senators heard allegations that the Indian Office misused tribal funds for personal and administrative purposes. Nationally, half of the annual $25 million Congressional appropriation was "consumed in paying the salaries, expenses, and compensation of these thousands of regular and irregular employees."[81] And by requesting "lump-sum" appropriations from Congress, the BIA avoided specifying where it spent the money. In a confidential memo written March 15, 1929, Collier accused E. B. Meritt of testifying before Congress in such a manner as to keep legislators "in a state of darkness while the appropriations were run up to 31 million dollars, of which . . . more than half represents waste." At the same time, he said, government consistently cut needed food and education programs.[82]

R. T. Bonnin — Gertrude Bonnin's husband — testified, "to the casual reader . . . it appears that great sums of money are spent for the interests and benefits of the Indians, when in fact . . . very little of that money actually reaches the Indian."[83] In the case of Navajos, Washington doled out royalties to each district, but without explanation or guidelines.[84] Cheschilligi admitted that the tribal council never received calculations or an explanation of how companies or BIA personnel came up with amounts paid.[85]

Historian Lawrence Kelly maintains that Collier misrepresented the facts and became more fanciful as hearings went on. It is also clear that what most upset Collier was Hagerman's inability to also stand up for Pueblos during land decisions and Hagerman's association with Fall.[86] Nevertheless, although perhaps not a dishonest man, Hagerman was clearly a poor match for the position. As his responsibilities mushroomed, his effectiveness plummeted. On October 9, 1934, the BIA named William H. Zeh as acting administrator. The drastic decline in oil production and prices meant lease supervision was only a small part of the job Hagerman once held.[87]

Navajos Seek More Control

After Hagerman's departure, tribal councils were held twice each year; in 1933 delegates met in July and October. In October, Navajos passed a resolution to cancel all oil or gas leases, even those extended by council in 1926 and renewed in 1931. Council members discovered, however, that they could not cancel leases unless they proved breach of contract. So, thwarted, the council revoked power of attorney as granted under the resolution of July 7, 1923.[88]

Navajos also challenged royalty amounts, especially when Morgan pointed out that in 1932 income totaled $32,669, whereas in 1933 it was $12,875 despite Midwest's new wells. A stumbling block to Navajo independence, however, was a new set of regulations and lease forms adopted by the Interior Department in January 1934, primarily for allotted lands. To "protect" Indians, these regulations expanded Interior's jurisdiction and permitted leases to be abandoned only with government permission. Moreover, companies had to pay royalties immediately despite market prices, a move primarily to protect allottees from oil companies that might sign leases, drill and store oil, and then take years to pay the owners. An automatic one percent was deducted for impurities. More rigid equipment rules were imposed as well. The government received all rights to helium, and it appeared that the Rattlesnake site contained a substantial amount.[89] Nevertheless, in 1934, there was no attempt made to mine the helium.

Despite the new regulations, Navajos sought more control of natural resource development and freedom from BIA dependence. The Returned Students Organization grew rapidly and set up chapters across the reservation. When Franklin D. Roosevelt became president in 1932, the group endorsed

Henry Roe Cloud (Winnebago), graduate of Yale University and Auburn Theological Seminary and an ordained Presbyterian minister, as BIA commissioner. Morgan and the others joined Anglo and Hispano stockmen to counter land consolidation and expansion.[90]

In 1933, returned boarding-school students actively encouraged other educated Navajos to run for the tribal council, so as to strengthen their voices. Of twelve delegates elected that year, ten had attended boarding schools, including Tom Dodge, Chee Dodge's son, who was elected chairman. A dark horse candidate, Dodge won with Morgan's support. Dodge had practiced law in Santa Fe for six years, but agreed to return with his Anglo wife to live in Fort Defiance.

Ironically, Dodge ultimately neutralized the returned students' voices by persuading council to let alternates vote — only five of the twelve were educated. In addition, Dodge lacked leadership ability and resigned before the end of his term to become assistant superintendent under E. R. Fryer.[91] During his short term, Dodge appointed an executive committee and extra council members responsible for water projects, farming, natural resources, education, public health, employment, and chapter organization.

Such changes did not please Morgan's group, who saw too great an emphasis on land and sheep. Then, over their adamant objections, Roosevelt named John Collier BIA commissioner. Collier's goal, Morgan argued, was to make Navajos more, not less, "Indian," and his proposed New Deal programs became obstacles to assimilation. Indeed, when Collier addressed the tribal council in 1933, he cautioned, "you must not go back to the blanket . . . [but] you must not altogether become white."[92]

Morgan's curt response written to a Farmington newspaper set the tone for the next decade: "One sure thing, the writer is not going back to the blanket, but will stay in the ways of the white man and never hang on to the inheritance of his ancestors."[93] In 1933, oil took a back seat to New Deal and other initiatives.

 # DEPRESSION AND DESPAIR: 1932–1949

... An old lady sits to the place of fire
Asdzáá Dibé Łizhini slowly turning over
the sizzling sheep intestines
with a sharpened oak twig

Sick and in numbness
her grandchild lies under
the shade of the Summer shade house
the Song of Hunger hidden
in her eyes
eyes glistening glossy
in the child's mind
missionary songs and punch
sing song with no rituals

Sick child smells the sweet odor
of the cooking achii and azid
craving for freshness of meat
even makes the inner self starve

Asdzáá Dibé Łizhini says so herself
so then she butchers and feeds
the Fire flames
to outwit the crafty skinny
Old Hunger.[1]

Even before the United States plunged into depression, the oil market was so unstable that some industry leaders favored outright federal regulation, and the American Petroleum Institute (API), the industry's primary trade association, officially endorsed conservation as a policy.[2] Overproduction remained such a problem that Interior Secretary Ray Lyman Wilbur cautioned

President Herbert H. Hoover that catastrophe loomed if something were not done, and done soon.

Navajos leased no new tracts after 1928, but Hogback, Rattlesnake, and Table Mesa operated steadily, earning $147,268 in royalties in 1929.[3] Although prices elsewhere plunged to 10 cents per barrel or less, during the 1930s, Navajo royalties, which often topped $1 per barrel, remained extraordinarily high by comparison. Even so, total royalties for Rattlesnake dipped to $26,554 in 1931 and remained at about that level through 1936; the price-per-barrel fluctuated.[4]

This was a bad decade for Navajos in other ways as well. Winter 1930–31 had brought devastating blizzards that destroyed two hundred thousand or more sheep, the loss of which also left many Navajos without the resources to hire singers or medicine men for religious and curing ceremonies.[5] Then came a drop in lamb and wool prices, which actually began in 1929, but got worse as the depression progressed.

The months between Franklin D. Roosevelt's election in November 1932 and his inauguration in March 1933 were perhaps the most dismal in history for Americans as a whole. Hoover, who refused to regulate oil or endorse conservation measures, remained ineffective. The oil industry sank into a state of utter demoralization.[6] Other businesses — especially banks — panicked as well, and by the time Roosevelt took office, people across the country felt desperate. As humorist Will Rogers quipped, "I don't know what additional authority Roosevelt may ask, but give it to him, even if it's to drown all the boy babies."[7]

New Deal Oil Programs

During his first hundred days, Roosevelt turned the federal government into a treasure trove of New Deal relief. Congressional legislation and presidential executive orders generated agencies to administer the new programs. One of these was the National Industrial Recovery Act (NIRA), whose central aim was to stabilize industrial prices and offer some minimal guarantees to organized labor by authorizing management and labor leaders within each industry to formulate codes of fair competition. Oil production and employment concerns were included. The NIRA, in turn, spawned an agency called the National Recovery Administration (NRA), headed by Hugh Johnson. Assisted by the API, the NRA drafted an industry-wide code and named Secretary of the Interior Harold L. Ickes its administrator. The code included, among other things, provisions for monthly state quotas. Ickes wanted to fix prices, too, but small producers still concluded that any regulations at all would put them out of business, and so the industry refused to endorse price-fixing.

At a Dallas meeting of API, Ickes addressed those who wanted government out of private business altogether. "If I were not as polite as I really am," he snapped, "I might remark that if private initiative is so wonderful and so self-efficient, how did it happen that the oil industry got into such a mess . . ."[8] Ickes also argued that unless everyone adhered to the codes, chaos would continue.

On January 7, 1935, the Supreme Court's decision *Panama Refining Co. v. Ryan* declared the federal enforcement of state quotas invalid, and in May of that year *Schechter v. U.S.* unanimously struck down the NRA. But the industry decided to take steps on its own to control waste and stabilize the market. Still, independents feared collapse if forced to slow production.[9] On January 8, Ickes proposed "hot oil" legislation to outlaw shipments of contraband oil, one way small companies avoided quotas. On August 27, 1935, Congress approved the Interstate Oil Compact to help coordinate production between states, although states could decide whether to become part of it.[10]

Some of the largest oil-producing states had already tried in vain to control oil locally. Texas, for example, struggled to limit production in its eastern fields through the Texas Railroad Commission. Similarly, in 1926 Oklahoma tried to stabilize oil by using its only regulatory body, the Oklahoma Corporation Commission, to impose barrel limitations.[11] Unsuccessful and besieged with violence after these agencies attempted to halt production, the two states came together in 1931 to create an interstate compact. However, this compact could not curb overproduction. Thus Texas, Oklahoma, and other oil-producing states joined the Interstate Oil Compact in 1935 and the Oil Conservation Commission organized by states in 1936.[12]

New Deal programs eventually made inroads toward stabilizing oil. By 1940, voluntary cooperation, interstate regulations, hot oil legislation, and new Bureau of Mines monthly production forecasts curbed much of the waste and cutthroat competition. In fact, some producers chose to remain federally regulated after 1940 and even following the end of World War II. On Indian lands where government had always controlled oil, however, Ickes encouraged production. He approved 194 new sites on reservations in ten states, including tracts on Table Mesa, Hogback, and Rattlesnake.[13] Hence, in 1933, while the state government of New Mexico challenged its allocated daily production rate set by the oil code, producers on Rattlesnake and Table Mesa were encouraged to increase output as part of a program of balancing production and consumption.[14] Nevertheless, despite Ickes's efforts, oil production on the Navajo reservation remained slow; profits were small albeit relatively steady, and companies attempted no significant exploration.

In 1934, Conoco (Continental's parent company) ran nationwide radio advertising to promote tourism and petroleum use. But the oil industry did not recover until World War II, and on the Navajo reservation improvement took much longer.[15] Records show that the tribal council seldom discussed oil after 1933. Yet the depression and war years are so significant to Navajo modern history that the major events cannot be overlooked.

Navajo Land Extensions Revisited

Of Hagerman's unfinished business, land was most important. After the government failed to obtain land in 1931, Secretary Wilbur withdrew four million acres of public domain in Arizona and New Mexico until the situation could be straightened out. Senator Carl Hayden wrote legislation in 1934 to settle the Arizona border, while James M. Stewart, land management director for the Indian Service, drafted a bill to annex 2.5 million acres in San Juan, McKinley, and Sandoval counties, New Mexico. Both settlements came with the understanding that once boundaries were established, Navajos could obtain no more off-reservation allotments, exchanges, or purchases. Thus, the legislation was intended to solve the problem forever.

The Arizona bill passed, and at first it appeared New Mexicans would go along as well. With Senator Bronson Cutting in favor, the state delegation seemed pro-extension. Local stock association leaders even met on June 30, 1933, in Gallup, and reached "an understanding," but newly appointed commissioner John Collier was so involved with his Indian Reorganization Act (IRA) that he neglected to secure a quick vote on the New Mexico extension, giving stock owners time to muster forces and allowing the bill to die in committee.[16]

Local New Mexicans left out of the June 30 meeting lobbied the governor.[17] The San Juan Basin Livestock and Grazing Association, for instance, denounced the proposed extension.[18] Taxpayers informed Governor Clyde Tingley, "We are sure 90% are opposed [to the legislation]."[19] *Colliers* later suggested the problem was simply that New Mexicans "hadn't the courage" to do "anything displeasing to a dozen big-hatted, high-booted, romantic-looking stockmen, whose pockets are very deep, whose trigger-fingers are very nervous, and whose political influence is so elastic that it stretches easily from Santa Fe to Washington."[20] But like many other Westerners, these New Mexicans resented federally held land and wanted it returned, not more land transferred for federal, non-taxable purposes.

In 1935, Cutting died in a tragic airplane crash, and protesters found a true friend and ally in Dennis Chavez, appointed to fill the empty seat. As Chavez sought to please white and Hispanic landowners, he assured constituents, "I'll let the Indian Bureau know that all the people in New Mexico are not Indians."[21] Chavez received valuable support from J. C. Morgan, who believed the extension would simply defeat his goal of economic development for Navajos. "A foreigner has a better chance than we have of enjoying the American dream," Morgan wrote.[22] Moreover, since citizenship in 1924, we have been led to believe . . . that the Bureau would grant us our personal freedom, yet . . . [the Indian Office] has continued to segregate the Indian, keep him an Indian . . . [and] cut him off from the greatest education for citizenship, namely personal contact with American life.[23]

Ironically, Morgan was so pro-assimilation and opposed to whatever made Navajos "more Indian" that he resisted anything he believed would isolate Navajos from white society even if that was more land.

In August 1934, Morgan's zeal led him to the right-wing American Indian Federation [AIF], which blended anti-government zeal with super-patriotism and Christianity.[24] Morgan's interest waned, however, when he discovered some of the organization's leaders were peyotists — a practice he abhorred. But his flirtation with the AIF and his affiliation with Chavez reveal tremendous resentment against John Collier's philosophy of cultural pluralism. It must be noted that some Navajos recalled Morgan with a sense of pride, while others accused him of selling out to Chavez and resorting to dirty politics.[25]

Although the New Mexico bill faltered, Congress added the Paiute Strip or Aneth Extension in Utah in 1933. House Resolution (H. R.) 11735 was introduced in 1932, but fearing trouble from Blanding-area stockmen, Governor George H. Dern personally talked with locals and extracted their approval. The Paiute Strip appended 500,000 acres to the reservation.[26] The arrangement reserved 37½ percent of future oil and gas royalties to Utah Navajos to be administered by the state; 62½ went to the Navajo Nation.[27]

In 1936, Collier finally turned his attention to the New Mexico boundary bill, which was stalled in committee. The Senate, stinging with the barbs of loud anti-boundary rhetoric, decided to investigate reservation conditions before going any further. Thus, senators took testimony in New Mexico during summer 1936. White stockmen and Morgan followers crowded in to hurl their resentment at the BIA, land extension plans, and Collier himself. By February 1937, the New Mexico bill again went to committee. Chavez told members "he had no objection to receiving it as an expression of the bureau's attitude," but assaulted the legislation so brutally that it died in committee a second time.[28]

Ironically, Howard Gorman, a member of the Returned Students Organization, headed the Navajo Eastern Boundary Association in 1937, which favored extension. Some whites heaped condemnation upon stock owners and Chavez alike. One recalled, "Chavez came to Thoreau about a year ago. He saw one person and then announced that the town was against the extension bill."[29] The opposition proved more powerful, however, and successfully blocked expansion, resulting in the loss of vast acreage to Navajos. It can thus be said that regarding land extensions, Collier fared no better than had

Hagerman. Moreover, historian Peter Iverson noted that failure of the New Mexico extension bill was a major blow to Navajos and crystallized sentiment against Collier.[30]

Navajos, Stock Reduction, and Tribal Reorganization

In 1933, Roosevelt had named the BIA's most vocal critic its new commissioner. Collier's immediate goals were to direct New Deal money to tribes, end allotments, and reawaken traditional Indian culture. During his tenure, Collier would also initiate Indian preference in hiring for BIA jobs. He sponsored legislation (Johnson-O'Malley Act of April 16, 1934) that allowed the Secretary of the Interior to contract with state or local agencies for services such as education and enlisted the Public Health Service to assist in Indian medical care. As such, he began to loosen the Indian Office's hold over tribes.[31]

Although many Native Americans across the country—as well as whites—heralded the commissioner as a welcome change from men like Burke and Rhoads, some of Collier's aims guaranteed the enmity of Navajos, especially educated Navajos. When Collier launched his controversial stock reduction program, he provided opponents with ammunition. A 1930 Bureau of Indian Affairs (BIA) Forestry Division survey affirmed that Navajos owned a surplus of sheep and goats on badly overgrazed, eroded land. The tribal council had formally identified the problem in 1924 and in 1928 imposed a grazing fee on all herds over one thousand. Few Navajos, of course, owned such large herds, but those who did—most of them from the Fort Defiance area—refused to pay, and neither the council nor Indian Office was able to enforce the fees.[32]

Navajos blamed the problem on drought, which they argued was cyclical and not, as federal authorities insisted, caused by too many sheep. The dry cycle had begun about 1900, and it would likely continue for several more years. In fact, had Navajos witnessed the devastating dust bowl that left farmers in Oklahoma, Kansas, Nebraska, and the Dakotas without crops, they might have pressed their convictions even more strongly. Regardless, as summer cloudbursts ate deeply into the soil and washed grass away, BIA employees saw a deteriorating situation.[33] Indeed, government had helped Navajos for the past decade breed and expand herds. They purchased and distributed thousands of pure bred rams, and most of the Navajo flocks showed improvement by 1930.[34]

But in October 1933, Collier proposed a 400,000-head reduction and vowed to supplement losses with wage work. He also promised to reduce herds on a percentage basis: families with subsistence herds would lose none. The tribal council reluctantly endorsed the plan when Collier told them reduction could ensue with or without delegates' permission. Most large stock owners refused to cooperate or merely culled their herds of old sheep called gummers and shells. Small owners, on the other hand, often lost entire herds. Chee

Dodge made himself the exception: he voluntarily reduced his herd from 200,000 to 700 and sharply criticized the BIA for kowtowing to a few.[35]

Complicating matters was the manner in which stock reduction occurred. Some officials asked Navajos to bring sheep to a central location and agreed to purchase them. But according to one worker "the process . . . proved to be nothing less than mass confusion."

> Several of us were detailed to do the paperwork as well as examine the sheep. . . . It was a nightmare. Thirsty sheep on all sides pushed toward the water. . . . From dawn through dusk without a break, the world was madness. Then it was over. . . . It haunts me now, more than a half century later, and it still haunts the Navajos even more profoundly.[36]

Collier announced a 150,000–goat reduction in March 1934, then raised the amount to 200,000 without informing Navajos.[37] This event was especially callous. Agents went to herds and often shot the animals before the eyes of astonished, grieving families. In some instances, agents gave fresh goat meat to families or had it canned and sent back to them. In other instances, goats rotted in fields or had gasoline poured over the carcasses and were partly cremated.[38]

The Soil Conservation Service (SCS), a division of the Department of Agriculture, created to solve the dust bowl problem, began a program of land control "convinced that their cause was just, that God was on their side, and that they really did know all there was to know."[39] However, both the BIA and SCS absolutely missed the significance Navajos placed on their sheep. As an elderly Navajo told authorities, "each year he harvested wool and a lamb from each of his ewes, and at the end of the year he still had the ewes." Money, he demonstrated with gestures, sifted through his fingers and vanished.[40]

Collier's wage work seldom materialized to the extent needed. Although some Navajos obtained jobs through the New Deal Civilian Conservation Corps (CCC), thousands needing wage work did not. As one Capiton Benally put it,

> After I reduced my sheep I asked for a job, and the other Navajos asked for work; but the U.S. officials told us there were no jobs. . . . the jobs they had talked about had been just fakes.[41]

Additional livestock reductions were announced after 1935, continuing through 1945. Many Navajos lost their livelihood altogether and were forced to accept government subsidies for the first time. Navajos who refused were often jailed and/or humiliated by having their hair cut off.

Two additional insults were heaped upon Navajos in 1936 and 1937. Congress had approved an irrigation farming project near Fruitland, Morgan's region, in 1931. Work began in 1933, and the goal was to create twenty-acre sub-sistence farms for landless Navajos. In April 1936, Collier cut the per-family acreage to ten acres, although judging by official correspondence, the BIA continued to debate the issue. In 1938, for instance, Fryer wrote "I believe that it would be very unwise politically and economically to make a flat change in our policy of land assignments to 20 from 10 acres." He added, "It would certainly hand Morgan a complete victory," a common worry for the Collier administration.[42]

The second insult was a stock limit of 350 or the equivalent (meaning fewer sheep if families also owned goats and horses). BIA and tribal officials distributed permits, and many ended up in places that clearly illustrated the Navajo attitude toward them. For example, *chindi* hogans were sometimes stuffed with stock permits. Capping the number of sheep a family could own also broke down social status based upon amount of livestock and undermined commodity stock raising, which whites had tried to encourage.[43]

Stock reduction was heaven-sent for anti-Indian Office Navajos like Morgan. It meshed with their desire to promote education and business development. But Morgan hated other Collier programs like closing boarding schools in favor of day schools, consolidating the tribal government at Window Rock, and implementing the IRA or Wheeler-Howard Act, which reversed the assimilation policy. Stock reduction was political dynamite. So, as Chee Dodge advocated compliance, Morgan expanded his popularity by upbraiding the hated policy. His attack did nothing to stop it, but allowed him to seriously challenge Collier and Wheeler-Howard, and to maintain a cloud of suspicion over nearly every New Deal policy.[44]

Eli Gorman of Nazlíní probably voiced the opinion of many when he admonished Collier: "He had taken a large part of our sheep, goats and horses. And he acted just like this was nothing." Furthermore, Collier grew frustrated with Navajos. Gorman recalled that during a Window Rock meeting "The Diné really were debating with him and chasing him around. Then he [Collier] got in his airplane saying, 'I am going back to Washington, D.C.'" Then, he "got into his plane, made a few rounds overhead and disappeared."[45]

E. Reeseman Fryer, who became superintendent in March 1936, was an easy target of Morgan's wrath and sheep owners' animosity. Fryer was generally considered "forceful, not subtle" in his approach. A Mormon from the Salt River Valley region in Arizona, Fryer had successfully implemented stock reduction programs among other Indian groups, namely the Laguna and Acoma — and it is interesting to note that such programs were not peculiar to Navajos. Nevertheless, Fryer quickly became an object of ridicule among Navajos.[46] By his own admission, the 35-year-old Fryer found youth a deterrent in dealing with elders, who lifted his hat and noted, "No, he doesn't have any gray hairs."[47] Dan Yazzie of Many Farms called Fryer "an ugly white man" and found some of Fryer's mannerisms particularly irritating:

He [Fryer] told Navajos at a meeting in Crown point, "I want no 'no' answer; I want a 'yes' answer," and when they finally agreed . . . he was very happy. He ran around slapping his rear end. He thanked us for accepting his stock reduction proposal.[48]

After Tom Dodge resigned as tribal council chairman in 1936 to become Fryer's assistant, some Navajos turned against him as well, especially since Dodge began to espouse the advantages of stock reduction.[49] Morgan, who had originally endorsed Dodge as chairman, considered him as just another Indian turned bureaucrat. Nevertheless, in his new position, Dodge remained actively interested in the tribal government.

On March 12, 1934, Collier presented the IRA to Navajos at a special tribal council session. He explained that the law repealed allotments, offered tribes and individuals loans through a $10 million revolving fund, and provided an education "that [would] equip an Indian to hold any position in the Indian Service." The IRA established lower courts and a higher Court of Indian Affairs, with judges "appointed by the President and confirmed by the Senate."[50] Most important, he said, the legislation gave Indians self-government. Navajos, like other tribes, could set up local governments ruled by a constitution and bylaws. Once approved by the Congress, these could not be destroyed by the BIA or Interior Department, Collier emphasized.[51]

Collier reasoned that without oil the tribal council as it existed in 1934 had little purpose. Besides, it had never represented Navajos overall. "None of [the council's] early actions affected the lives of the Navajo people . . . and many said they had never heard of it."[52] If anything, chapters, introduced in July 1927 by Leupp Agency Superintendent John G. Hunter, were more effective in solving local problems. Tribal councils usually attracted at least several hundred people, and Indian Office employees encountered difficulties providing food and facilities for them. Chapters were smaller and more easily managed. These meetings also gave individuals a voice, especially women, who were seldom if ever elected as delegates to the council.

Traditionals like Chee Dodge and Little Silversmith advocated chapters so strongly that when the Indian Office transferred Hunter to the Southern Navajo Agency in 1928, they encouraged him to initiate the system there. Educated Navajo Howard Gorman transported the idea to Ganado and Crownpoint. Thus, chapters sprang up across the reservation.[53] They worked well with the extended family units and clan structures because they encouraged entire groups to participate. While the council addressed matters raised by the dominant society — like oil royalties — chapters dealt with internal or local issues. Unfortunately, the upheaval caused by stock reduction undermined, even destroyed, many chapters, although others grew stronger and served as rallying points for the opposition.[54]

Reluctance to embrace the first tribal council led Collier to conclude that Navajos might be receptive to his IRA. Besides, in the councils, progressives had steadily gained control, debating topics in English and excluding older, less schooled men.[55] Many tribes would ultimately take advantage of the IRA. Some of the smaller New England tribes, the Algonkians in particular, reorganized under an IRA constitution. When Wheeler-Howard was expanded in 1936 to include Alaskan natives, the Aleuts adopted the new system. Moreover, the Oklahoma Indian Welfare Act of 1936 extended similar provisions to the Five Tribes. The Creeks even petitioned for recognition of their existing constitution under the IRA.

Navajos faced a different situation. For instance, one has only to read Collier's address to the tribe to see how poorly he explained the provisions. Page after page was devoted to topics like allotment, which Collier admitted even as he spoke, had nothing much to do with Navajos. Instead of a broad overall plan, Collier presented IRA in such minute detail that it proved almost impossible to fathom. In addition, whereas New England and Oklahoma tribes spoke fluent English, fewer than ten percent of all Navajos spoke English at all in 1934. Thus, everything was, by necessity, translated, making comprehension even harder.

Debate over the IRA raged into spring 1935. Navajos felt confused: "We thought our leaders knew what it was, but it appeared that even they didn't know what was going on." One compared the meetings and discussions to the moccasin game, where a "person hides the ball and others guess where it is."[56] IRA required a referendum with a majority of all adult voters to pass, and this vote was delayed twice.

Worse, many Navajos associated IRA with failed land extensions and especially stock reduction. Would rejection of IRA prevent further livestock deaths, they asked?[57] Morgan's Returned Students Organization told Navajos that Wheeler-Howard gave control of tribal affairs to the Indian Office. Confusion only aided their cause. Missionaries split, too. Catholics endorsed IRA as a Navajo passport to self-government, as did most Fort Defiance leaders.[58] Protestants, though, feared self-government might ultimately ban them from the reservation. Christian Reformed and Baptists predicted the IRA would permit medicine men to teach tribal culture in Navajo day schools.[59]

On June 15, 1935, Navajos rejected IRA by 7,679 to 8,197, a very close vote. Agents charged "Navajos [do] not care to assume responsibilities of home rule" and cautioned that "danger of dissipation of Navajo tribal lands, oil, and timber rights" could result.[60] Morgan crowed,

The Indian commissioner has met more than a match in the young progressive Navajos who want the benefits of civilization for themselves and their children . . . [schooled Navajos] were afraid this self-government idea would result in the loss of those cherished rights of equal citizenship with their white brothers.[61]

IRA foe and tribal leader Roger Davis justified the vote: "We do not wish to be held back by the power and rule of Indian Bureau . . . We will never go forward and will never take our place in our great American Government."[62]

The vote, however, reflected confusion more than any referendum for or against Collier. Moreover, many Navajos believed that a rejection of IRA would also end stock reduction. It is important to note, too, that although Collier felt a particular fondness toward the Pueblos of New Mexico, only Santa Clara Pueblo initially accepted the IRA. Later, five more voted in favor, but thirteen Pueblo groups rejected the European-structured model. Still, the Navajo tribal council remained inadequate, and so in 1936, Navajos voted to reorganize.[63]

Navajos Create A New Tribal Council

On November 24, 1936, the Navajo tribal council turned to chapters for assistance. Delegates agreed to reorganize and determined that Navajo headmen should draft the constitution and bylaws based on traditional values.[64] Then, council members voted to disband. Morgan asked Chavez, "Are we going to let this work of Tom Dodge, Fryer and Collier be okayed?"[65] But from December 4, 1936, to March 6, 1937, a committee made up of former council delegates and Father Berard went to chapters and visited allotments, collecting the names of elders who might serve as members of the constitutional assembly.

Navajos received the group warmly, except in Shiprock, where Morgan was circulating a petition advocating separation of the New Mexico from the Arizona reservation and annexing each to its respective state. Robert Young contends that this was yet another extension of the earlier fight over oil royalties and of the Shiprock/Fort Defiance rivalry.[66] Hostile Shiprock Navajos chose Morgan to represent them. By March 6, 1937, the committee had 250 names, which they culled down to seventy in time for the April 9–10 assembly. Compromising, the committee kept Morgan on the list, and when the meeting opened, Morgan was named chairman. His response was to call those in the assembly "crooked long-hairs" and then to depart.[67]

By September 29, delegates completed the draft and presented the constitution and bylaws to Fryer. The document resembled an IRA constitution, but with more autonomy to the tribe.[68] The bylaws proposed a seventy-four-member council, twenty at-large delegates, and fifty-four apportioned among land management districts. Cañoncito and Puertocito (Alamo) each received one delegate.[69] Bylaws also stipulated a president, vice president, and executive committee comprising both of these plus the at-large delegates. The document clearly delineated officer powers and responsibilities, with special attention paid to natural resources. Collier proved reluctant to approve the document since Navajos had already voted down IRA.

Compounding the upheaval, Collier had recently dismantled the six Navajo agencies that had existed for thirty years. In their place, he created nineteen land management districts, which some Navajos resented and which afforded yet another opportunity for dissent.[70] He also centralized BIA and Navajo offices at Window Rock, designating the new district "tribal headquarters." Although Collier apparently liked the Window Rock location, many Navajos hated it. Thus, before disbanding, the tribal council delegates had met outside of their regularly scheduled meeting to discuss these changes beyond the range of Anglo eyes and ears.[71] Window Rock was far from population centers, and again Shiprock Navajos feared Fort Defiance Navajos and Catholics would wield disproportionate influence.

A number of whites, especially traders, also disliked the new headquarters, apparently believing consolidation would hurt business. Hence, Collier heard tales that made Gallup sound like a regular Sodom or Gomorrah, stories that Governor Tingley admitted were fanned by the Hubbells, who had land to sell the government at Ganado. Other traders were perhaps trying to give Gallup a black eye so that government officials would keep Navajos from going there and spending their money in that town instead of in reservation trading posts.[72]

So, as the constitutional assembly hammered out its constitution and bylaws and Navajos protested the Window Rock location, Morgan called the first meeting of the Navajo Progressive League in Farmington. The League censured Collier and the IRA and dubbed Senator Chavez "a real, true, and honest friend of the Indian."[73] The group rejected the draft constitution and endorsed an unrealistic program of self-government with Navajos in control of their land, schools, hospitals, and irrigation. Whereas Catholic friars sanctioned the constitution, Protestants attended the Progressive League meeting. *Aztec Independent* editor George Bowra called the gathering old-fashioned, town-hall democracy at its finest and praised progressives as working to free themselves from the whims and foibles of every passing Indian Department commissioner.[74]

Yet according to Chee Dodge, the Progressives were more alarmists than democrats, and Morgan used stock reduction to coerce money from even the poorest Navajos. Collier mused that once Morgan had been one of the

strongest and sanest leaders of the tribe, but "has completely reversed himself."
He "fights without logical reasoning every constructive move of the tribe and
of the government [and] opposes the reorganized Tribal Council."[75]

Protestant missionary J. H. Boscher agreed that Morgan was difficult.[76] But
Bowra later decided the real problem was "too many White Men helping bake
the pies in the kitchen."[77] One such baker was Farmington attorney Paul
Palmer, an outspoken Collier critic, who on June 4, 1937, accompanied Morgan to Washington.[78] Collier apparently listened to complaints for three days,
but found few constructive ideas. Fryer thought Palmer dishonest: "he got
money from the Navajos on promises of services that he knew at the time he
couldn't possibly deliver."[79] Palmer eventually experienced personal problems
and thankfully withdrew from reservation affairs.

In the end, Collier rejected the constitution, fearing Navajos might use it
to counter federal programs like stock reduction. Navajos had removed the
1923 ruling allowing councils to meet only when called and with agents present.[80] Collier reinstated it. Finally, the Indian Office revised the document
and promulgated "Rules for the Navajo Council" on July 26, 1938. "Rules" established a new tribal council, but neglected to fully spell out its powers or responsibilities as the draft constitution had done.[81]

The reorganized tribal council met for the first time on September 24, 1938.
Morgan attended, as usual, and was elected chairman; Gorman was chosen
vice chairman. Collier and Fryer clearly worried about the outcome. Technically, Morgan lived off the reservation, which disqualified him. But to deny
him a leadership role would only strengthen his faction and "throw back in
our faces the policy of self-determination." Plus, Navajos might think Collier
feared Morgan's influence. Fryer recommended that they simply accept the
outcome; besides, Morgan was less potent as chairman "than as a frustrated
raving maniac on the outside."

> I believe if he were Chairman, given an office at Window Rock, and
> brought into our discussions that in time we could bend him in our
> direction. He is a pathological paranoic who demands recognition of
> his leadership. Give him an occasional dose to inflate his ego and tho I
> may be unduly optimistic, I believe he can be made more of a help than
> a hindrance.[82]

They might alienate Dodge, but as Fryer concluded,

> Chee will pretend to be with us only as long as there is an advantage in
> being pro-government. When the shoe starts pinching Chee, he will stop
> at nothing to preserve his huge livestock interests and land monopoly.[83]

Fryer made Morgan's installation "as much of an occasion as possible" to "impress upon the Chairman and the Council members the greatness of their responsibility." Morgan's acceptance speech in English was "completely inoffensive," Fryer reported, although Gorman admitted that the Navajo translation included barbs not included in his English version. "It is a Morgan council," Fryer wrote, composed of missionaries and returned students "who have not been able to make cultural adjustments." Few owned property. Several had jail records. All spoke English. None were "long hairs." Moreover, "not a single stockman of any consequence is represented."[84] As expected, the council had no knowledge of the limits of its authority, and "appears to believe that it is all-powerful."[85]

Tom Dodge feared the Morgan council symbolized a turning point in Navajo history, with white interests solidly represented. "The old is on its way out and this is the beginning of an irresistible movement . . . to acculturation." But Fryer thought the election represented little more than a revolt against stock reduction and "everything in fact that has been done on the reservation for the past six years." Of the seventeen thousand votes cast, Morgan's eight thousand votes did not represent a majority viewpoint.[86]

Fryer's prophecy proved correct. The chairman quickly fell in line with Indian Office policies. As Navajos grew increasingly upset with stock reduction, they also became disillusioned with Morgan and his "clique."[87] Sadly, Navajos generally agreed that Morgan was rapidly turning into "a member of the Window Rock gang" with a good salary.[88]

With Morgan safely in the BIA fold, new factions formed. Cheschilligi established the Navajo Rights Association (NRA), which within a short time attained an estimated membership of five thousand.[89] The NRA opposed stock reduction and even favored returning to a policy of upgrading herds "to maintain the tradition of [the] self-supporting Navajo Nation."[90] Members endorsed boarding schools, Public Health Service hospitals, and Navajo supervision of natural resources.[91] They accused the BIA of appropriating tribal money to purchase employee airplanes and radios while neglecting irrigation and housing.[92] Morgan threatened to remove NRA sympathizers from the council, but because of growing resentment against him, Morgan lost the 1942 election for tribal chairman to old rival Chee Dodge. Ironically, by this time, Morgan was upholding the BIA party line, while Dodge emerged as Collier critic and NRA spokesman.[93]

The NRA weakened after September 21, 1945, with the end of federally-mandated stock reduction and the Collier administration. Furthermore, a Farmington deputy sheriff discovered Deshna allegedly drunk and passed out in a ditch. Arrested and taken to jail, Cheschilligi was found dead hours later of a blow to the head.[94] The white policeman was acquitted, but sadly Navajos lost a pioneer member of the first tribal council, who believed that the organization could be more than yes-men.

Interest in oil and Natural Gas is Rekindled

In January 1938, Continental Oil, Stanolind, and Standard Oil applied jointly for a 25,000-acre exploratory lease on Tocito, Beautiful Mountain, Chimney Rock, and Bitlabito. Red Butte Oil Company asked Navajos to reinstate its Stony Butte lease as well. Claiming "Washington can not afford to continue spending money to help us," acting chairman Henry Taliman appointed a five-person committee to consider the requests.[95]

Oil revenues took on increased importance in 1938 although they did not provide much additional income. With the New Mexico boundary bill a dead issue, the BIA proposed setting aside $750,000 to purchase land, claiming Indians could repay the loan from future royalties. Moreover, stock reduction combined with inadequate wage work left many Navajos impoverished. Hesitant to fully endorse oil exploration, the committee recommended the exploratory and Red Butte Oil leases only, although Morgan approved a lease to small operator George Goodrun to prevent corporate monopolies.[96] While production nationwide was still subject to monthly quotas and temporary shutdowns, Navajo wells were not.[97]

In 1938, Congress passed the Omnibus Tribal Leasing Act, which would dictate mineral and oil leasing on Indian lands until 1982. Oil and gas leases still required competitive bidding, but the Secretary of the Interior could set aside bids and readvertise or negotiate leases with tribal consent. Tribes not organized under IRA, like the Navajos, needed specific authority to control mineral development on their land.

Although oil production remained minimal, Morgan made it a point to advance tribal enterprises during his term. Locals predicted success for the new $75,000 Fort Defiance sawmill, the flour mill built at Round Rock, and the slaughterhouse and cannery near Many Farms.[98] Yet oil hardly provided sufficient funds to encourage investments in natural resource development, and a 1932 assessment of off-reservation formations even speculated that perhaps there was little oil left in northwestern New Mexico.[99]

Some companies initiated exploration with the onset of World War II, recalling that oil drilled on Navajo land in the 1920s had generally come from shallow sands. Despite Hagerman's repeated demands to deep-test, for the most part, few had. Now firms possessed sophisticated means by which to seek oil at deeper levels. Phillips Oil arrived in November 1943 with a seismograph, which allowed geologists to trace underground characteristics by setting off a series of subterranean explosions and measuring the "waves" as they traveled downward and struck successive rock formations. By calculating the intensity of waves and time intervals, geologists obtained a good idea of what lay below the surface.[100] As one author explained it,

> Imagine an inverted triangle with equal sides. The scientist uses a dynamite shot and recording instrument to measure the distance from the triangle's base (earth's surface) to its apex, the reflecting point on the structure, far underground. Where the structure is highest, oil may be found.[101]

In 1947, Gulf Oil used an electronic bird.[102] This was actually a C-47 airplane equipped with magnetometer (magnetic dip-needle or dip-compass) to perform aerial mapping. Introduced to the oil industry in 1946, it was particularly useful in mapping remote areas. Gulf Oil plotted ten thousand square miles in New Mexico, Colorado, and Arizona, seeking oil, gold, nickel, silver, and iron.[103]

A major discovery during the 40s was helium. In July 1942, Conoco struck gas on Rattlesnake that contained a chemical used in the manufacture of explosives. For security reasons, the military released no information, but reports indicated that underground pressure was so intense wells threatened to run wild.[104] Santa Fe Company and Continental still owned the lease, so in March 1943, the government negotiated with them for rights, allowing the companies to keep the oil, but turning helium production over to the Bureau of Mines. On July 10, 1943, the tribal council approved the helium plant.[105]

Hudson Construction erected a processing plant and forty employee houses for the Bureau of Mines near Shiprock. Natural gas from several San Juan fields was piped in to operate the processing plant. The helium was piped from Rattlesnake to the Shiprock plant, then trucked to railroads in Gallup and Farmington. Ickes named the structure the Navajo Helium Plant.[106]

By 1944 there were two helium projects; one was on the original 1923 4,080-acre lease co-owned by Santa Fe Company and Continental Oil, and the other on a 3,720-acre lease owned by Continental alone and acquired by the federal government. Since the companies involved were only interested in the oil, the Bureau of Mines agreed to an arrangement whereby the government would obtain rights to the helium and the companies could retain the oil.[107] Production halted in 1945, but in June 1947, Congress authorized the Interior Department to take over the entire 7,800-acre helium gas lease.[108] In August 1952, the Bureau of Mines reactivated the plant, making it a continuous, day-and-night operation.[109] Most of the helium continued to come from the Rattlesnake and Table Mesa sites. The United States controlled helium production worldwide, and the Navajo plant was one of only five plants.[110]

There was still no official geological survey of the Navajo reservation, but when Western Natural Gas offered to fund one, the BIA informed the company that it was not authorized to accept the money from the lessee for this purpose.[111] Nor did the Indian Office have sufficient money to conduct a survey. So again, an impasse arose between the need for such a survey and how to fund it.

Royalty questions also arose. In 1932, the BIA had agreed to establish royalties for Navajo oil at fifteen cents above the highest mid-continent price for oil of 44-degree gravity or less. Now, with prices on the increase and dramatic changes in the oil industry overall, some believed it was time to review the arrangement. But, at this point, nearly all Navajo oil was still marketed locally, quelling temporarily the urgency for surveys or royalty reviews.[112]

The Impact of the Depression and War Era

The reform impulse that brought Collier into the BIA was spent by the time World War II began. Because of the war, Native Americans were thrust into the background of national concerns, and the federal government redirected resources. Navajos, like thousands of other native peoples from across the United States, joined the military and, like whites, sought war work in cities. Only after everyone returned were the full implications of stock reduction realized. As historian Richard White so aptly explained in his groundbreaking study of dependency, the once self-sufficient Navajos faced starvation or welfare after 1945.[113]

Women, who had always cared for the great flocks of sheep and goats, were also greatly affected mentally and physically by the abuse of their stock and isolated by a program whose only compensation went to men in the form of wage work. Stock reduction pitted women against the BIA and even some tribal leaders.[114] Navajo women who never heard the term "depression" or to whom the date 1934 had no meaning often had much to say when asked about Collier. So, too, could these mothers and grandmothers later elaborate on how they felt when "the sheep were taken away."[115] One Navajo woman explained that in addition to all the other problems it caused, stock reduction accelerated alcohol use among both sexes and helped erode family life on the reservation.[116]

Historians have asked how Collier could have misunderstood Navajos so completely, especially since stock reduction rivaled the Long Walk in its devastating consequences. But Navajo reactions to Collier and his New Deal policies hinged in large part on how a Navajo identified as Navajo. Educated Navajos who dreamed of total assimilation into white society feared cultural pluralism. Traditionals ardently rejected stock reduction, but often favored IRA. In 1947, former Interior Secretary Wilbur said, "Collier put the Indians back under the blanket and then took the blanket away."[117] This was only one view of the Collier era.

Scholars tend to view the first tribal councils, which met between 1923–1936, as ineffective. True, members faced tremendous frustration as they dealt with oil company and BIA antics. It was undoubtedly difficult for them to forge a tribal political entity given their brief annual meeting schedule and their limited authority. Moreover, it is probably true that delegates were chosen by agents rather than fellow Navajos. But leaders employed this forum to discuss a wide range of matters and used their single weapon — lease approval — as best they could. Navajos relegated royalties to the tribe, not individuals — a farsighted choice — and nobody can read council minutes without gaining tremendous insight into Navajo values. Factions aired disagreements and forced compromises. Navajos sought ways to invigorate their economy and laid the framework for the natural resource development that would occur after 1969.

6 NEW DISCOVERIES, 1950–1959

In a letter written to the federal government, a Navajo man said: "Beauty and Harmony are the heart of the Navajo way of life. This harmony comes from the eternal and natural balance of the Male Mountain (Lukachukai) and the Female Mountain (Black Mesa). The singers and traditional religious leaders have stated that if these mountains, the sources of harmony are damaged, the Navajo Way will be destroyed. I do not agree with this mining." [1]

Navajos call the years immediately following World War II the "starving time." The return of nearly three thousand servicemen and ten thousand war workers combined with ten years of stock reduction created widespread malnutrition and disease among Navajo people. Federal handouts proved inadequate.[2] "After all the hue and cry," wrote one newspaper editor, "nothing has been done to help the Navajos . . . schools remain closed and the hospitals are but a sham."[3]

In 1946, the government began what it did best: it launched a series of studies. In one of these, industrial consultant Max M. Drefkoff pointed out, "Our former enemies—the German people are now being provided with 1500 calories a day," while Navajos struggled along on less than 1,200 calories. He recommended business development, especially oil, helium and coal mining, and lumbering and wool processing to solve their poverty.[4] Another report also stressed oil development, emphasizing existing wells at the Rattlesnake site and noting a recent bonus of $180,000 paid to the tribe.[5]

Surveys underscored the need for education, health care, and water development. A March 1948 report initiated by Secretary of the Interior Julius Krug formed the basis for the Navajo-Hopi Rehabilitation Act of April 1, 1950, which authorized $88.5 million for a ten-year program of basic improvement. These improvements included $25 million for schooling, plus funds designated for soil conservation, irrigation, industrial development, and off-reservation employment assistance. It is noteworthy that the Navajo-Hopi Act came just as a nationwide conservative backlash attempted to overturn the Collier reforms and launch an all-out assault on Indian property across the country.

As early as 1944, the National Council of Churches had condemned Collier's focus on tribalism and religious freedom that tolerated peyote. In 1947, Congress considered legislation, albeit unsuccessfully, to repeal the Indian Reorganization Act (IRA) and dismantle the very governments Collier had told tribes were untouchable. Eighty-seven bills urging issuance of unrestricted patents to all allotments were introduced, along with other legislation detrimental to Indian welfare. Even the Navajo-Hopi bill, first passed in 1949, contained provisions so objectionable that President Harry S Truman vetoed it.[6]

John Collier resigned in 1945; successors included his own handpicked man William A. Brophy, whose poor health prevented him from carrying out his duties and forced early resignation, and John R. Nichols.[7] Both continued Collier's policies, but without Congressional support or zeal. In May 1950, Dillon S. Myer was named commissioner. Previously in charge of wartime Japanese-American internment camps and postwar resettlement programs, Myer was staunchly anti-reservation and turned government's attention to ending federal responsibility for native peoples. In his 1952 annual report, Myer proudly announced that oil and gas leasing on reservations was again underway.[8]

The Quest for Economic Independence

The cast of players changed dramatically on the Navajo reservation after the war. Reform officials either resigned or were discharged. J. C. Morgan disappeared from tribal politics, and on January 10, 1947, Chee Dodge died following a long illness. Vice chairman Sam Ahkeah of Shiprock (Tódích'íinii or Bitter Water Clan) assumed the role of chairman. Ahkeah had as a youth contracted tuberculosis, worked on a Colorado ranch to regain his health, and returned to the reservation in 1930. He started his own herd, which in 1934 numbered six hundred, but was reduced to thirty-nine in 1935, making Ahkeah an outspoken Collier critic.[9] As chairman, Ahkeah called for Navajo emancipation from government and greater latitude for self-determination.[10]

The problem was that termination, as the new federal Indian policy was called, and tribal self-determination were not as closely aligned as they sounded. In many instances government simply withdrew services and programs, while states, which were supposed to pick up the slack, neglected to do so or could not. A relocation program accompanied termination, and thousands of Native Americans were promised housing, vocational education, and jobs to leave their reservations. Although termination did not immediately apply to Navajos, many were indeed relocated. Prior to 1950, for example, members of the Five Oklahoma Tribes made up the largest Indian population in Los Angeles; after relocation that shifted to Navajos and Sioux.[11]

Ahkeah favored oil and gas development on the Navajo reservation, but also exhibited concern for tribal funds, which he hinted did not always go to pay for schools, hospitals, or roads.[12] In 1949 the tribal council authorized the position of secretary-treasurer in part to keep financial records straight and to report on funds, resources, and tribal enterprises.[13] In a speech printed in the *Farmington Times Hustler*, Ahkeah noted that Navajos desperately needed medical care, job opportunities, and schools: "So many promises have been made and broken, that we don't know who or what to believe."[14]

Moreover, Ahkeah traveled to Washington, where he met with former assistant U.S. Attorney General Norman M. Littell. On July 10, 1947, the tribe hired this University of Washington Law School graduate as its general legal counsel.[15] In 1935, Littell had been employed as assistant solicitor for the Interior Department and special assistant to the U.S. Attorney General. By 1939, he was in charge of the Justice Department's Land Division, with responsibility for land and natural resources on the public domain.[16] In 1944, Littell went into private practice in Washington, D.C. Littell blamed Collier for many tribal woes, and one of his first moves in their employ was to help Navajos formally end federal stock reduction.

During the twenty years Littell remained legal counsel, his goals for Navajos included encouraging more individual involvement in tribal politics for the people and a better deal for Navajos in regards to their land and natural resources. In 1959 Littell and his staff won *Williams v. Lee*, a very important case for Navajos because it allowed them to regulate tribal affairs free from state interference. Robert Young dubbed Littell "the sparkplug in tribal political development."[17] Certainly, he was one of the most important public figures in reservation politics after 1947.

Assistant Bureau of Indian Affairs (BIA) Commissioner William Zimmerman, Jr., belittled Littell, claiming he had not previously shown any interest in Indian Affairs except as concerned him when he was in the Department of Justice.[18] Commissioner Myer wrote new criteria on June 22, 1951, regarding Indian Office review of contracts between tribes and their attorneys. Although the ruling did not affect Littell, it angered Ahkeah, who snapped, "the Bureau has made a lot of mistakes. We will make them, too, but we prefer our own mistakes."[19]

Also in 1947, the council organized a nine-member advisory committee to serve as Washington liaison and economic advisor to the tribe. The committee and Littell's appointment came at the dawn of America's post-war love affair with oil, and Navajos had every reason to believe that if oil still existed in commercial quantities under their land, it would provide a lucrative source of revenue for them. Oil companies had recently drilled 35,000 new oil wells across the United States, and the nation used as much oil in one year as the entire world had utilized in 1938. Motor vehicle registrations rose by one-half, and petroleum consumption soared.[20] President Truman's 1948 budget requested $211,491,000 for military fuel.[21] By 1960 there would be 860 wells on Navajo land producing over thirty-four million barrels, but in 1950 the boom hardly made a splash in northwestern New Mexico, especially with increased activity in the southeast quadrant of the state near the Texas border.[22]

On non-Indian lands in the San Juan Basin, developers sought natural gas, not necessarily oil. In January 1952, there were 300 producing gas wells serving local markets, but ten years later, there were 5,608 wells providing natural gas for customers on the West Coast. Natural gas development in the San Juan region averaged 200 to 650 wells per year, and Farmington, a quiet agricultural town in 1950, saw its population soar, as did populations in nearby Aztec and Bloomfield.[23]

The major stumbling blocks to oil or natural gas development on the reservation, as before, were the lack of geological surveys, few pipelines, virtually none of which headed out of the area, and a transportation problem little changed since 1923. In fact, poor conditions—paved roads were still almost non-existent, for example—caused some companies eager for Navajo leases to cancel them almost immediately.[24] Companies had sold oil locally during the 1930s and 40s, and although the arrangement kept prices somewhat immune from the national economic roller coaster, it was not useful in establishing royalty rates overall.[25] By 1950 rates needed revision, but nobody knew exactly how to tackle the problem.[26]

Allotments presented yet another difficulty. These leases clearly stipulated that successful bidders secure the signatures of Indian owners after ownership status was determined by the government. But approximately one-half of all Navajo allotments were in an inheritance status, making special field investigations mandatory and cumbersome.[27] The problem was compounded when several allotments were combined into a single lease. This situation caused nightmares for all involved. More than three years sometimes elapsed between the sale and official approval. In at least one case there were six hundred individual heirs to locate.[28] The Branch of Realty and Probate handled heirship investigations, and seventeen overworked federal employees responsible for the Navajo reservation found their work multiplying rapidly after 1950.[29]

Once owners and heirs were sorted out, bonuses, royalty, and rental fees were sent to the tribal superintendent (later Mineral Management Services) and divided among all of those entitled to a share.[30] Trader Bill Richardson of Gallup recalls that sometimes superintendents made Navajos explain why they wanted their money before they could receive it.[31] "Yes, it was terribly paternalistic," Young agrees, "but was done so as to avoid the mess that occurred among the Osages, when they lost almost all of their money."[32] Navajo Frank Toledo added that a number of Navajos escaped poverty because they owned allotments containing oil or uranium.[33]

New Demands, New Discoveries

Some of the problems associated with oil and gas development began to get solved after 1950. By late 1951, El Paso Natural Gas Company completed a gas pipeline to California, thereby creating the area's first major market for natural gas. The line immediately boosted the local, off-reservation economy. It also stimulated exploration and drilling throughout the San Juan Basin and Four Corners.[34] Although Senator Dennis Chavez opposed the pipeline on the grounds that exportation would exhaust New Mexico's supply within twenty years, proponents prevailed. The pipeline included a 240-mile stretch across Navajo land, and so natural gas became a commodity sought there. The largest pools, however, were off the reservation, northeast of Aztec and Farmington and into Rio Arriba and Sandoval Counties. Ninety-five percent of natural gas development in the region has taken place since 1951.[35]

Oil development, on the other hand, remained slow until 1957. Still, the federal government hired the universities of New Mexico and Arizona to finally conduct mineral surveys on the Navajo reservation during summer 1952, and afterward, lease demands mounted.[36] The government also contracted with the New Mexico School of Mines in 1954 for a survey. Despite these studies and others done by corporations, large areas remained relatively uncharted.[37] In 1957, El Paso Company constructed a new oil refinery at Ciniza and built a sixteen-inch pipeline to California, which began shipping oil in early 1958. Again, an expanded market set off an explosion of activity.

Hence oil exploration increased, especially in Utah and along the Utah-Arizona border. Here surface mapping of anticlines had remained the primary exploration tool until 1952.[38] But Texas Company drilled a huge discovery well in the Aneth field in spring 1956 as a result of wildcatting. The well soon flowed 1,704 barrels per day.[39] By November, Superior Oil, Gulf Oil, and Carter Oil reported discoveries in the region, and in May 1957 Sun Oil, Pure, and Ohio Company paid $8 million in bonuses for Aneth tracts.[40] In fact, Aneth became the most significant field in the Rocky Mountain region, particularly when another sixteen-inch pipeline, completed in 1958, carried oil from that field to Jal, New Mexico, and connected with a larger line there. Others — Akah and Boundary Butte in Utah, Walker Creek and East Boundary Butte in Arizona, and Bisti in New Mexico — also received much attention.[41]

At one lease sale alone, Navajos received over $28 million, more than bonus bids received for leases on all the other Indian reservations.[42] Soon, the number of producing wells soared. But although pipelines made it possible to move oil, transportation for equipment and crews remained burdensome. There were no paved roads into Aneth; the closest pavement was thirty miles away in some places and as far as seventy miles from other active spots. The few gravel roads were rough and impassable during wet spells.[43] The *Oil and Gas Journal* warned potential drillers of the adverse weather conditions and difficulty with rock formations; holes caved in easily, tools got stuck, and El Paso Company was forced to develop an experimental rig to tackle conditions.[44] The problem for Navajos was that even though leaders like Ahkeah invited the increased activity and welcomed large bonuses, those not directly involved or individuals with misgivings about development had little or no voice in the process.

Navajos Diversify Their Economy

In 1953 Glenn L. Emmons, Gallup businessman and banker, replaced Myer as commissioner. Before the 1952 elections, Myer had already implemented regulations allowing tribes broader access to bank loans and other credit institutions, which allowed them to more easily mortgage their land, or as some described it, "just one more easy road to land alienation."[45] Myer had also initiated termination legislation, which Emmons and Interior Secretary Douglas McKay ardently embraced.

In August 1953 Congress passed Public Law (PL) 280 giving states the power to extend civil and criminal law over Indian reservations. Ironically, it was a section of the Navajo-Hopi Rehabilitation Act extending state law over these two tribes that had caused Truman to veto the initial bill.[46] President Dwight D. Eisenhower had no trouble signing PL 280, but asked Congress to amend the legislation giving consent to the Indians affected. This was not accomplished until April 11, 1968. In all, the 83rd Congress passed six termination laws.

Navajos were deemed unfit for termination because of widespread English illiteracy and low education levels. Many, however, were relocated to Albuquerque, Phoenix, Denver, Los Angeles, and Chicago. In 1958, the BIA extended relocation services to include nearby communities, where more industrial employment existed.[47] So, too, were Navajos directly affected by Senate Bill 809, passed in 1955 to encourage development of reservation industries. Believing government paternalism made Indians less, not more, self-reliant, Emmons initiated programs to "wean" them from federal dependency.[48]

A cornerstone of his program was the American Indian Research Fund (AIRF), a non-profit organization to promote tribal surveys to determine their economic potential.[49] Following these surveys, Emmons anticipated using the information to encourage natural resource development, vocational training, corporate cooperation to build factories on or near reservations, and improved agricultural and livestock programs.[50] Emmons quickly found, however, that corporate America resisted the program because it considered Indians incompetent.[51] Moreover, white workers feared cheap Indian labor. On top of that, AIRF proved almost completely ineffective.[52]

But Navajos as a tribe endorsed the program. The tribal council even contributed $447,563 in money borrowed from the United States under the credit program and $16,000 of their personal funds to encourage creation of small business ventures by Navajos.[53] Emmons worked with new chairman Paul Jones (Ta'neeszahnii or Scattered Tree Branches Clan from Naschitti, New Mexico) to draw up a contract with Baby Line Furniture Corporation of Los Angeles, manufacturers of juvenile furniture, for a plant near Gallup.[54] Lear, Inc., opened an electronics assembly plant in Flagstaff, and Arizona Pulp and Paper Company also attempted a subsidized training program, which failed due to inadequate capital. The council approved a number of tribal facilities such as the Navajo Tribal Sawmill, the largest of approximately twenty enterprises operated by the Navajo Tribe.[55] Between 1956–1960 the tribe established Navajo Tribal Utility Authority, First Navajo National Bank at Window Rock, a series of tribal trading posts, tourist campgrounds, and a tribal park.[56]

The council took additional steps to assure a better future for Navajo people. In 1955, for instance, delegates supported a bill (House Resolution [H.R.] 1591, No. 3141) introduced by then-Congressman Stewart L. Udall (D-AZ) to set aside "10% of monies received by the Federal Government from the mineral sub-soil resources . . . as the Indian Education and Rehabilitation Fund" to provide loans to all native peoples for college.[57] Even so, Navajos were not entirely happy with the arrangement; they wanted grants and scholarships, not just loans. And they wanted these made available to Navajos without a high school diploma as the bill stipulated.[58]

In 1954 Paul Jones replaced Ahkeah as chair. Jones, born October 20, 1895, attended the Christian Reformed mission school at Tohatchi as a youth, then lived in Chicago and New York City before returning to the reservation in 1938. He was an interpreter for the tribal council for many years and was serving as a delegate in 1954 when elected chairman.[59] The BIA had found Ahkeah difficult and domineering; Emmons called his leadership "myopic."[60] The animosity was probably caused because Ahkeah and Littell sought more tribal autonomy and challenged the entire process of federal review, approval, and control of funds. In Paul Jones, Emmons found a leader more willing to work with government: "In my opinion, the tribal officers have consistently demonstrated the very best qualities of statesmanship, responsibility, and dedication to the tribal welfare," Emmons stated after four years of Jones's direction.[61]

In 1955 the council hired Martin Bennett as oil consultant to oversee oil and gas leases. It authorized the chairman to delay or withdraw tribal consent to leases. Delegates also hired two geologists, Forrest Sur and Ralph Arnold, to make studies of potential oil and gas properties on Navajo land.[62] In a report, Sur and Arnold recommended that Navajos replace existing lease arrangements with partnerships, and in response, the council declared a moratorium on new leases, a move Littell called "legal pioneering." In late 1956, the Advisory Council and Littell drew up a contract with Delhi-Taylor Oil Company of Dallas for five million acres of reservation land to extend over a 25-year period. The company agreed to explore the leased area and to develop whatever sites they might discover. Delhi-Taylor and the tribe would split any profits on a 50–50 basis.[63]

Navajos declared the joint venture valid by the inherent power of the Navajo tribe as owner of the lands. Secretary of the Interior Fred A. Seaton called it "risky," probably illegal, and forbade it.[64] Jones blamed the denial on "a response to a well-organized publicity campaign" by the oil industry, designed to destroy Delhi-Taylor's advantage.[65] Seaton asked the Advisory Council to draft a proposed amendment to the Navajo-Hopi Rehabilitation Act to, in essence, provide for piecemeal termination in terms of leasing. Congress, however, delayed, especially when Navajos requested 99-year leases as well. The immediate reason was to assure development of a coal-based industrial complex south of Fruitland that the sponsor, Utah Construction Company, threatened to abandon unless it obtained long-term land tenure. But Navajos also entertained the possibility of a similar arrangement with oil and gas companies.[66]

Navajos got a small boost on August 6, 1957, when a bill supported by the National Council of American Indians (NCAI) passed, allowing lessees to suspend production for up to two years to obtain higher rates. Congress also approved legislation that placed the initiative for leases in the hands of the tribal council, but retained Secretary of the Interior approval.[67] In 1958, Littell negotiated an increase in royalty rates from 1/8 to 1/6 except on the most remote lands, thereby increasing Navajo income.[68] In 1959, NCAI asked Congress for funds to hire qualified engineers to survey natural resources on Indian lands across the United States and make recommendations for development, something that would not be done, however, for another twenty years.[69]

By 1959, bonuses for leases on Indian lands overall topped $45 million; $33.7 million went to Navajos.[70] Thus Jones found himself facing a quandary: he had worked hard to change the negative Navajo image, even appearing on television in San Francisco after local celebrity Don Sherwood called Navajos "a picture of wholesale death and degradation." Now, Jones walked a tightrope.[71] Despite newspaper headlines pronouncing multi-million-dollar bonuses, conditions on the reservation were not prosperous. Federal dollars were all that stood between many Navajos and starvation, and average annual income was $900 versus $3,921 for whites. "The public mistakenly thinks that the Navajo people are now oil-rich and need no more appropriation," council members remarked.[72] Gorman noted further, "the Tribe has a few dollars in the Treasury [and] the government [is] determined to spend it."[73] It must be noted, however, that the period between 1956 and 1959 has often been called the "Golden Years" on the Navajo reservation.[74]

Finally, the tribe took the federal government and the Arizona Highway Commission to task for their lack of interest in improving roads. In general, the oil boom brought about a road-building revolution, but this provided nowhere near all of the needed highways.[75] Senator Chavez, chairman of the committee on Public Works, endorsed a $10 million bill providing roads in important regions; the Atomic Energy Commission built thirty-two miles of road from Shiprock to the Arizona border.[76] In 1957, Senator Clinton Anderson (D-NM) obtained additional highway funds, which permitted the completion of a Shiprock-to-Tuba City highway and Route 666 between Gallup and Shiprock, which had been started years earlier but not finished. By the end of fiscal year 1961, 291 miles of bituminous-surfaced highway and 360 miles of graveled road were added.[77] Usually oil companies funded their own roads. But none was paved in the Aneth region until after 1960.

Navajos used their income to generate even more improvements and achieve quasi-autonomy. Unhappy with the limited nature of Udall's 1955 legislation to create a loan fund, Navajos established a $5 million scholarship fund in 1957 to pay for college. The fund was subsequently increased in 1958 to $10 million. The capital was invested and the interest used for scholarships.[78]

Royalties also meant money for the needy and for irrigation, drought relief, and soil conservation.[79] Jones personally oversaw the revitalization of chapters and the rebuilding or renovation of chapter houses, many of which were in sorry states of disrepair. Glenn R. Landbloom was appointed general superintendent on October 6, 1958, and three days later, Littell announced that there was so much business confronting the tribal legal department that he needed more personnel. In August 1959, the council reorganized its executive branch to incorporate a Resources Division, with six departments, including an Oil and Gas Department. This reorganization was approved in 1960.[80]

So, before he left office in 1962, Jones proudly announced that total in-the-black treasury figures stood at $86 million.[81] A new nine-member advisory committee, with notables like Henry Taliman, and a fourteen-member budget committee led by Roger Davis, Howard Gorman, Annie Wauneka — Chee

Dodge's daughter—among others, were put in place to help the tribal government make better-informed decisions and to function when the council was not in session.

But problems still existed. It was into this general arena of expansion that old animosities resurfaced, most visibly between the so-called Old Guard like Annie Wauneka and Howard Gorman and the younger, college-educated leaders, who called themselves the Navajo Rights Association (NRA). The NRA challenged Old Guard control of council and advisory committee. Much of this battle focused on Littell, who had endeavored in vain to compose a tribal constitution and whose hands-on participation in tribal politics angered some, although Old Guard delegates generally wanted even more of Littell's time dedicated to the tribe.[82]

Jones had supported Littell, but Raymond Nakai, chairman in 1962, vehemently objected to the general counsel's influence and had during the election vowed to replace him. *Navajo Times* editor Marshall Tome shared Nakai's opinion.[83] On the other hand, Littell criticized Nakai and referred to him as Secretary Udall's "puppet."[84]

The new chairman irked the Old Guard almost from the start. In April 1963, Nakai announced that he intended to eliminate the post of executive secretary held for many years by Maurice McCabe; Nakai's followers claimed McCabe's hold on the budget and finance committees and his responsibility for signing tribal documents created an administrative bottleneck. The Old Guard, however, was convinced Nakai's real goal was more power for himself.[85] Their beliefs seemed substantiated when Nakai then asked Interior Secretary Udall to investigate charges against Littell—misappropriation of funds in particular—and to terminate his contract.[86] Littell appealed his firing, and Federal Judge Joseph C. McGarraghy ruled in his favor. Then, in May 1965, Littell won an injunction from U.S. District Court Judge John J. Sirica.[87]

Nakai, however, ejected Littell from the council chambers in February 1964, ordering the sergeant-at-arms to escort him outside. A U.S. Court of Appeals overturned Sirica's injunction in 1966. Littell petitioned the U.S. Supreme Court this time, but on January 9, 1967, justices declined to review the appeal. Old Guard delegates took a pro-Littell vote of confidence on January 26, but the advisory council—now aligned with Nakai—refused it, and Navajo public relations director Perry Allen suggested "the Navajo Tribal Council is getting tired of having Littell as the center of controversy."[88] Littell resigned in February 1967, and the council narrowly approved hiring Nakai's personal attorney Harold Mott. The Littell crisis illustrates continuing divisions within Navajo leadership. The Old Guard, in turn, resented Udall and wondered if the government would try to undermine council authority altogether.[89]

Nevertheless, many ordinary Navajos resented the council altogether, dubbing delegates "employees of the administration." Regular Navajo citizens had remained relatively silent for years, and now their voices grew louder. A group of Navajo veterans called the body "ineffective," with a chairman who "cannot speak for himself," in general, "an Edgar Bergan — Charlie McCarthy situation."[90] A pervasive belief was "tribal council members get everything . . . they don't give much back to the people."[91] Or, "Navajos who oppose oil have nowhere to turn." Navajos could "complain to their neighbors, but that was about all they could do."[92] Discontent over natural resource development increased as exploitation burgeoned and expanded to include natural gas, uranium, and coal.

Expansion Brings New Funds and New Problems

The 1956 decision to build a trunk pipeline from the Four Corners to Los Angeles had an electrifying effect upon companies doing business in the Paradox and San Juan Basins. Shell Oil, Standard Oil of California, Gulf Oil, Continental, Richfield Oil, and Superior Oil all announced that they were part of the project, and Shell Pipe Line Corporation was chosen to construct and operate the $50 million project. The pipeline would cross three major rivers, run entirely underground, and initially carry a seventy-thousand-barrels-per-day capacity, with three pumping stations anticipated, two on the reservation. Completion was anticipated by April 10, 1958, and Joe T. Dickerson, president of Shell Pipe Line Corporation, pointed to the development as heralding "a new and better life for the 88,000 Navajos."[93]

Yet such expansion created upheaval among some Navajo residents. On February 18, 1958, for example, Aneth-area delegate Bill Hatathly urged the tribal council to pass a resolution promising to restore land and paying residents for damage done to structures and stock. Members finally agreed that the Navajo government would make it their responsibility to fill in or fence abandoned or dangerous areas left unprotected if companies failed to so do, and to bill these companies for the work done. Even so, former chairman Ahkeah argued, "Window Rock has spent $34 million and still 13,000 of our children are without schools." BIA employees — both Navajo and white — were guilty of wasting Indian money and neglecting the people, Ahkeah accused.[94]

There were other dissenting voices. When in 1959 Paul Jones discussed building a bombing range on Navajo land with the Defense Department, retired U.S. General Herbert C. Holdridge allied with disgruntled Navajos to accuse Emmons, Chavez, the departments of Interior and Defense, and the tribal council of a "gigantic [oil] swindle." They blocked Jones's driveway on the morning of April 30, placed him under citizens' arrest, and declared an independent Navajo Nation.[95] Holdridge — diagnosed as "psychoneurotic" with mild depression—accused Jones of helping whites embezzle millions in oil royalties.[96] Although some Anglo owners of oil land received up to 37½ percent royalties, Navajos generally got only 12½ percent (and sometimes 16 percent), and allottees often received nothing, he said.[97] Udall dubbed the man a "crackpot," but Holdridge was correct about one thing: Navajos did not acquire the money to which they were entitled.

Uranium and Coal on Navajo Land

It is necessary to mention at least briefly other natural resources, particularly uranium and coal. Oil earned Navajos larger royalties, but uranium often inspired the sensational headlines. Pioneers to the region had known that the uranium-bearing rocks existed just as they had spotted oil years before it became commercially important. Trader and archeological explorer John Wetherill, in fact, staked the first claim in San Juan County, Utah, in 1898, seeking not uranium, but carnotite, which contains uranium and vanadium, a metallic element used to harden steel.[98] War generated a demand for vanadium. The Tribal Leasing Act of 1938 gave the tribal council authority to approve or disapprove leases; the base royalty was ten percent.

With the advent of the Manhattan Project in 1942, uranium became valuable. By 1944, about one thousand tons of ore had come from the Colorado Plateau, including the Navajo reservation. In 1948 the U.S. government announced a program to buy even more uranium.[99] In 1951, Paddy Martinez, a Navajo living near Grants, showed geologists a uranium-bearing ore deposit on railroad land in the Navajo Checkerboard. This dramatic find led to others around Gallup, but as with oil, Navajos received limited benefits. They got unskilled, minimum wage jobs. Skilled and supervisory positions went to whites, who often received company housing as well, while Navajos got neither housing nor subsidized meals. Worse, Navajos were exposed to dangerous levels of radiation and radon, and when they went home covered with mine dust, so too, were their wives and children.[100] Not until 1990 was there any move to identify and offer compensation to those Navajos diagnosed with cancer or respiratory ailments as a result of this work.

In addition, mining damaged the land. Radioactive tailings were piled as waste, and sometimes these leached into ground water. When companies shut down operations, they often abandoned the buildings, mines, mills, and radioactive debris. Thus contaminated dust blew freely across communities, found its way into rivers, and was ground at times into concrete slabs used to build schools and public buildings. Grazing areas frequented by sheep and goats also received large doses of the radioactive waste.[101] Children sometimes fell into the old uranium mines. These workings were frequently exposed, even used as temporary shelters by unsuspecting herdsmen or livestock.

One might anticipate hefty compensation for such abuse, but income from uranium and vanadium from 1950 to 1960 brought Navajos just over $6.5 million; oil income totaled $76.5 million.[102] Income on allotted land was just over $1 million for uranium; oil and gas brought $7.4 million. Wage work in the uranium industry surpassed that of oil, but given the accompanying health problems, this seems no bargain.[103] Royalty agreements seldom favored Navajos; when in 1977, uranium prices rose from $10.70 to $41 per pound nationwide, the price paid to Indians remained at about $4.45.[104]

Similarly, coal contributed to Navajo income. In 1953, the tribe issued a permit to Utah Mining and Construction to explore, and in 1957 signed a lease with that company to mine. In 1964, Pittsburgh-Midway Coal Company obtained a lease to mine between Window Rock and Gallup, and Peabody Coal negotiated a lease for Black Mesa in 1966. Thanks to federal attorneys, who were either incompetent or unconcerned, Navajos did not receive adequate recompense. Furthermore, once the leases were negotiated and in place, corporations could muster tremendous legal power to make certain they remained unaltered.[105] The Black Mesa lease, which also involved the Hopi tribe in Arizona, became the basis of lawsuits and a Senate investigation. More recently, in 1992, evidence surfaced revealing that attorney John S. Boyden of Salt Lake City represented Peabody at the same time that he was legal representative for the Hopis and Utes.[106]

But in 1959, the oil market experienced a temporary downturn and reduced demand. Whereas Navajos leased 382,373 acres in 1958, that fell to 109,323 acres one year later. Despite a record bonus of $5,505 per acre on January 13, 1959, oil revenues declined again, both in New Mexico and across the United States.[107] Government subsidized the domestic oil industry, but not the lease owners.[108]

It is telling that despite the gains made, few Navajos qualified for the skilled mining jobs despite having asked the Bureau of Indian Affairs (BIA) for assistance in this area since the 1920s. It is also noteworthy that government never even entertained the notion of helping the tribe take over mining, processing, or sales, finding it easier to lease to outsiders. When Navajos asked for a bigger role in their own economic development after World War II, the BIA had encouraged such enterprises as piñon nut packaging and a playpen manufacturing plant that hired nineteen people, while ignoring more lucrative possibilities. The economic innovations and educational advances came largely through Navajo, not federal initiatives. Hence, as oil income waned, Navajos justifiably grew more and more protective of their funds.

In August 1959, Superintendent Landbloom cautioned the council to begin planning programs and budgets with an eye to lower oil and gas revenues. Wauneka estimated that Navajo funds on reserve might last only seven more years. Oil consultant Martin Bennett said although he believed Navajos could anticipate a relatively steady annual income of $15 million from oil and gas, they could hardly expect the high bids of 1958 and 1959 to continue.[109] By the 1960s, Navajo leaders sought more control and alternative ways to fund their programs, and at the same time discovered that there was a growing number of Navajo people who felt alienated from the Window Rock hierarchy.

NAVAJO SOLUTIONS, 7 1960–1982

On March 13, 1978, eighteen-year-old Peter Benally went in search of his family's herd of sheep and goats. Upon reaching the top of a mesa, the young man heard laughter and the bleating of a goat in the valley below. He rode his horse to the edge of the cliff and peered down to find three oil company workers at a pumping unit torturing one of his goats. They dragged it a distance, picked it up, then tossed it about among one another. Peter shouted for the men to stop, but they bellowed obscenities and told him to "get [his] god'damn goats out of here." Benally protested; his goats had every right to graze where they wished. At this point, an oil worker ran for his truck and got a pistol. He pointed the gun and shot at Peter's horse, causing it to rear. In all, four shots were fired.[1]

Seventeen days later, one hundred Navajo residents of the Aneth region staged a takeover of a Texaco pumping station and shut it down. Obviously, some Navajos resented oil exploitation and development.

The clash between traditional Navajos and those who saw promise in technology and scientific land use was undoubtedly heard for years in chapter houses and between neighbors, but the former are largely absent from documents until the late 1950s. By that time, a sizable number of traditionals had already lost ground to "younger and more educated Indians," particularly in the tribal government. There was also a significant regional gap.[2] In San Juan County, Utah, for example, residents still lacked running water and electricity despite the millions in oil taken from beneath their land. Families there believed Window Rock delighted in this wealth, but was not interested in spending revenues on residents; Chairman Paul Jones resisted demands to divide all funds on a per-capita basis in Aneth and focused instead on improving chapter houses, increasing education, and extending electrical services to residents through Navajo Tribal Utilities Authority. "Spread over 80,000 people on a per-capita basis," explained tribal council secretary Maurice McCabe, the money "would pay grocery bills and liquidate a few debts. Then we'd be back where we started."[3]

Still, as the American public filled its chrome-laden gas-guzzlers for a couple of dollars per tank and warmed suburban homes with cheap energy, Utah Navajos in particular continued to live in extreme poverty. Even the scholarship fund did little to help since often their children were too ill-prepared to meet university admissions requirements.[4]

Utah Navajos Make Demands

Utah Navajos had long felt isolated from the rest of the reservation. It was there that many eluded Kit Carson's soldiers and escaped the Long Walk in 1864. Utah Navajos were sometimes excluded from tribal plans as a whole.[5] Some joined the Native American church and used peyote, customs adopted from their close proximity to Utes. J. C. Morgan had found both abhorrent, and under his leadership the council outlawed peyote.[6] Beyond these influences, Mormon missionaries converted large groups in this region, further contributing to their isolation and sense of alienation.

In 1956 alone, the Aneth oil field brought in $34.5 million in royalties and bonuses. Area residents, however, experienced little improvement in their lives. The growing animosity toward oil companies and their Window Rock "conspirators" finally came to a head on September 1, 1963, following a radio broadcast from Cortez, Colorado. The announcer claimed that the state of Utah "had a lot of money at Salt Lake City" to use for the benefit of Navajos living on the Aneth Extension and related areas, and thus far had done nothing to administer the money. In fact, Navajos knew nothing about the fund, which was the result of the 1933 extension agreement that granted 37½ percent of all royalties to Utah.[7] At the time, Navajos had so desperately wanted the land that Herbert J. Hagerman acquiesced rather than risk losing the extension. Furthermore, he rationalized that the tribe "was not much interested in oil prospects there," and it was generally believed that the strip contained no oil anyway.[8]

But there was oil, and after its discovery, Utah created an Indian Affairs Commission to deal with the funds. Three members were appointed by the governor: by law, appointments had to include one resident Navajo, plus one member from outside the tribe and region, and an at-large member. Attorney John S. Boyden of Salt Lake City was the at-large member and its chairman.[9]

By September 1961, a total of $3.8 million was paid to the state of Utah, but the money remained unspent because the 1933 act specified that funds pay for tuition for Navajo children. In 1963, most attended public schools, and the Federal Impacted Area Aid Program picked up the tab.[10] What Navajo children really needed was books and transportation, but commissioners said they hesitated to expand the language of the legislation without clarification. The law also stipulated that the state consult Navajo residents regarding the use of funds for other purposes, but in this instance, commissioners argued that they could not delineate between permanent and seasonal occupants. The court also insisted that the commission canvas Navajos regarding the expenditure of oil revenues for other purposes.[11]

According to the *Navajo Times*, although the commission required a legal decision to expand the meaning of tuition, it had no difficulty handing over chunks of money to a Monument Valley mission and an Oljato trader for a private airstrip. Members were allegedly on the verge of appropriating $500,000 for an off-reservation tourist road when in February the court stepped in and ordered the state to spend nothing without the consent of Navajos in Aneth, Montezuma Creek, Navajo Mountain, and Oljato. So, the new commission called a hasty meeting at Oljato, met with a handful of Navajos, and sped home.[12]

On June 29, Aneth Navajos hired their own attorney and drew up a list of priority purchases, including a cattle ranch, houses, stores and motels to attract tourists, water and soil conservation projects. Utah stalled. This time, the state wanted Congress to amend the 1933 legislation. The hearing was held in 1966, and by this time Utah held $5 million in Navajo oil funds. The commission proposed using these funds to reimburse state welfare and public health programs.[13]

Navajos charged that the commission kept expanding in size and now consisted of five people — only one Navajo. Its mission had also swelled to include the administration of Indian affairs generally in the state of Utah.[14] One Navajo testified that as the original definition expanded, so, too, did the bureaucracy, and every new department, bureau, commission, and division wanted something to say about the use of the oil money.[15] Could these funds be placed into a private foundation — free of political influence — Navajos asked?[16]

Thomas Billie of Montezuma Creek and Herbert Clay of Oljato blamed at least part of the dilemma on the Window Rock government and, in particular, on Norman Littell, who kept in close contact with the Utah Commission.[17] Senate hearings before a subcommittee of the Committee on Interior and Insular Affairs also revealed differences of opinion between tribal government and Utah residents. While Window Rock agreed that the money should be spent generally for "health, education, and general welfare" and "in the greater area of San Juan County," some Utah residents wanted royalties used to purchase grazing land and even proposed a communal cattle ranch.[18]

About the same time, Hopis protested abuses on their land and in June 1964 closed the Sunlight Baptist Mission road to prevent Superior Oil Company from completing a wildcat well. Badly divided between pro- and anti-oil forces, the Hopi council had hesitantly awarded Superior Oil a lease. But before the council could even complete the lease, company representatives offered $50 to the mission for mineral rights underneath their land. Outraged, Hopis moved to halt the unauthorized drilling, and many Navajos — especially those in Utah — pointed to the incident as proof of corporate ill will toward Indians.[19]

Navajos Grapple with Federal Incompetence and a New World Market

Against rising displeasure among rank-and-file Navajos, the tribal government underwent growth and change. The Navajo Nation was the largest tribe with land still intact and had dealt with oil companies and pro-development Bureau of Indian Affairs (BIA) officials since 1921. Thus Navajos, perhaps more than any other Native American group, exemplify how difficult it is to grow economically yet survive culturally.

The Diné could boast several major advantages. They had their own attorney, oil consultant, and vast leasing experience. Since the 1950s, the tribal Executive Branch had contained a Resources Division, which included Departments of Oil and Gas and Mining, to deal with government and corporations even though ultimate decision-making rested with the Secretary of the Interior. Navajos established an Environmental Protection Administration to deal with oil spills, uranium tailings, and other potential hazards. Navajos established their own bank in 1960, which by 1962 generated several branches. Navajos hired their own geologists, and few tribes were able to gather as much geologic information. In 1959, the tribe even owned its own utility operation — Navajo Tribal Utilities Authority.[20] Still, Navajos faced myriad roadblocks in their quest for tribal self-determination and control of natural resource development on their land.

Hopis, on the other hand, were relative newcomers to mining. In another example, oil-producing lands under the Blackfeet and Fort Peck reservations in Montana were 90 percent allotted, making their situations extremely complex. In all cases, the BIA lacked sufficient funds to supply technical and legal expertise to tribes, much less individuals. Moreover, in the case of Arapahos and Shoshones on the Wind River Reservation in Wyoming, oil theft grew so rampant that Amoco, for one, "failed to account for more than 1.38 million barrels of allottee oil from 1971 to 1982."[21]

Monitoring presented a major stumbling block for all Native Americans. The U.S. Geological Service (USGS) oversaw production on both tribal and allotted lands. However, because it lacked sufficient staff, USGS employed an honor system.[22] Even when its few field investigators found evidence of oil piracy, government-imposed punishments were usually nothing more than a small fine, or at best, lease cancellation.

In 1981, an FBI investigation agreed that USGS was understaffed and its inspectors poorly trained, but concluded that stolen oil was more often the result of accounting practices. In some instances, companies overestimated the amount of impurities or sold good oil as junk. At other times companies transferred crude from a lease paying higher royalties to a lower-paying one or waited a few days before announcing a newly completed well so as to obtain several days' worth of free product. Like the USGS, the U.S. General Accounting Office found it hard to keep track of oil on federal land.[23]

Navajos eventually began their own monitoring program, but smaller tribes could not afford such an expense.[24] And even with the geological survey, Navajos still did not know the full extent of their oil deposits or the depletion rates.[25] To solve these pressing problems and insure adequate revenues, Navajos explored pan-tribal options.

The world oil market changed dramatically throughout the 1960s. The Organization of Petroleum Exporting Companies (OPEC) and Organization of Arab Petroleum Exporting Companies (OAPEC) were two groups that emerged to protect their resources from the grasp of western nations.[26] At about the same time, Charles Lipton, director of an independent New York City consulting firm, told energy-resource tribes that they, too, should stop accepting "trinkets and lollipops," and like Third World nations, force companies to grant fair deals.[27]

Navajos Join CERT

In 1975, Peter MacDonald, who had replaced Raymond Nakai in 1970 as council chairman, joined the Council of Energy Resource Tribes (CERT), a consortium of twenty-five energy-producing tribes determined to be included in formulating national energy policy. These tribes were eager to use their potential wealth to industrialize, educate their people, and free themselves from BIA domination. Edward Gabriel of the Federal Energy Administration was named executive director in Washington.[28]

MacDonald was an enigma in many ways. Some Navajos detested his leadership; others believed there was no more forward-looking chairman. Grand-nephew of former chairman Deshna Clah Cheschilligi, MacDonald was college educated and entered the tribal government in 1965 through President Lyndon B. Johnson's Great Society programs. The Office of Navajo Economic Opportunity (ONEO) was created in 1965 to distribute the government funds, and Chairman Nakai appointed MacDonald its director. "Where poverty was deepest on the reservation, ONEO appeared with money and jobs"; MacDonald transformed the directorship of ONEO into political clout and was elected tribal chairman in 1970.[29]

MacDonald and Phoenix-based former Wall Street attorney George Vlassis set about to renegotiate energy contracts with companies like Kerr-McGee, Exxon, and El Paso Natural Gas, only to discover that in many instances the Interior Department had removed the automatic twenty-year adjustment clauses.[30] MacDonald was outspoken against power brokers like BIA officials, state governors, and legislators.[31] Superintendent Landbloom was a typical example. According to MacDonald, Landbloom held the only key to council chambers; "No Navajo could use the chambers without first going to [his] office and requesting the key." If council delegates debated an issue too long, Landbloom would "throw every one of us out, put a padlock on the council chamber, and not let us back in until we learned to behave like adults."[32]

Some Navajos applauded MacDonald's outspoken tactics, but many criticized his $55,000 salary, Lincoln Continental, airplane, and extravagant home, when Navajo per-capita income was a mere $2,900. Although a primary goal was mineral development, by MacDonald's second term, which began in 1975, many Navajos from impacted areas bitterly spoke against further exploitation. Younger Navajos formed groups like the Coalition for Navajo Liberation and in some instances managed to slow development. MacDonald's deals, critics said, seemed to come at the expense of the "poorest of the poor."[33]

CERT was not the first pan-tribal attempt to discuss mutual energy-related problems. In 1974, twenty-six Northern Plains tribes met and formed the Native American Natural Resources Development Federation (NANRDF). The group wrote a declaration of Indian rights, which stressed protection of land, water, and minerals. Tribes of the Southwest began to meet with NANRDF. CERT, however, garnered the political and financial support of government leaders, and as it increased its influence, NANRDF lost its federal funding and ceased to exist.[34]

CERT was quickly dubbed "Indian OPEC" by opponents, and MacDonald was derisively called "the Shah of the Navajos." Corporations feared CERT might collectively turn the screw on the society that had exploited them for centuries.[35] The BIA resented the organization because of its influence with tribes and because of its federal funding. After members sent their mission statement to FEA—later Department of Energy (DOE)—CERT received $250,000 in funds for a survey of Indian resources, which the BIA tried to block. The problem was made worse when NANRDF's principal founder, Thomas Frederick, was nominated as Assistant Secretary of the Interior in 1980, and CERT allegedly blocked confirmation.[36]

The CERT survey was conducted and revealed that 30 percent or more of the West's coal, 4 percent of remaining U.S. oil reserves, and 50 percent of the nation's uranium lay on Indian land. CERT opened its offices in 1977; in 1979, the organization hired Ahmed Kooros, previously Iran's prime minister of economics and oil, as its chief economist. Of course, a barrage of letters to the Interior Department charged that Kooros's employment was unpatriotic. But MacDonald maintained that Indian tribes merely sought self-sustaining economies; how could this be deemed un-American?[37] By 1980, CERT employed twenty-three people in Washington and forty-two in its Denver office. MacDonald asked the federal government in 1979 for $600 million — one-half of one percent of the amount President Jimmy Carter earmarked for energy security — to finance CERT projects. DOE gave CERT $24 million, but left future funding up in the air and specified how the sum was to be used.[38]

Nevertheless, four founding tribes left CERT, citing pressure to develop their resources and naming MacDonald as one source of that pressure. Some members criticized the financial marriage between CERT and government.[39] Others feared that whites would come to see a rich Indian image, which was certainly not the case for the vast majority. The American Indian Movement (AIM) shunned CERT's entrepreneurial objective: "He's [MacDonald] being sodomized by the multinationals and the U.S. government and he's enjoying every second of it; I pity him," AIM co-founder Russell Means stated in 1982.[40]

Yet pan-tribal efforts seemed the only way to improve bargaining power.[41] CERT attorneys discovered and canceled inactive or abandoned leases — many on Navajo land. With *Dinébéiina Nahilnabee Aghaditahee* (DNA), established in 1966 as an OEO-sponsored legal aid program for Navajos, CERT filed a class action suit in 1983 on behalf of 14,500 Navajo allottees accusing the federal government of holding back mineral rights.[42]

At the request of Navajos and Southern Utes, CERT began a project, *Shii Shi Keyah*, to monitor production and royalties for allottees. Albuquerque lawyer Alan Taradash, also of DNA, headed the project. Taradash filed suit against the Interior Department in October 1984 to force prompt royalty payments, and in 1988 hired an independent accounting firm, claiming it cost less than using the federal system. CERT also used its lawyers to renegotiate a pipeline deal between Navajos and Atlantic Richfield in which BIA had settled for a $280,000 easement.[43]

CERT got Navajos $70 million over twenty years, and helped Jicarilla Apaches to obtain total ownership of producing oil and gas wells, the first tribe to accomplish such a feat. The Northern Cheyennes permitted a survey of oil and gas on their land, while other western tribes made similar moves. In 1977, CERT also opened talks with OPEC, again generating concern over possible Middle East collaboration.[44]

In 1982, Peterson Zah beat MacDonald for the Navajo chairmanship. An environmentalist and former DNA attorney who was not entirely in favor of oil development, Zah refused at first to even attend CERT meetings. In fact, he threatened to withdraw Navajos from the organization entirely, claiming that MacDonald's involvement in CERT led to the former chairman's neglect of reservation troubles. But Zah's staff intervened, convincing him that Navajos indeed needed the technical and legal expertise that CERT provided. In 1983, Zah announced that the Navajo tribe would remain a member.[45]

A major blow to CERT came with a budget cut during President Ronald Reagan's administration and BIA's threat to withdraw support. The Environmental Protection Agency (EPA) continued to provide funding, however, and Congress pressured BIA to resume assistance. CERT, headquartered in Denver, Colorado, continues to survive despite financial woes.[46] This organization's attempt to pull native leaders together into a single endeavor is something that historically tribes have found difficult. By 1994, membership stood at forty-nine energy tribes. Hopefully, tribes will soon direct and fully benefit by whatever energy development they wish to pursue.

Navajos Face the Energy Crisis

In October 1973, OPEC imposed an oil embargo on the United States in large part to protest American support of Israel in conflicts with Arab nations. The United States at this time used one-third of the world's energy resources, two-thirds of which came from the Middle East. As a result of the embargo, oil and gas prices rose and domestic production accelerated. What should have been a boon for Navajos actually undermined their bargaining power because government wanted to develop oil and natural gas rapidly, and Native Americans were still subject to federal review and approval.[47]

President Carter ran into immediate trouble with western tribes when he neglected to consult them, causing outspoken Mescalero Apache chairman Wendell Chino to challenge tribal leaders to demand control.[48] CERT vowed not to "turn into an energy cartel," but warned that if the United States refused to commit to Indians, it might explore other options.[49] Associate director of the National Indian Youth Council, John Redhouse, called Carter's energy policy the "moral equivalent of war."

> **We knew then that the Indian wars were not yet over and we must battle the bureaucratic cavalry and the corporate cavalry in order to protect our land.**[50]

The energy crisis brought Navajo tribal responses as well. In 1978, the tribal council provided chapters with the power to pass ordinances to govern their land and offered them planning expertise. Council members even discussed incorporating chapters in order to enable them to impose a severance tax on minerals taken from their land, but obstacles stood in the way of fully implementing such local control.[51] Navajos in 1980 declared a brief moratorium while they completed a comprehensive economic development program.[52] The tribal government sunk more into investments and claimed autonomy in the management of internal affairs.[53] Also in 1980, the council established the first Comprehensive Employment and Training Program under the Navajo Division of Labor. The program emphasized technological and mining training, increasing Navajo employment, and establishing Navajo-owned mines "through total development, performance, and service contracts, or purchase of existing mining activities."[54]

Congress also reacted to the oil crisis, and in 1982 passed the Indian Mineral Development Act, the first significant piece of legislation since 1938. It permitted joint ventures and other innovative arrangements between tribes and energy corporations for exploration, extraction, processing, or other development. Leases were still subject to Secretary of the Interior approval, but forced a decision within 180 days.[55] Former Secretary Udall said although the new law did not alter the 1938 Mineral Act as significantly as Indians had hoped, it did expand their options, clearly spelled out the Interior Department's authority, and would help meet rising energy demands in the United States.[56]

According to Robert Billie, Aneth-area delegate to the tribal council, whereas the Omnibus Indian Mineral Leasing Act of 1938 had discouraged maximum economic and social benefits, the new legislation encouraged both through flexibility and allowing the Navajo government to "vertically integrate" its energy projects. Billie added that in 1980, the tribal council adopted a reservation-wide energy policy and created Navajo Energy Development Authority to carry it out, but had been unable to function under the BIA's leasing-only policy. Even so, the BIA upper echelon continued to remain uneasy about the new arrangements, favoring instead a continuation of competitive bidding.[57]

By 1982, however, the oil crisis boom had peaked. Once the decline set in, there was no projected use for coal after the year 2000, and uranium, too, was becoming obsolete.[58] Thus, by the time Congress acted, companies were no longer lined up at the tribes' doors.[59] But Navajos suspected that the boom would not last—booms never did—and had already explored taxation as one way to bolster tribal coffers.

we can see that the State of New Mexico has collected $2,466,309.84 in taxes on oil and gas produced in the Navajo Nation in the years 1972–1974 alone. . . . [and] the total amount of taxes collected by non-Navajo governments from within the Navajo Nation is a great deal more.[60]

Navajos realized that they must begin to tax non-Navajos working on the reservation and businesses to help fund tribal government and environmental protection projects. Passage in 1982 of the Indian Tribal Government Tax Status Act helped; CERT actively lobbied for the legislation. As early as 1928, the State of New Mexico had taxed oil companies doing business on the reservation, and in 1957 Arizona placed an income tax on allottees.[61] States and counties within which the Navajo Nation was located reportedly collected more taxes from energy-producing companies than Navajos received in royalties, rents, bonuses, and wages.[62]

DNA also noted that tribal income between 1958 and 1972 was $279,726,652, but expenses totaled $296,498,357, suggesting the tribe might do well to seek additional revenue sources.[63] But when Jicarilla Apaches placed a moderate severance tax on oil, corporations filed suit and newspapers filled with venomous — and racist — attacks.[64] In 1982, the Supreme Court upheld the Jicarillas' authority to impose a severance tax on oil and gas production if funds were used to support government and services.[65] Because Interior approval was required, government immediately began to draw up tax guidelines and procedures. CERT protested when it discovered that government asked industry for assistance in writing the guidelines.

In 1978 Navajos enacted property and business-activity taxes, and energy companies immediately challenged. In autumn 1978, a Phoenix federal court ruled that Navajos had an inherent right under tribal sovereignty to tax.[66] But it was the 1985 case *Kerr McGee Corp. v. Navajo Tribe* — one of two lawsuits filed by Superior Oil — that affirmed Navajos' right to tax non-Indians. While it left the door open to future congressional action, Navajos had a new revenue source.[67] With the court decision, the tribal government was able to discuss joint taxation and tax-sharing programs with state and local governments as well.

There is a footnote to Peter MacDonald's story. Reelected chairman in 1986, he blamed Navajos for their own poverty and accused opponents of trying to turn the clock back to John Collier.[68] He launched new development initiatives, including purchase of a ranch, with a controversial $100 million financing plan. His activities earned him a U.S. Senate investigation, which tore the Navajo Nation into pro- and anti-MacDonald factions.[69]

In 1991, MacDonald was convicted of embezzlement, income tax evasion, and accepting bribes, and sentenced to federal prison. During his term, he sent Navajos a message of self-determination that offered hope for some, disappointed others who found him long on rhetoric and short on solutions, and insulted dissidents. Hence, MacDonald was perhaps the most controversial Navajo leader in Navajo history. It was even suggested that his administration caused an increase in federal intervention into tribal affairs in the 1980s and 90s.[70]

Navajos Challenge Oil Corporations and Utah

While the Navajo tribal government achieved a degree of autonomy, residents became increasingly angry. Scholar David Aberle told the U.S. Commission on Civil Rights, "economic development is not simply a question of how the reservation can most profitably be milked by outside interests."[71] Unemployment remained high, with Navajo workers the first laid off or fired and the lowest paid.[72] Jobs generated a sort of us-versus-them competition with the unemployed growing weary of intrusion and those working for the energy corporations in favor of development. Wilber Yazzi, a pumper and handyman at the Dineh bi Keyah field on Lukachukai Mountain, for instance, earned $3.31 per hour in 1967 and told newspaper reporters, "my oldest daughter is in junior high school . . . and if my work holds up, I plan to send her to college."[73]

At the opposite pole were allottees, who often faced corporate trickery when they negotiated leases and bonuses.[74] Fifty-year-old Kenneth Willie told the *Denver Post* that to get a lease, Mobil Corporation "rushed me like a police officer giving me a ticket."[75] Navajos who spoke little or no English were urged to place thumbprints on contracts before they could consult with anyone. A 1980 University of New Mexico Indian Law Center report noted:

Allotted lands and resources, valued at millions of dollars, are leased without Indian owners being provided the benefit of technical and legal assistance and advice to assure the best bargain possible.

As one Albuquerque attorney snapped, "No one has ever done a damn thing for the allottees." The chasm between Navajos widened.[76]

Reservation residents reported property damage and resented tribal leaders, whom some claimed, "get everything." "They [tribal leaders] won't even pay attention to the people." Moreover, "the ordinary Navajo probably had as much say in their government as you do with the state or federal government, actually less. Most are ignored."[77] Navajo rancher Raymond Arviso reported that when crews drilled in full sight of his home "nobody even did [me] the courtesy of telling me that they would be on my property."[78] Richard Hughes of DNA asserted, "whether or not we are willing to acknowledge it, [the] traditional Indian belief is under assault."[79] Anthropologists Klara Bonsack Kelley and Harris Francis recalled how 81-year-old Bessie Adakai Morgan wanted an oil company to leave her grazing area and to stop clearing the land because "she collects herbs for her medicine from the spot, and she also uses the soil from there for sandpainting for various ceremonies."[80]

Disgruntled Navajos eventually took action. Fifteen years after the Utah Indian Affairs Commission was launched, residents still had no running water or electricity.[81] They experienced vandalism and cruelty to stock. Elsie Peshlakai saw crews invade family graves, strip timber, and dewater aquifers. "We weren't a political family before . . . but we are now."[82] With the advent of oil and uranium development, she noted, Navajo families broke up more often and child and spousal abuse and alcoholism increased. "In a very real sense . . . the

Navajo family, the social structure and the values that underlie both are in danger of being torn apart." Her husband Walter Peshlakai agreed: "energy companies are concerned with projects, not impacts, and the land and people will be ruined if that is allowed to go on."[83] Council delegate Andrew Tso charged that "oil companies have been lax in cleaning up their sites or compensating Navajos" and began to pressure for change.[84]

Navajos and Hopis first challenged Peabody Coal and the secrecy surrounding company-tribal decisions. In 1971 Black Mesa Defense Fund convinced Congress to investigate, and Hopis attempted to sue the Secretary of the Interior. These events sparked Navajo activism. Affected chapters began to pass anti-development resolutions, and by 1978, Navajos and the National Indian Youth Council sued to halt a strip mine near Burnham, New Mexico. When the suit failed, Navajos took over the mine and were arrested by tribal police.[85]

The Utah Navajo Development Council (UNDC) came under fire in the 1970s. Incorporated as a private, non-profit agency in 1971, its primary duty was to administer the Navajo trust fund on behalf of San Juan County Navajos for the Utah Division of Indian Affairs.[86] The agency rapidly evolved into a complex organization with six non-profit divisions and a subsidiary, Utah Navajo Industries, which operated diverse businesses including an educational materials publishing company.[87]

In February 1977, San Juan County Navajos filed suit against UNDC, and on September 8, the District Court in Salt Lake City ordered a full audit of the council's accounting and management practices plus an investigation of its transactions. In addition, the court ordered Utah to inform Navajos of all expenditures. The audit was completed in January 1978. The report accused chapter officials of using trust money for personal savings or checking accounts and some board members of appropriating funds for "real estate, underwriting the publishing of private manuscripts, and loans . . ."[88]

The audit found that UNDC's profit-seeking ventures suffered from mismanagement. In fact, the *Navajo Times* reported that in 1977 only one venture avoided "drastic losses." The Utah Division of Indian Affairs was charged with mismanaging funds and blatant conflicts of interest. In one instance, plumbing contractor Don Smith — serving on both the UDIA and UNDC boards — received a $200,000 contract without competitive bidding for fiscal year 1976–77.[89]

MacDonald and other tribal officials reportedly received kickbacks and "various kinds of gratuities" from companies seeking to do business on the reservation. Everett Kenneth, manager of Henry Hillson Company, admitted that loans were written off and gifts were commonly given to tribal officials.[90] A Navajo who signed his letter simply "A Concerned Diné" charged UNDC with "nepotism, religious bias," and giving Anglos top administrative positions while college-educated Navajos were consistently relegated to inferior positions and lower pay. He added, "Let's unite as one people to solve this problem."[91]

At about the same time, New Mexico Navajos described the ills associated with rapid population explosion to Senator Pete Domenici (R-NM). Councilmen Frank Chee Willeto and Edward T. Begay worried about taxes and how to stretch existing services to provide adequate health care, housing, and electrical power to newcomers. "Non-Indians are moving in with energy companies. They are welcome . . . but they are creating problems . . . "[92] According to tribal vice chairman Wilson Skeet, Crownpoint's population had doubled in ten years and was expected to double again in another decade. In addition to these problems, new road construction was an absolute necessity.

By early 1977, Navajos grew increasingly irritated with oil companies, pollution, and livestock deaths. Although MacDonald agreed to create a committee of oil agents, tribal officials, and government leaders, residents felt their complaints were generally being ignored.[93] On March 30, a group of at least fifty Navajo men, women, and children from Aneth and Montezuma Creek — and led by AIM spokesman Larry Anderson — set up a roadblock leading to the Texaco pumping station at Montezuma Creek and shut down operations there. Within a short period of time, that number grew to more than one hundred. Eventually, they closed all oil operations in the Aneth oil field.[94]

Texaco held a meeting on April 5, with about one thousand Navajos attending. The protesters issued their demands, among these reparations for damage done to Navajo land and stock and grievance committees to hear complaints.[95] The Diné accused tribal officials and the state of Utah of pocketing royalties. Furthermore,

> the people of Aneth and Montezuma Creek say the underground wealth of their land has not meant a better or easier life. Instead it has killed their cattle, destroyed their environment, and disrupted their lifestyle.[96]

Within two weeks, the occupying force — led by the Utah chapter of the Coalition for Navajo Liberation (CNL) — swelled to one thousand. The group issued a resolution declaring, "We are sick and tired" of damaged grazing lands. . . . These oil problems are polluting our air, mother earth, and our spiritual way of life."[97]

Now the protesters demanded renegotiation of all leases with a maximum term of ten years. They wanted harsh penalties for companies that failed to implement reclamation programs. In addition, the Navajos wanted new procedures drawn up to include locals in the decision-making process. They asked that companies police their crews, particularly since many had the reputation of provoking the Navajo people and harassing or stealing their livestock. Finally, the Aneth Navajos insisted that they receive electricity, company-financed health programs, housing, and education plans. Moreover, they wanted tribal programs extended to Utah.[98]

Ella Sakizzie, an elderly Navajo woman, reported, "the land has gotten dryer and less green ever since the companies have started drilling," while another resident said, "when it rains or snows, the oil and chemicals from drilling sites get mixed up with the water and drains all over the land."[99] MacDonald traveled to Aneth, where he heard stories of finding white chemicals in the stomachs of dead livestock, Navajo women molested by oil employees, and families offered liquor and drugs in exchange for their daughters. Residents emphasized that, in addition, area unemployment stood at 90 percent.[100]

Seventeen days later, the occupation ended. Oil companies agreed to prohibit alcohol and firearms on the reservation and promised to reseed and restore the land. They vowed to protect burial sites and demand that their non-Indian employees respect Navajo families. Companies acquiesced to donating $5,000 to an education fund and to extending power lines and natural gas to residents, but refused to renegotiate their leases.[101]

Despite the seeming victory, Aneth Navajos grew increasingly hostile when oil companies failed to uphold the new agreements. By June, the *Navajo Times* reported residents throwing rocks at oil representatives and at visiting tribal leaders, claiming they had been betrayed. Texaco, Phillips, Superior, and Continental had all resumed operations, but protesters saw few changes.[102] On July 5, Red Mesa Chapter passed a resolution against new oil drilling, claiming they would "use guns if necessary to enforce the agreement."[103] By August, tribal EPA and other officials feared traveling around Aneth, Montezuma Creek, and Red Mesa because of threats of violence. The Navajo EPA established $145,000 in claims against oil firms by this time, but residents declared that new development was in the works without their approval.[104]

In November, Montezuma Creek Navajos staged a 250-mile walk to protest continuing problems in their area. "We are not walking for the fun of it. We pray together, eat together, walk together, and we are doing this for our elders, young ones, and the Navajo people's future generation."[105] The walk, they said, was to promote awareness of Mother Earth and threats against her, express concern over continuing mismanagement of tribal funds, and make clear the views of Navajos regarding UNDC. Protests continued throughout the 1970s, but none proved as dramatic as the sit-in or the Navajo walk.[106]

Nor was the situation with the state of Utah solved. Although Utah reportedly held $180 million in a trust fund, a 1991 audit conducted by the auditor general discovered only $9.2 million.[107] The audit also suggested that Window Rock was returning only a fraction of the royalty money to local chapters as it was required to do. According to San Juan County Commissioner Ty Lewis, "The leaders of the Navajo Tribe have ripped off the tribe for millions." Fellow commissioner Calvin Black noted, "About $1 billion [*sic*] in royalties has been collected by the tribe from the Utah [section] and I'm aware of no improvements on the Utah portion of the reservation."[108] Craig Moody, Utah legislator [R-UT], who requested the investigation, added, "The audit reads like a cheap novel . . . The sad thing is it's true."[109]

Dependency or Safety Net?

In *The Roots of Dependency*, Richard White laid out the steps by which Navajos went from a self-sufficient people sustained by a herding and barter economy to dependency. Destruction of their traditional way of life meant that Navajos could no longer depend upon themselves for food and clothing and for the first time in their lives were forced to purchase almost everything from traders or merchants. Like so many other Native Americans, Navajos were integrated into a capitalist system in ways disadvantageous to them. White primarily blamed stock reduction, and claimed that because of the federally-mandated program, the Navajo economy after 1945 came to resemble a welfare state.[110]

Oil could have provided a safety net; it should have eased Navajos into the mainstream economy, but fell far short of expectations. Government and industry must shoulder most of the blame. Despite all the assimilationist rhetoric of the late nineteenth and twentieth centuries, Indians were denied integration into U.S. society even as they were being stripped of land and other valuable resources. In the case of Navajos, from 1923 forward, the Interior Department repeatedly failed to maximize revenues. Officials consistently auctioned Navajo oil resources to the highest bidders and in return failed to monitor production or royalties.[111] The BIA neither prepared Navajos to assume the more lucrative aspects of oil development like exploration, drilling, refining, or sales, nor trained them for higher-paying jobs. Navajos achieved most of their success through their own devices, with government at times actively hindering them. As Lorraine Turner Ruffing, formerly with American Indian Policy Review Commission, accurately observed, "the BIA has consistently favored one method of exploiting Navajo resources — leasing resources to non-Indians."[112] The result has been underdevelopment and dependency. Yet, sadly, the U.S. Commission on Civil Rights concluded in 1975 that despite its shortcomings, "the BIA, in the view of the Navajo Tribe, must continue to exist for the protection of Indian rights."[113]

In all fairness, the BIA has long occupied the lowest tier of the Interior Department hierarchy and suffers from a persistent lack of appropriations.[114] It has historically been in charge of one group Americans prefer to ignore.

Hence a public that for two hundred years has tried to wish away American Indians and questioned their cultural tenacity must share the responsibility. It is always easier to blame government than an insatiable capitalistic system eager to gobble up resources but hesitant to share the wealth. Americans have taken pleasure at the low at-the-pump cost of gasoline and oil without much regard for who was actually paying the bills. Neither have state and local governments conveyed much concern about native peoples within their borders. Thus, Peter MacDonald accurately stated the Navajo dilemma when he remarked,

> The Navajo Nation has arrived at a fateful point in history; those [energy] resources can be totally wiped out in a 25-year period . . . those resources, and the land on which they lie, are the only assets we have. They hold our only chance for a future; we are either at the point of a new beginning or this is simply the beginning of the end.[115]

Corporations have clearly contributed to the problem as well. Since 1922, oil companies have repeatedly demonstrated little sense of liability or concern for reclamation, relocation, health problems, or cultural disintegration unless forced to pay these costs.[116] Local oil men in the Four Corners area agree that many more individuals and companies lost money than made it in their quest for oil riches, and certainly Rattlesnake, Table Mesa, and Hogback were quite small as oil fields go.[117] Yet, some corporations profited handsomely. Navajos have long watched *bilagáanas* nose around their reservation seeking land, gold, and later oil, natural gas, coal, and uranium. Who knows what they will seek next? But Navajos know it will be something, and chances are, industry will continue to demonstrate the same sense of impunity.

It must be noted that while most Navajos never lived under the shadow of a derrick, oil played a significant role in their lives, and sometimes that role was positive. The demand for leases in 1923 gathered Navajos from across the reservation and created a government that formed the core of the future Navajo Nation. Royalties offered some hope for those desperate for more grazing land. During the stock reduction years, Navajos faced three alternatives — try to recapture their subsistence economy, relocate, or attempt to modernize.[118] Oil allowed them to choose the third.

Oil also generated a college scholarship fund and millions for water development, irrigation, flood control, and reclamation. Bonuses and royalties encouraged tribal businesses and lured small industry to the reservation.[119] Under Paul Jones, this income was used to build new chapter houses and refurbish old ones. The need to accommodate oil crews produced a transportation revolution. In addition, petroleum and natural gas produced some jobs and provided badly needed income for allottees.

But oil altered Navajo society in negative ways, too. In combination with stock reduction, it helped undermine the roles and status of women, who, as Ruth Roessel claims, lost much of their pride and control in the economic transition. Compounding the situation was a rise in alcohol consumption and a decrease in spirituality among both men and women.[120] Still, college gave women an alternate route.

Oil contributed to environmental misuse. Crews unearthed aquifers, providing new drinking and stock water sources, but they also destroyed burial grounds and sacred areas and displaced families and herds. More devastating, exploitation altered the entire Navajo concept of land. In 1921, most Navajos believed that Dinétah was valuable not for its underground riches, but because it housed ancestor spirits and provided everything Navajos held sacred. Since that time, a significant number of Diné men and women have adopted the bilagáana message that land is mere commodity. Whether this denotes disintegration of Navajo culture in favor of mainstream American materialism remains to be seen.

Still, Navajo society has never been static. It was changing when Navajos traded, warred, and married into Pueblo, Apache, and Spanish societies, and when bilagáanas arrived. To entertain the notion of an unchanging native culture at any period is severely short-sighted. Oil generated tremendous change, but has not destroyed Navajo culture or obliterated the stories that hold them together as a people. It may in the long run strengthen them. As Navajo poet Luci Tapahonso wrote:

You are here.
Your parents are here.
Your relatives are here.
We are all here together.

It is all this: the care, the prayers, songs,
and our own lives as Navajos we carry with us all the time.
It has been this way for centuries among us.
It has been this way for centuries among us.[121]

Navajos still live between the four sacred peaks of their land. And the *yé'ii* continue to encircle them.

NOTES

Chapter One

1. Ethelou Yazzie, ed., *Navajo History*, vol. 1 (Many Farms, Ariz.: Navajo Community College Press, 1971), 83.

2. Ibid. W. Matthews, "A Part of the Navajo's Mythology," *American Antiquarian* 5 (July 1883): 207–24, says First Man and First Woman encountered other Indian peoples in the third world, and at first everyone spoke the same language. Later their "tongues became twisted."

3. Peter Iverson, *The Navajo Nation* (Westport, Conn.: Greenwood Press, 1981). Robert W. Young, *A Political History of the Navajo Tribe* (Tsaile, Ariz.: Navajo Community College Press, 1978). For a Navajo view, see Clyde Benally et al., *Dinéjí Nakee' Naahane': A Utah Navajo History* (Monticello, Utah: San Juan School District, 1982).

4. James M. Goodman, *The Navajo Atlas: Environments, Resources, People, and History of the Diné Bikéyah* (Norman: University of Oklahoma Press, 1982), 45.

5. Donald L. Baars, *Navajo Country: A Geology and Natural History of the Four Corners Region* (Albuquerque: University of New Mexico Press, 1995), 2–3.

6. Emily Benedek, *Beyond the Four Corners of the World: A Navajo Woman's Journey* (New York: Alfred A. Knopf, 1995), 4.

7. Edward T. Hall, *West of the Thirties: Discoveries Among the Navajo and Hopi* (New York: Doubleday, 1994), 104.

8. Clyde Kluckhohn and Dorothea Leighton, *The Navajo* (Cambridge, Mass.: Harvard University Press, 1946), 177.

9. Leland C. Wyman, *Blessingway*, Trans. by Father Berard Haile (Tucson: University of Arizona Press, 1970, 1975), 8.

10. David J. Weber, *The Spanish Frontier in North America* (New Haven, Conn.: Yale University Press, 1992), 47.

11. Zaraté Salmeron, *Relaciones*, trans. by Alicia Ronstadt Milich (Albuquerque: Horn & Wallace, 1966), 94.

12. Weber, *Spanish Frontier*, 98.

13. David M. Brugge, *Navajos in the Catholic Church Records of New Mexico, 1694–1875*, Research Reports No. 1 (Window Rock, Ariz.: Research Section, Parks and Recreation Department, Navajo Tribe, 1968), 39.

14. Raymond Friday Locke, *The Book of the Navajo* (Los Angeles: Mankind, 1986), 195.

15. Gerald Thompson, *The Army and the Navajo* (Tucson: University of Arizona Press, 1976), 3.

16. Brugge, *Catholic Church*, 67.

17. Ibid., 70.

18. Grant Foreman, ed., *A Pathfinder in the Southwest, The Itinerary of Lieutenant A. W. Whipple During his Explorations for a Railway Route from Fort Smith to Los Angeles in the Years 1853 and 1854* (Norman: University of Oklahoma Press, 1941), 126.

19. Testimony of Colonel Kit Carson, "Conditions of the Indian Tribes," Senate, Report of the Joint Special Committee, Appendix, 39th Cong., 2d Sess., No. 156 (Washington: GPO, 1867), 97.

20. Frank D. Reeve, "The Long Walk," in *New Mexico Past and Present, A Historical Reader*, ed. Richard N. Ellis (Albuquerque: University of New Mexico Press, 1971), 136.

21. Thompson, *The Army and the Navajo*, 157.

22. Louise Lamphere, *To Run After Them: Cultural and Social Basis of Cooperation in a Navajo Community* (Tucson: University of Arizona Press, 1977), 30.

23. James F. Downs, *Animal Husbandry in Navajo Society and Culture* (Berkeley: University of California Press, 1964), 85.

24. Eleanor D. MacDonald and John B. Arrington, *The San Juan Basin: My Kingdom Was a County* (Denver: Green Mountain Press, 1970), 58.

25. Frank McNitt, *The Indian Traders* (Norman: University of Oklahoma Press, 1962), 299–300.

26. MacDonald and Arrington, *My Kingdom Was a County*, 35.

27. T. M. Pearce, ed., *New Mexico Place Names: A Geographical Dictionary* (Albuquerque: University of New Mexico Press, 1965), 56. Also, Robert W. Young and William Morgan, *The Navajo Language: A Grammar and Colloquial Dictionary* (Albuquerque: University of New Mexico Press, 1980), 708.

28. Leon Wall and William Morgan, *Navajo-English Dictionary* (Washington: BIA, 1958; New York: Hippocrene, 1994), 77, 151.

29. Jim Bob Tinsley, *The Hash Knife Brand* (Gainesville: University Press of Florida, 1993), 53–58. Zane Grey popularized the Hash Knife in a 1929 serial, "The Yellow Jacket Feud," which became *The Hash Knife Outfit* (Harper, 1933). Aztec Land investors purchased 1 million acres from Atlantic and Pacific Railroad but gained more by appropriating land from Navajos and white farmers.

30. Charles S. Peterson, *Take Up Your Mission: Mormon Colonizing Along the Little Colorado River, 1870–1900* (Tucson: University of Arizona Press, 1973), 169–70.

31. Janet Smith, "History of San Juan County," March 10, 1936, WPA Reports, San Juan County File, New Mexico State Records and Archives, Santa Fe, New Mexico (NMSRA).

32. McNitt, *Indian Trader*, 322.

33. Martha Austin and Regina Lynch, eds., *Saad Ahąąh Sinil: Dual Language, A Navajo-English Dictionary*, rev. ed. (Chinle, Ariz.: Rough Rock Press, 1990), 36.

34. Frank McNitt, *Navajo Wars: Military Campaigns, Slave Raids, and Reprisals*

(Albuquerque: University of New Mexico Press, 1972), 246–47; Lawrence C. Kelly, *Navajo Roundup: Selected Correspondence of Kit Carson's Expedition Against the Navajo* (Boulder, Colo.: Pruett, 1970), 27.

35. Eleanor Delong, "Gallup," June 12, 1936, WPA, McKinley County File, NMSRA.

36. Eleanor Delong, "Ramah," July 3, 1936, Ibid. Also see Pearce, T. M., ed., *New Mexico Place Names: A Geographical Dictionary* (Albuquerque: University of New Mexico Press, 1965), 129.

37. McNitt, *Indian Traders*, 46.

38. Albert H. Kneale, *Indian Agent* (Caldwell, Idaho: Caxton, 1950), 372.

39. C. F. Hauke to Rachel Lufkin, April 14, 1913, Record Group (RG) 75, Central Classified Files (CCF), 53637-13, National Archives (NA).

40. Smith, "San Juan County."

41. Baars, *Navajo Country*, 123.

42. Smith, "San Juan County."

43. "Seventy Million Gasser in Aztec-La Plata Oil Field," *Aztec Independent*, April 27, 1923.

44. Baars, *Navajo Country*, 149.

45. "Treaty Between the United States of America and the Navajo Tribe of Indians," June 1, 1868, as quoted in *Treaty Between the United States of America and the Navajo Tribe of Indians: With a Record of the Discussion That Led to its Signing*, ed., Martin A. Link (Flagstaff: K.C., 1968), 23.

46. Lawrence Kelly, *Assault on Assimilation: John Collier and the Origins of Indian Policy Reform* (Albuquerque: University of New Mexico Press, 1983), 181.

47. Baars, *Navajo Country*, 152.

48. M. S. Hart to L. Miller, November 2, 1895, and Hart to Miller, January 2, 1897, Territorial Archives of New Mexico (TANM), Microfilm, Reel 26, NMSRA.

49. Gerald D. Nash, *United States Oil Policy 1890–1964* (Pittsburgh: University of Pittsburgh Press, 1968), 13.

50. C. V. Koogler and Virginia Koogler Whitney, *Aztec: A Story of Old Aztec from the Anasazi to Statehood* (Fort Worth, Tex.: American Reference, 1972), 105.

51. Baars, *Navajo Country*, 155.

52. Peter Paquette to Commissioner of Indian Affairs (CIA), June 12, 1912, RG 75, Box 91, CCF 61343-12, NA.

53. Berard Haile to E. R. Fryer, November 7, 1936, Berard Haile Collection (BHC), Box 6, Folder 7, Special Collections, University of Arizona, Tucson, Arizona (UA).

54. Richard Van Valkenburgh, "The Government of the Navajos," *Arizona Quarterly* 1 (Winter 1945): 72. Aberle, 34.

55. Berard Haile to John Collier, April 16, 1934, BHC, Box 6, UA.

56. John L. Kessell, "The Navajo Tribal Council in the 1920s," Unpublished court report, presented in Albuquerque, N. Mex., June 24, 1981, 2.

57. "Will Open Navajo Reservation," *Farmington Times-Hustler*, March 14, 1907.

58. Kessell, "Navajo Tribal Council," 4.

59. "Will Open . . . ," *Times Hustler*, op. cit.

60. Minutes of the Tribal Council (Fort Defiance, Ariz.), November 9, 1901, RG 75, Letters Received (LR) 69825–01, 2, NA.

61. Ibid.

62. Peter MacDonald, *The Last Warrior: Peter MacDonald and the Navajo Nation*, ed. Herman J. Viola, (New York: Orion Books, 1993), 9.

63. Minutes of Council (Fort Defiance, Ariz.), July 16, 17, 1901, RG 75, LR, 40301–01, 10, NA.

64. Ibid., 16.

65. Ibid., 22.

66. Abbott to A. B. Fall, July 5, 1913, RG 75, Box 91, CCF 83033–13, NA.

Chapter Two

1. Paul G. Zolbrod, *Diné Bahane: The Navajo Creation Story* (Albuquerque: University of New Mexico Press, 1984), 92.

2. Russell Lord, *The Wallaces of Iowa* (Boston: Houghton Mifflin, 1947), 228. Articles like "The Menace of Fallism" showed up in journals across the country by 1922, and the term continued long after Fall's resignation.

3. David H. Stratton, "New Mexico Machiavellian: The Story of Albert B. Fall," *Montana, the Magazine of Western History* 7 (October 1957): 14.

4. A. B. Fall to F. H. Abbott, July 2, 1913, and Abbot to Fall, July 5, 1913, Record Group (RG) 75, Box 91, Central Classified Files (CCF) 32083033–13, National Archives (NA).

5. U.S. Congress, Senate, *Congressional Record*, 63rd Cong., 2d Sess., February 11, 1914, 3318.

6. "Forest Reserve to Become Pike's Peak National Park," *Colorado Springs Gazette*, September 29, 1921.

7. Albert Bacon Fall, *The Memoirs of Albert B. Fall*, David H. Stratton, ed., Southwestern Studies Series, vol. 4 (El Paso: Texas Western Press, 1960), 7.

8. David H. Stratton, *Tempest Over Teapot Dome: The Story of Albert B. Fall* (Norman: University of Oklahoma Press, 1998), 211.

9. U.S. Department of the Interior, *Annual Report of the Secretary of the Interior for 1921* (Washington: GPO, 1921), 8.

10. Samuel P. Hayes, *Conservation and the Gospel of Efficiency: The Progressive Conservation Movement, 1890–1920* (Cambridge, Mass.: Harvard University Press, 1959), 36.

11. "Last First Americans," *Santa Fe New Mexican*, December 2, 1922.

12. Albert B. Fall to Seldon Spencer, *Bulletin of the National Parks Association* 20 (n.d.), Merritt C. Mechem Governor Papers (MCM), Correspondence File, New Mexico State Records and Archives (NMSRA).

13. Frederick Lewis Allen, *Only Yesterday: An Informal History of the 1920s* (1931; New York: Harper & Row, 1964), 148.

14. Roger M. Olien and Diana Davids Olien, *Easy Money: Oil Promoters and Investors in the Jazz Age* (Chapel Hill: University of North Carolina Press, 1990), 30.

15. Allen, *Only Yesterday*, 116–17.

16. Norman E. Nordhauser, *The Quest for Stability: Domestic Oil Regulation 1917–1935* (New York: Garland, 1979), 7.

17. John A. DeNovo, *American Interests and Policies in the Middle East, 1900–1939* (Minneapolis: University of Minnesota Press, 1963), 169.

18. Gerald D. Nash, *United States Oil Policy 1890–1964* (Pittsburgh: University of Pittsburgh Press, 1968), 48. The event precipitated a minor diplomatic crisis during the Harding administration.

19. Lawrence C. Kelly, *The Navajo Indians and Federal Indian Policy, 1900–1935* (Tucson: University of Arizona Press, 1968), 42.

20. Ibid., 57. Kelly says this occurred after the General Land Office rejected Harrison's prospector permit on the grounds that the GLO had no jurisdiction and the 1891 Indian Mineral Leasing Act applied only to treaty reservation.

21. Evan W. Estep to Commissioner of Indian Affairs (CIA), October 11, 1921, in U.S. Senate, Subcommittee of the Committee on Indian Affairs, *Survey of Conditions of the Indians in the United States*, 71st Cong., 3rd Sess., January 30–31, and February 3, 5, 1931 (Washington: GPO): 4789. Hereafter designated as *Survey*.

22. Lawrence C. Kelly, "Charles Henry Burke, 1921–29," in *The Commissioners of Indian Affairs, 1824–1977*, eds. Robert M. Kvasnicka and Herman J. Viola (Lincoln: University of Nebraska Press, 1979), 251–61.

23. CIA to Estep, April 14, 1922, in Herbert J. Hagerman, "A Report, by Herbert J. Hagerman," June 28, 1924, RG 75, Box 30, Item 150, Folder 1, CCF, p. 23, NA; also Herbert J. Hagerman Collection (HJH), Reel 1, Item 1, Center for Southwest Research (CSWR). The Hagerman Collection originals are located at NA, RG 200.

24. Estep to CIA, January 11, 1921, RG 75, Box 92, CCF 322–4292–21, NA.

25. U.S. Department of the Interior, *In the Matter of Applications for Oil and Gas Leases . . .* , Hearing, June 13, 1925, RG 75, Box 92, CCF 322–93658–22, pp. 7–8, NA.

26. Robert W. Young, "The Rise of the Navajo Tribe," in Edward H. Spicer, ed., *Plural Society in the Southwest* (New York: Interbook, 1972), 185.

27. E. B. Meritt to Estep, March 3, 1921, RG 75, CCF 322–4292–21, Box 92, NA.

28. "Proceedings of the Tribal Council (Shiprock)," May 7, 1921, Ibid.

29. Interior, *Applications*, 9.

30. "Proceedings," May 7, 1921, op. cit.

31. John L. Kessell, "The Navajo Tribal Council in the 1920s," unpublished court paper, June 24, 1981, 12.

32. Interior, *Applications*, 14.

33. *Survey*, 4785.

34. Ibid.

35. Estep to CIA, November 22, 1921, RG 75, Box 92, CCF 322–83819–21, NA.

36. Hagerman, "Report," 18. (See note 23)

37. "Mining Lease of Tribal Lands," August 15, 1921, RG 75, Box 97, CCF 322–68–1924, NA.

38. Robert O. Anderson, *Fundamentals of the Petroleum Industry* (Norman: University of Oklahoma Press, 1984), 116–17.

39. Hagerman, "Report," 16–17.

40. Estep to CIA, November 22, 1921, op. cit.

41. *Survey*, 4790.

42. Hagerman, "Report," 22.

43. *Survey*, 4789.

44. Hagerman, "Report," 24.

45. Ibid., 25. June Foutz was not Navajo. He was the eldest son of a Mormon trading family. Estep no doubt knew him, and it is likely that Hagerman misunderstood. See Frank McNitt, *The Indian Traders* (Norman: University of Oklahoma Press, 1972), 300.

46. F. G. Bonfils to Fall, September 6, 1923, RG 75, Box 93, CCF 320–77371–23, NA.

47. Hagerman, "Report," 27.

48. Curtis A. Betts, "How Fall Revolutionized Navajo Tribe to Control Their Oil Lands," in *Survey*, 4778.

49. Hagerman, "Report," 32.

50. Estep to CIA, November 22, 1921, op. cit.

51. *Survey*, 4780. In 1923, the name was spelled "Yakima," but today the preferred spelling is "Yakama."

52. Estep to Hagerman, December 10, 1923, (HJH), Reel 5, Item 28.

53. "Chee Dodge Case Meets Dismissal," *Gallup Herald*, October 17, 1925. Represented by son Tom Dodge, Dodge sued Gregory Page and John J. Emmons for $28,500, claiming bank stock sold to him was fraudulent. The case was dismissed.

54. David M. Brugge, "Henry Chee Dodge: From the Long Walk to Self-Determination," in *Indian Lives: Essays on Nineteenth- and Twentieth-Century Native American Leaders*, eds. L. G. Moses and Raymond Wilson (Albuquerque: University of New Mexico Press, 1993), 93.

55. Robert W. Young, *A Political History of the Navajo Tribe* (Tsaile, Ariz.: Navajo Community College Press, 1978), 45.

56. Francis Borgman, "Henry Chee Dodge, The Last Chief of the Navaho Indians," *New Mexico Historical Review* 23 (April 1948): 91. Borgman says he was baptized on December 4, 1932, when he was very ill.

57. Richard White, *The Roots of Dependency: Subsistence, Environment, and Social Change Among the Choctaws, Pawnees and Navajos* (Lincoln: University of Nebraska Press, 1983), 232.

58. Clyde Kluckhohn and Dorothea Leighton, *The Navajo* (Cambridge: Harvard University Press, 1946), 177.

59. Donald L. Parman, "J.C. Morgan: Navajo Apostle of Assimilation" *Prologue* 4 (Summer 1972): 87.

60. Young, *Political History*, 56.

61. Edwin T. Hall, *West of the Thirties: Discoveries Among the Navajo and Hopi* (New York: Doubleday, 1994), 142.

62. Chee Dodge to Berard Haile, December 12, 1922; George E. Cranmer to Haile, March 7, 1923, Berard Haile Collection (BHC), Box 2, Folder 1, Special Collections, University of Arizona, Tucson, Arizona (UA).

63. Haile to Marcellus Troester, April 9, 1923, BHC, Box 3, Folder 3.

64. George E. Cranmer to Haile, March 20, 1922; McPhee McGinty Building Materials to T. D. Brophy, August 24, 1922, BHC, Ibid. Navajo Tribal Council, *Navajo Tribal Council Resolutions 1922–1951* (Window Rock: Navajo Tribal Council, n.d.), Lease to George Cranmer, January 26, 1922, 383; Lease to Gerald Hughes, January 26, 1922, 435; Lease to A. E. Wilson, January 26, 1922, 395.

65. Hagerman, *Memoirs*: "The Navajos," January 28, 1935, HJH, Reel 2, Item 9, p. 99.

66. D. A. Lyons to Fall, October 7, 1922, Albert B. Fall Collection (ABF), Box 7, Item 6, CSWR.

67. Estep to CIA, November 19, 1922, *Survey*, 4794.

68. H. Foster Bain to Fall, October 21, 1922, ABF, Box 1, Folder 4.

69. Herbert J. Hagerman, *Letters of a Young Diplomat* (Santa Fe: Rydal Press, 1937), 187.

70. Hagerman, "Navajos," 94.

71. Kelly, *Indian Policy*, 63.

72. Hagerman to Fall, February 9, 1923, HJH, Reel 5, Item 42.

73. Department of the Interior, BIA, *Regulations Relating to the Navajo Tribe of Indians*, January 27, 1923, *Survey*, 4379.

74. Ibid., 4780.

75. "Work Seeks Place in Harding Cabinet," *Rocky Mountain News*, January 15, 1922, Hubert Work File, Western History Collection, Denver Public Library (WHA).

76. Hagerman, "Navajos," 94.

77. George F. Bruington to Holm O. Bursum, March 28, 1923, RG 75, Box 92, CCF 322–27191–23, NA.

78. Ibid.

79. Telegram, Hagerman to Work, June 29, 1923, HJH, Reel 2.

80. Hagerman to Work, May 25, 1923, Ibid.

81. Robert W. Young, interview with author, August 20, 1997, Albuquerque, New Mexico.

82. HJH, Reel 1, Item 1.

83. Hagerman, "Navajos," 99.

84. HJH, Reel 1, Item 1.

85. *Navajo Tribal Council Resolutions*, 315.

86. "Minutes of the Navajo Tribal Council," July 7, 1923, HJH, Reel 1, Item 1.

87. Hagerman to Work, December 26, 1923, HJH, Reel 2, Item 6.

88. "More Oil Land," *Dallas News*, May 1923, HJH, Reel 5, Item 34.

89. Interior, *Application*, 2.

90. H. C. Bretschneider to Fall, July 30, 1923, ABF, Box 1, Folder 5.

91. Bretschneider to Work, August 28, 1923, HJH, Reel 3, Item 13.

92. Peter Q. Nyce to Work, Ibid.

93. Hagerman to Work, September 22, 1923, HJH, Reel 2, Item 6.

94. Mark Radcliffe to Hagerman, September 9, 1923, HJH, Reel 6, Item 46.

95. Hagerman to Mark D. Radcliffe, August 14, 1923, Ibid.

96. K. B. Nowels to H. H. Hill, September 28, 1923, HJH, Reel 3, Item 16.

97. K. B. Nowels, "Report on Development Accomplished in the Hogback Field . . ." October 15, 1923, Ibid.

98. Ralph C. Ely to Hagerman, September 11, 1923; Hagerman to Ely, September 19, 1923, HJH, Reel 5, Item 26.

99. Thomas Gorman to Hagerman, September 29, 1923, Ibid.

100. Radcliffe to Hagerman, August 11, 1923, HJH, Reel 6, Item 46.

101. Nordhauser, *Quest*, 9.

102. William M. Davis to Hagerman, October 12, 1923, HJH, Reel 3, Item 13.

103. Hagerman to Work, October 15, 1923, HJH, Reel 2, Item 6.

104. Work to Hagerman, October 29, 1923, Ibid.

105. Ibid.

Chapter Three

1. Edward T. Hall, *West of the Thirties: Discoveries Among the Navajo and Hopi* (New York: Doubleday, 1994), 107–8.

2. "Two Million Barrels of Oil Estimated," *Gallup Independent*, March 7, 1924. "Fifty Years Changed Desert to Garden," *Farmington Republican*, March 1, 1927.

3. *Albuquerque Herald*, April 29, 1925, Erna Fergusson Collection (EFC), Scrapbook 12, Center for Southwest Research, Zimmerman Library, University of New Mexico (CSWR).

4. Joseph Bruchac, "Four Worlds: The Diné Story of Creation," in *Native American Stories* (Golden, Colo.: Fulcrum, 1991), 18.

5. K. B. Nowels, "Report on Extent of Oil and Gas Development," Record Group (RG) 75, Box 30, Folder 12, Central Classified Files (CCF) 150, National Archives (NA).

6. Robert Young, interview with author, August 20, 1997.

7. Randolph C. Downes and Elizabeth Clark, "Navajo Report," August 1, 1946, 65, in Robert Young Personal Collection (RYC).

8. "Five Exploration Leases to be Let on Reservation," *Aztec Independent*, July 13, 1923.

9. Chee Dodge to Charles Burke, February 14, 1928, Franciscans, Province of St. John the Baptist, Records of the St. Michaels Mission (St.M), Box 42, Folder 2, Special Collections, University of Arizona, Tucson, Arizona (UA).

10. Herbert J. Hagerman (HJH), "Record of the Meeting of the Navajo Tribal Council (Shiprock)," July 7, 1924, Reel 1, Item 1, CSWR. Also, Navajo Tribal Council, *Navajo Tribal Council Resolutions, 1922–1951* (n.d.), July 7, 1924, 387.

11. Terry P. Wilson, *The Underground Reservation* (Lincoln: University of Nebraska Press, 1985), 134–46. Also, Dennis McAuliffe, Jr., *The Deaths of Sybil Bolton: An American History* (New York: Times Books, 1994); "The Osage Murders and Oil," in *The Invasion of Indian Country in the Twentieth Century: American Capitalism and Tribal Natural Resources*, by Donald L. Fixico (Niwot: University of Colorado Press, 1998), 27–53.

12. "Roseate with Oil Gas Illuminated," *Gallup Herald*, March 1, 1924.

13. Hagerman to Mrs. Willard Straight, March 10, 1925; Will Irwin, *Saturday Evening Post*, to Hagerman, November 16, 1925, HJH, Reel 5, Item 27.

14. U.S. Senate, Subcommittee of the Committee on Indian Affairs, *Survey of Conditions of the Indians in the United States*, 71st Cong., 3rd Sess., January 30–31, and February 3–5, 1931 (Washington: GPO, 1931), 4607 (hereafter cited as *Survey*).

15. Peter MacDonald, *The Last Warrior, Peter MacDonald and the Navajo Nation* (New York: Orion, 1993), 123.

16. Donald L. Parman, "J. C. Morgan: Navajo Apostle of Assimilation," *Prologue* 12 (Summer 1972): 83.

17. E. R. Fryer, interview with Donald L. Parman, July 21, 1970 (Santa Fe), American Indian Oral History Collection (OHC), Box 15, Folder 890, CSWR.

18. Klara B. Kelley and Peter M. Whiteley, *Navajoland: Family Settlement and Land Use* (Tsaile, Navajo Nation, Ariz.: Navajo Community College, 1989), 81.

19. Hagerman, "The Navajos," *Memoirs*, manuscript, January 28, 1935, HJH, Reel 2, Item 9, p. 120.

20. Executive Order No. 1284, in *Tribal Council Resolutions*, 690; Kelly, Lawrence C., *The Navajo Indians and Federal Indian Policy, 1900–1935* (Tucson: University of Arizona Press, 1968).

21. "Minutes of the Navajo Tribal Council, 1925," HJH, Reel 1, Item 1; Hagerman to Mrs. Willard Straight, March 10, 1925, HJH, Reel 5, Item 27.

22. *Navajo Tribal Resolutions*, July 7, 1925, 217.

23. J. H. Bosscher and Reverend Floris Vander Stoep, interview with Donald L. Parman, October 29, 1971, OHC, Box 15, Folder 880.

24. Mike Kirk to Berard Haile, July 15, 1924, Berard Haile Paper Collection (BHC), Box 2, Folder 1, Special Collections, UA.

25. Bosscher and Vander Stoep, OHC, op. cit.

26. Berard Haile to Hagerman, December 1, 1924, BHC Box 2, Folder 1, UA.

27. Deshna Clahcheschillige (*sic*) to Hagerman, September 19, 1924, HJH, Reel 5, Item 26.

28. Cheschilligi to Chee Dodge, February 11, 1926, St.M, Box 42, Folder 2.

29. Lawrence C. Kelly, *The Navajo Indians and Federal Indian Policy, 1900–1935* (Tucson: University of Arizona Press, 1968), 83; Felix Cohen, *Handbook of Federal Indian Law* (Washington: GPO, 1942), 249.

30. Work to Representative Snyder, January 15, 1924, as quoted in John Collier, "Shall White Men Confiscate Indian Money to Build Bridges!," February 22, 1926, John Collier Collection (JC), Reel 3, CSWR.

31. James A. Frear to Secretary of the Interior, May 28, 1929, JC, Reel 2; "For Whose Benefit?" *The Nation* 122 (March 10, 1926): 248.

32. John Collier, "Shall White Men Confiscate Indian Money to Build Bridges!" February 22, 1926, JC, Reel 3, p. 3.

33. Ibid.

34. *Congressional Record*, 69th Cong., 2nd Sess., January 11, 1927, 68, Part 2: 1434.

35. Kenneth R. Philp, *John Collier's Crusade for Indian Reform, 1920–1954* (Tucson: University of Arizona Press, 1977), 125. Also see items in HJH, Reel 1, Item 1.

36. "Hagerman Finds Indians Are Receiving Much Attention," *Santa Fe New Mexican*, April 2, 1926, 2. Also see items located in St.M, Box 30, Folder 7, UA.

37. Report of Deschna Clah Cheschilligi," in Extracts of Proceedings of the Navajo Tribal Council, Fort Defiance, July 7, 1926, St.M, Box 30, UA.

38. "Navajos Want 'Debt' to Uncle Sam Forgiven; Reimbursable Total Now Reaches over $700,000," *Santa Fe New Mexican* (*SFNM*), February 25, 1926; "Hagerman Finds Indians Are Receiving Much Attention," *SFNM*, April 2, 1926.

39. Burke to Hagerman, February 17, 1926, HJH, Reel 3, Item 12.

40. Philp, *Crusade*, 81.

41. Chee Dodge to Charles Burke, June 22, 1926; Hagerman to Dodge, June 26, 1926, HJH, Reel 3, Item 13.

42. W. H. Fergusson to Hagerman, May 19, 1926, HJH, Reel 3, Item 12.

43. Hagerman to W. H. Fergusson, June 25, 1926, HJH, Reel 3, Item 13.

44. Burke to Hagerman, February 17, 1926, HJH, Reel 3, Item 12.

45. HJH, "Council," Reel 1, Item 1.

46. Hagerman to Burke, July 30, 1926, HJH, Reel 3, Item 13.

47. Collier to Mrs. H. A. Atwood, April 8, 1926, JC, Reel 1.

48. Burke to Hagerman, February 17, 1926, HJH, Reel 3, Item 12.

49. Lawrence C. Kelly, *Assault on Assimilation: John Collier and the Origins of Indian Policy Reform* (Albuquerque: University of New Mexico Press, 1983), 360.

50. H. J. Hagerman, "Indians and Taxes in New Mexico: Address . . . University of New Mexico," January 16, 1925, as printed in the *Santa Fe New Mexican*, January 19, 1925.

51. "Governing Indian Land Leases," *Farmington Republican*, March 22, 1927.

52. "More Indian Lands for Oil Development," *Farmington Republican*, March 8, 1927.

53. Hagerman to Work, January 5, 1927, HJH, Reel 1, Item 1.

54. Superintendent Hopi Agency to Samuel F. Stacher, January 10, 1927, Ibid.

55. "Report of the 1927 Tribal Council," in *Indian Truth*, HJH, Reel 3, Item 18, p. 2.

56. J. C. Morgan to Hagerman, January 19, 1927, HJH, Reel 5, Item 41.

57. HJH, Reel 3, Item 18.

58. Hagerman to Dodge, May 5, 1927, Ibid.

59. Hagerman to E. B. Meritt, June 10, 1927, HJH, Reel 3, Item 13.

60. Dodge to Hagerman, May 14, 1927, Ibid.

61. "Report, 1927 Tribal Council."

62. "Minutes of the Sixth Annual Session of the Navajo Tribal Council (Leupp, Ariz.)," November 12–13, 1928, HJH, Reel 6, Item 47.

63. Deshna Clahcheschillige, "Indian Council Opposes Leasing Indian Oil Lands," *Farmington Republican*, August 7, 1928.

64. Hagerman to Work, December 26, 1923; Hagerman to Work, December 19, 1924, HJH, Reel 2, Item 6.

65. Hagerman to Work, October 23, 1923, HJH, Reel 3, Item 12.

66. "Denver Men Buy Indian Oil Leases at Public Auction," *Rocky Mountain News*,

October 16, 1923, 9. Also, Hagerman to Riley Drilling Company, October 23, 1923, HJH, Reel 2, Item 6.

67. Hagerman, "A Report by Herbert J. Hagerman, Commissioner to the Navajo Tribe, July 28, 1924, RG 75, Box 30, Folder 1, CCF 150, NA. Also HJH, Reel 1, Item 1.

68. Hagerman to Burke, Washington, November 5, 1923, HJH, Reel 3, Item 12.

69. Collier saw corruption in Hagerman's award of the Rattlesnake to Muñoz for $1,000 because Muñoz eventually resold his interest for $3 million. Yet Field, a long-time friend of Hagerman's, also obtained a prime site for $1,000, and Hagerman turned the bid down.

70. Hal Nabors, interview to Diana Olsen, May 18, 1984, transcript, Farmington Museum, Farmington, New Mexico (FM).

71. Van Fortune, "Royalties and Lease Rentals to Net State Large Income," *Albuquerque Journal*, May 17, 1925, EFC, Scrapbook 12.

72. "Bring Pipe Line to Albuquerque," *Albuquerque Herald*, April 29, 1925, Ibid.

73. Harold O'Brien, "History of the Oil and Gas Developments in San Juan County," 20, FM.

74. "Retarding Oil Industry," *Albuquerque Journal*, March 15, 1926, EFC, Scrapbook 13.

75. "San Juan Refinery Supplies All Near Filling Stations," *Santa Fe New Mexican*, April 3, 1925, EFC, Scrapbook 21.

76. O'Brien, "History," 12.

77. John Collier, "Navajo Reservation: Notes," 1931, JC, Reel 3.

78. S. C. Muñoz to Hagerman, October 28, 1924, HJH, Reel 3, Item 12.

79. Hagerman to Col. E. Walters, June 9, 1926, Exhibit in U.S. Senate, Subcommittee of the Committee on Indian Affairs, *Survey of Conditions of the Indians in the United States*, 72nd Cong., 3rd Sess., January 30–31, February 3, 5, 1931 (Washington: GPO, 1931), 4843.

80. "Pipe Line Projected 700 Miles East from this County," *Aztec Independent*, December 1, 1922.

81. Hagerman to H. C. Bretschneider, March 5, 1924, RG 75, Box 91, CCF 320–18541–1924, NA.

82. "Commissioner Hagerman to Navajoes (*sic*) Explains Oil Situation on Reservation in Full," *Santa Fe New Mexican*, June 6, 1924.

83. Arthur M. Johnson, *Petroleum Pipelines and Public Policy, 1906–1959* (Cambridge: Harvard University Press, 1967), 24–6.

84. Ibid., 145.

85. Hagerman to Burke, September 13, 1926, HJH, Reel 3, Item 12.

86. K. B. Nowels, "Oil Production in the Rattlesnake Field," *Oil and Gas Journal* 27 (June 7, 1928): 107.

87. "Midwest Boom City," *Aztec Independent*, December 29, 1922.

88. Nowels, "Oil Production," 106.

89. Hagerman to S. C. Muñoz, April 10, 1925, HJH, Reel 3, Item 12.

90. Hagerman, "The Navajos," *Memoirs*, Ibid.

91. Hal Nabors interview with Olsen. "Shouting out" was a custom among Navajos. One did not knock, but stayed outside and called to residents.

92. Hal Nabors, interview with Tom Dugan, June 16, 1989, FM.

93. Ibid.

94. News brief, *Farmington Republican*, October 10, 1928.

95. Hagerman to Fergusson, May 15, 1926, HJH, Reel 3, Item 13.

96. "Navajos Tap Oil Pipe Line," *Farmington Republican*, May 8, 1928.

97. Judson King, "Scheme Before Congress to Loot Rich Indian Lands," as quoted in Philp, *Crusade*, 77.

98. "Hoover Issues Call for Oil Conference," *New York Times*, May 23, 1929, 39: 2.

99. "Oil Conservation Conference Opens Today," *Colorado Springs Gazette*, June 10, 1928.

100. Gerald D. Nash, *United States Oil Policy, 1890–1964* (Pittsburgh: University of Pittsburgh Press, 1968), 45.

Chapter Four

1. Edward T. Hall, *West of the Thirties: Discoveries Among the Navajo and Hopi* (New York: Doubleday, 1994), 112.

2. "Oil Capital Know (sic) Us," *Farmington Republican*, December 27, 1927.

3. H. A. Moore, "Six Million Dollars Expended in Preliminary Exploration of San Juan Basin Oil Fields . . . " *Farmington Republican*, January 31, 1928.

4. Arthur M. Johnson, *Petroleum Pipelines and Public Policy, 1906–1959* (Cambridge, Mass.: Harvard University Press, 1967), 142–43.

5. "Continental Oil Company Among the Pioneers of Basin Area Development," *Aztec Independent-Review* (Magazine Supplement), May 18, 1934, 3.

6. Emery C. Arnold and Thomas A. Dugan, "Aztec Oil Syndicate Drilled 1st Commercial Well in 1921," *Western Oil Reporter* 28 (August 1921): 9.

7. Herbert J. Hagerman, "Report for 1925," July 16, 1925, Herbert J. Hagerman Collection (HJH), Reel 3, Item 12, Center for Southwest Research, Zimmerman Library, University of New Mexico (CSWR).

8. Hagerman to Charles Burke, September 13, 1926, HJH, Reel 3, Item 12.

9. Burke to Hagerman, July 18, 1924; S. C. Muñoz to Hagerman, October 28, 1924, HJH, Reel 3, Item 12; Hagerman, "Oil," *New Mexico Tax Bulletin* 8 (September 1929): 122.

10. Burke to Hagerman, July 18, 1924, HJH, Reel 3, Item 12.

11. Hagerman to Hubert Work, July 1, 1924, HJH, Reel 2, Item 6.

12. Burke to Hagerman, November 4, 1924, Ibid.

13. Hagerman to Burke, March 29, 1925, HJH, Reel 3, Item 12.

14. Hagerman to H. C. Bretschneider, November 24, 1923, Ibid.

15. Hagerman to Burke, December 10, 1924, Ibid.

16. Ibid.

17. E. B. Meritt to Hagerman, April 20, 1925, Ibid.

18. S. C. Muñoz to G. F. Smith (Continental Oil), May 15, 1925, Ibid.

19. There is much correspondence regarding pricing. For example, "Report by Herbert J. Hagerman for 1925," July 16, 1925, and other items in HJH, Reel 3, Items 12–14.

20. Hagerman to J. W. Elliott, August 4, 1925; W. H. Fergusson to Hagerman, May 10, 1926, Ibid.

21. Hagerman, "Memorandum Relative to Oil and Gas," October 16, 1928, HJH, Reel 6, Item 47.

22. Hagerman to Burke, April 25, 1927, HJH, Reel 3, Item 12.

23. Hagerman to Ray Lyman Wilbur, April 24, 1929, HJH, Reel 4, Item 21.

24. "Report on Oil Prices," Dennis Chavez Papers (DCP), Box 81, Folder 7, CSWR.

25. "Oil Update," *Aztec Independent*, July 14, 1933, 3.

26. "Navajo Indian Tribal Council at Fort Wingate Puts in Busy Session," *Farmington Times Hustler*, July 10, 1931.

27. "Conditions of Indians in the U.S.," February 8, 1933, 72nd Cong., 2nd Sess., Document 214 (Washington: GPO, March 3, 1933), in HJH, "Dietrich Papers/General Indian File," Reel 8, Item 7, p. 72. There is no mention, however, of Hagerman's car, which Hubert Work purchased for the special commissioner in 1923.

28. Ibid.

29. "Minutes of the 10th Annual Session of the Navajo Tribal Council," (Fort Wingate), July 7–8, 1932, in HJH, Reel 4, Item 22.

30. Hagerman to Mark W. Radcliffe, September 18, 1923, HJH, Reel 6, Item 46.

31. Herbert J. Hagerman, "The Crownpoint Exchanges," n.d., HJH, Reel 1, Item 14.

32. A. A. Jones to Hagerman, April 20, 1923, HJH, Reel 1, Item 3.

33. "Minutes of the Advisory Council on Indian Affairs," December 12–13, 1923, 2–3, Governor Papers: James Hinkle, Correspondence: 1923–1924, Department of the Interior and Indian Affairs, New Mexico State Records and Archives, Santa Fe, New Mexico (NMSRA).

34. "Wood Growers Upheld Policy . . . Debate Navajo Extensions," *Albuquerque Herald*, February 8, 1924; Hagerman to Chee Dodge, March 26, 1924, HJH, Reel 3, Item 37.

35. Hagerman to E. B. Meritt, October 18, 1927, HJH, Reel 5, Item 39.

36. Senator Bronson Cutting to Hagerman, March 16, 1928; S. F. Stacher to CIA, April 4, 1928, HJH, Reel 5, Item 19. A copy of S.R. 3159, February 13, 1928, is also contained here.

37. Memo, "Collier-Frazier Inquisition, 1932," HJH, Reel 2, Item 10; Rupert F. Asplund to Hagerman, January 30, 1930, Ibid.

38. Hagerman to Burke, July 6, 1927, HJH, Reel 1, Item 3.

39. Stacher to General Hugh L. Scott, September 5, 1921; Cato Sells to Thomas K. Andreon, Special Agent, January 22, 1915, HJH, Reel 1: Crownpoint Exchanges.

40. Hagerman to Rhoads, June 16, 1933, HJH, Reel 4, Item 4.

41. U.S. Senate, Subcommittee of the Committee on Indian Affairs, *Survey of Conditions of the Indians in the United States*, 72st Cong., 3rd Sess., January 30–31, February 3, 5, 1931 (Washington: GPO, 1931), cover page. Hereafter cited as *Survey*.

42. Lawrence C. Kelly, "Charles James Rhoads, 1929–33," in *The Commissioners of*

Indian Affairs, 1824–1977, eds. Robert M. Kvasnicka and Herman J. Viola (Lincoln: University of Nebraska Press, 1979), 265.

43. Collier to Haven Emerson, March 10, 1931, John Collier Collection (JC), Reel 1, CSWR.

44. James A. Frear to the Senate Subcommittee, *Survey*, 4494.

45. John Collier, "The Indian Bureau's Record," *Nation* 135 (October 5, 1932): 304. James A. Frear to Lynn J. Frazier, January 29, 1931, JC, Reel 2.

46. "Herbert J. Hagerman's Record as a Whole," JC, Reel 7.

47. *Survey*, 4745.

48. Oliver La Farge, "A Gross Injustice," *New York Times*, January 28, 1931, 20. Hagerman's duties were expanded and his title changed to special commissioner to negotiate with Indians in 1929.

49. Clara True to R. H. Hanna, May 17, 1931, JC, Reel 3; Hagerman to Burke, May 2, 1926, HJH, Reel 5, Item 37.

50. *Survey*, 4527.

51. William N. Davis to Hagerman, October 12, 1923, HJH, Reel 3, Item 12.

52. "Navajo Reservation," memorandum, n.d., JC, Reel 3, p. 2.

53. K. B. Nowels to H. H. Hill, September 28, 1923, *Survey*, 4821.

54. Kenneth B. Nowels, "Report on Development Accomplished . . . ," October 13, 1923, *Survey*, 4823–28.

55. Kenneth R. Philp, *John Collier's Crusade for Indian Reform, 1920–1954* (Tucson: University of Arizona Press, 1977), 70–74; Philp, "Albert B. Fall and the Protest from the Pueblos, 1921–1923," *Arizona and the West* 12 (Autumn 1970): 237–54.

56. "Navajo Reservation," Memorandum, n.d., JC, Reel 3.

57. Clara D. True to R. H. Hanna, JC, Reel 7.

58. *Survey*, 4743.

59. Ibid., 4753.

60. "Hagerman's Record," JC, Reel 7.

61. Lawrence C. Kelly, *The Navajo Indians and Federal Indian Policy, 1900–1935* (Tucson, University of Arizona Press, 1968), 120–25.

62. "Hagerman's Record," JC, Reel 7.

63. *Survey*, 4478.

64. Ibid., 4375.

65. Ibid., 4539.

66. Herbert J. Hagerman, *Letters of a Young Diplomat* (Santa Fe: Rydal Press, 1937), 187.

67. H. B. Hening, ed., *George Curry, 1861–1947: An Autobiography* (Albuquerque: University of New Mexico Press, 1958), 193.

68. William A. Keleher, *Memoirs: 1892–1969, A New Mexico Item* (Santa Fe: Rydal Press, 1970), 261.

69. Hagerman to Roberts Walker, June 26, 1926, HJH, Reel 2, Item 7.

70. Collier to Dr. Haven Emerson, April 4, 1931, JC, Reel 1.

71. Hagerman to Robert Dietz, January 23, 1931, HJH, Reel 4, Item 25.

72. "Washington Congressional Party Meets Farmington People at Chamber of Commerce Banquet," *Farmington Times Hustler*, May 1, 1931; "United States Senate Committee Guests of Farmington Chamber of Commerce Thursday," Ibid., May 15, 1931.

73. U.S. Senate, Hearings before a subcommittee of the Committee on Indian Affairs, *Survey of Conditions of the Indians of the United States* (S. Resolution 79, 308), 71st Cong., 3rd Sess., Part 18: Arizona and New Mexico, April 27-May 20, 1931 (Washington: GPO, 1931), 9304. Hereafter cited as *Survey 2*.

74. Ibid., 9228.

75. Ibid., 8929.

76. John Collier to Howard Gans, May 20, 1931, JC, Reel 2.

77. Collier to Senator William H. King, May 26, 1932, JC, Reel 3.

78. *Congressional Record*, 72nd Cong., 1st Sess., in HJH, Reel 2, Item 10. *Survey* records contain correspondence about Hagerman's dismissal as governor. He claimed to know nothing about charges against him. Still, his dismissal came primarily through pressure from Old Guard Republicans like Fall, who targeted the young progressive. So perhaps his confusion was valid.

79. C. S. Rhoads and J. Henry Scattergood to Senate Committee on Indian Affairs, April 17, 1931, *Congressional Record*, Senate, 72nd Cong., 1st Sess., March 16, 1932, in HJH, Reel 2, Item 10, Frame 193. Two months before the investigation concluded they wrote a note rejecting future negative findings of the committee. It was approved by Wilbur.

80. Howard Gans to Collier, May 26, 1931, and Collier to Edward B. Burling, June 26, 1931, JC, Reel 2.

81. Speech by William H. King, HJH, Reel 8, Item 7.

82. "Record of Assistant Commissioner of Indian Affairs, E. B. Meritt in its Bearing on the Future," March 15, 1929, JC, Reel 7.

83. *Survey*, 4748.

84. *Survey 2*, 8929.

85. Ibid., 9787.

86. Kelly, *Indian Policy*, 193.

87. Collier to William H. Zeh, October 9, 1934, JC, Reel 18.

88. Resolution of October 31, 1933, *Resolutions*, 317. A good description of the meeting is contained in "No Action Probable on Cancellation of Navajo Oil Leases," *Aztec Independent*, November 10, 1933, 3.

89. "Stricter Rules Made on Indian Leases," *Farmington Times Hustler*, January 12, 1934, 6.

90. "Navajo Reservation Enlargement Taken Up at Aztec Meet," *Farmington Times Hustler*, November 10, 1933.

91. Elizabeth Shepley Sergeant, "Chief Dodge of the Navajos," JC, Reel 31, p. 5.

92. J. C. Morgan, "News Of Navajo Tribal Council Week at Fort Wingate," *Farmington Times Hustler*, July 21, 1933.

93. Ibid.

Chapter Five

1. Nia Francisco, "The Song of Hunger," in *Blue Horses for Navajo Women* (Greenfield Center, N.Y.: Greenfield Review, 1988), 71.

2. Gerald D. Nash, *U.S. Oil Policy, 1890–1964* (Pittsburgh: University of Pittsburgh Press, 1968), 97.

3. Report of oil royalties, Dennis Chavez Papers (DCP), Box 1, Folder 7, Center for Southwest Research, Zimmerman Library, University of New Mexico (CSWR).

4. Navajo Service, "Statement showing production of crude in barrels and royalty receipts on leases from the Rattlesnake, Table Mesa and Hogback oil lands . . . ," March 30, 1937, Record Group (RG) 75, Box 98, Central Classified Files (CCF) 322–15529–37, National Archives (NA).

5. "Herbert J. Hagerman's Record as a Whole," John Collier Collection (JC), Microfilm, Reel 7; Collier to Dr. Haven Emerson, January 16, 1932, Reel 1, CSWR.

6. Nash, *U.S. Oil Policy*, 111.

7. James T. Patterson, *America in the Twentieth Century: A History* (1976; New York: Harcourt Brace, 1994), 219.

8. Richard O'Connor, *The Oil Barons: Men of Greed and Grandeur* (Boston: Little, Brown, 1971), 311.

9. Nash, *U.S. Oil Policy*, 144–47.

10. Robert O. Anderson, *Fundamentals of the Petroleum Industry* (Norman: University of Oklahoma Press, 1984), 30.

11. Keith L. Bryant, Jr., "Oklahoma and the New Deal," in *The New Deal: The State and Local Levels*, John Braeman et al., eds. (Columbus: Ohio State University Press, 1975), 167–68.

12. Nash, *U.S. Oil Policy*, 151.

13. "Oil Pools in State Get OK," *Aztec Independent*, May 18, 1934; "Ickes Releases 194 New Pools for Development," *Aztec Independent*, "Review: Magazine Supplement," 3.

14. "Report: Oil Code," Governor Papers: Arthur Seligman, (Seligman), Folder: Washington Oil Conference, July 1933, New Mexico State Records and Archives (NM-SRA), Santa Fe, New Mexico. Also, "Ickes Releases . . . ," Ibid.

15. "Conoco Broadcast Will Help Local Tourist Business," *Farmington Times Hustler*, February 16, 1934.

16. Harold L. Ickes to Arthur Seligman, August 31, 1933, Seligman, Folder: Navajos, Proposed Extension, 1933.

17. Clarence Iden to Governor A. W. Hockenhull, November 8, 1933, Governor Papers: A. W. Hockenhull (Hockenhull), Folder: Navajos, Proposed Extension, 1933–1934, NMSRA.

18. C. L. Russell, San Juan Basin Livestock and Grazing Association, "Statement," n.d., Governor Papers: Clyde Tingley (Tingley), Folder: Navajos—Proposed Extension of Reservation, 1935–1938, NMSRA.

19. Taxpayers Association, Fruitland, New Mexico, to Tingley, April 11, 1935; Fruit-

land Trading Company to Tingley, April 3, 1935; E. H. Davis to Tingley (telegram), April 21, 1935, Ibid.

20. Owen P. White, "Low, the Poor Indian," *Colliers* (February 6, 1937): 13, in Tingley, Folder: Indian Matters, 1935–1936.

21. Donald L. Parman, *The Navajos and the New Deal* (New Haven, Conn.: Yale University Press, 1976), 138–44.

22. J. C. Morgan, "Morgan Makes Speech Against New Indian Self-Rule Measure," *Farmington Times Hustler*, April 20, 1934.

23. J. C. Morgan, "Navajos Object to Policies of John Collier," *Farmington Times Hustler*, June 21, 1935.

24. Parman, *New Deal*, 70.

25. J. C. Morgan to Dennis Chavez, April 12, 1937, DCP, Box 81, Folder 7.

26. Herbert J. Hagerman, "Memorandum for Commissioner Rhoads's Personal Use at 1932 Navajo Council Meeting," June 14, 1932, Herbert J. Hagerman Collection (HJH), Microfilm, Reel 1, Item 4, CSWR.

27. "Navajos Will Get Paiute Strip Back," *Farmington Republican*, August 3, 1932.

28. "Official Prophecies of Bloodshed Between Navajos and Whites"; "Collier Offers a New Navajo Boundary Bill," *Farmington Times Hustler*, June 5, 1936, February 5, 1937.

29. "Navajo Tribal Council Asks for Boundary Extension," *Farmington Times Hustler*, January 21, 1938.

30. Peter Iverson, *The Navajo Nation* (Westport, Conn.: Greenwood Press, 1981), 33.

31. Ibid., 63.

32. J. C. Morgan, "Wants Navajos to Pay Stock Assessment," *Farmington Republican*, June 3, 1931.

33. William Pickens, "The New Deal in New Mexico," in Braeman et al., *The New Deal*, 318.

34. "Minutes of the Tenth Annual Navajo Tribal Council (Fort Wingate)," July 7–8, 1932, HJH, Reel 4, Item 22, p. 8.

35. Francis Borgman, "Henry Chee Dodge: The Last Chief of the Navajo Indians," *New Mexico Historical Review* 23 (April 1948): 89–90; Virginia Hoffman and Broderick H. Johnson, "Henry Chee Dodge," *Navajo Biographies* (Rough Rock, Ariz.: Diné and Board of Education, Rough Rock Demonstration School, 1970), 210.

36. Edward T. Hall, *West of the Thirties: Discoveries Among the Navajo and Hopi* (New York: Doubleday, 1994), 136.

37. "Minutes," Navajo Tribal Council (Fort Defiance, Ariz.), March 12–13, 1934, Tribal Organization Records, Navajo File, RG 75, Item 150, NA. Also, Robert W. Young, "The Rise of the Navajo Tribe," in Edward H. Spicer and Raymond H. Thompson, eds., *Plural Society in the Southwest* (New York: Interbook, 1972), 196.

38. David H. Aberle, *The Peyote Religion Among the Navajos* (Chicago: AlDiné, 1966), 57.

39. Hall, *West of the Thirties*, 129–30.

40. Ibid.

41. Ruth Roessel and Broderick H. Johnson, *Navajo Livestock Reduction: A National Disgrace* (Chinle, Navajo Nation, Ariz.: Navajo Community College Press, 1974), 31.

42. E. R. Fryer to Collier, October 15, 1938, RG 75, Box 10, CCF 054–44151–1938, NA.

43. "Monk Tells of Work Among Navajos After Living 52 Years with Tribe," (1952), Berard Haile Collection (BHC), Box 1, Folder 1, Special Collections, University of Arizona (UA).

44. Interview with Howard Gorman, in Roessel and Johnson, 42.

45. Interview with Eli Gorman, Ibid., 26–27.

46. Parman, *New Deal*, 108.

47. Interview, E. R. Fryer to Donald L. Parman, July 21, 1970 (Santa Fe), American Indian Oral History Collection (OHC), Box 15, Folder 890, p. 16, CSWR.

48. Interview with Dan Yazzie, Roessel and Johnson, 91.

49. Ibid., 50.

50. "Minutes of the Special Session of the Navajo Tribal Council," March 12–13, 1934, JC, Reel 30, Item 512.

51. Collier to Thomas Dodge, February 4, 1935, JC, Ibid.

52. Robert Young, interview with author, August 20, 1997, Albuquerque; Young, *Plural Society*, 192.

53. Aubrey Willis Williams, Jr., "The Function of the Chapter House System in the Contemporary Navajo Political Structure," Ph.D. diss., University of Arizona, 1964, 119.

54. Young interview.

55. Young, *Political History*, 74.

56. Roessel and Johnson, 28.

57. Beulah Francis Wilson to Dennis Chavez, January 1937, DCP, Box 81, Folder 7.

58. Berard Haile to Collier, April 16, 1934, BHC, Box 6, Folder 7.

59. Parman, *New Deal*, 69.

60. "Navajos Reject Wheeler-Howard Reorganization Act," *Farmington Times Hustler*, June 21, 1935.

61. J. C. Morgan, "Editorial," *Farmington Times-Hustler*, June 21, 1935, 6.

62. Roger Davis to Dennis Chavez, February 6, 1937, DCP, Box 81, Folder 7.

63. The Tribal Council was formally dissolved November 7, 1938, by resolution; *Navajo Tribal Resolutions*, 583.

64. "With the Reorganization Committee of the Navajo Tribal Council, 1936–1937," April 9, 1937, Franciscans, Province of St. John the Baptist of the St. Michaels Mission, Arizona, 1868–1978 (St.M), Box 44, Folder 2, UA.

65. Jake Morgan to Dennis Chavez, April 19, 1936, DCP, Box 81, Folder 7.

66. Young interview.

67. "Taliman Denounces Morgan Activities," *Gallup Independent*, May 14, 1937, clipping, DCP, Box 81, Folder 7.

68. Wayne Holm (Navajo National Literacy Project), interview with author, May 22, 1995, Albuquerque, New Mexico.

69. Young, *Political History*, 106.

70. "Morgan Says John Collier Wants 19 Navajo 'States'," *Farmington Times Hustler*, July 3, 1936.

71. "Navajos Oppose Collier's Plan to Create 19 Districts," *Farmington Times-Hustler*, July 24, 1936, 6.

72. Charles H. Kern to Clyde Tingley, August 23, 1935, Tingley, Folder: Proposed Extension of Reservation, 1935–1938.

73. J. C. Morgan, "Morgan Says Chaves Is Friend of Navajos," *Farmington Times-Hustler*, July 23, 1937.

74. Orval Ricketts, "Says Navajos Want Voice in All Tribal Affairs," *Farmington Times-Hustler*, July 30, 1937.

75. Chee Dodge to Carl Hayden, June 1, 1937; John Collier to Carl Hayden, June 4, 1937, RG 75, Box 34, CCF 155–34609–37, NA.

76. Interview, J. H. Boscher and Reverend Floris Vander Stoep, to Donald Parman, October 29, 1971, Box 15, Folder 880, OHC.

77. George B. Bowra, "Advises Immediate Federal Probe of Navajo Controversy," *Farmington Times Hustler*, August 13, 1937.

78. "Navajo Indian Delegation," *Farmington Times Hustler*, June 4, 1937.

79. Fryer to Parman, OHC, 10.

80. "The Navajos and the Land: The Government, the Tribe, and the Future," Bulletin 26, February 1937 (New York: National Association on Indian Affairs and American Indian Defense Association [AIDA]) 13, HJH, Reel 4, Item 82.

81. Young, "Navajo Tribe," 205.

82. E. R. Fryer to John Collier, September 7, 1938, RG 75, Box 10, CCF 054–33133–1935, NA.

83. Ibid.

84. E. R. Fryer to Collier, October 5, 1938; E. R. Fryer to Collier, November 15, 1938, RG 75, Box 10, CCF 054–44151–38, NA.

85. Ibid.

86. Ibid.

87. Editorial, *Farmington Times Hustler*, April 26, 1940.

88. Editorial, *Aztec Independent*, July 26, 1940.

89. "Navajo Indians Organize Ass'n," *Aztec Independent*, November 22, 1940; Kenneth R. Philp, *John Collier's Crusade for Indian Reform, 1920–1954* (Tucson: University of Arizona Press, 1977), 193, says NRA claimed more than six thousand members.

90. Deschna C. Cheschilligi to Dennis Chavez, March 10, 1941, DCP, Box 82, Folder 11; Philp, 194, claims Cheschilligi wrote to Eleanor Roosevelt giving Navajo Rights Association (NRA) views.

91. "Navajo Rights Ass'n members Will Study New Stock Program . . . " *Aztec Independent*, March 21, 1941.

92. George B. Bowra, "Rips and Tears," *Aztec Independent*, January 19, 1945.

93. Fryer to Parman, July 21, 1970, OHC, Box 15, Folder 890.

94. "Navajo Leader is Dead," *Aztec Independent Review*, September 21, 1945.

95. "Navajo Tribal Council Asks for Boundary Extension," *Farmington Times Hustler*, January 21, 1938.

96. Navajo Tribal Council, *Navajo Tribal Council Resolutions 1922–1951* (Window Rock, Ariz.: Navajo Nation, n.d.), 322.

97. Governor Papers: John Miles (Miles), Folder: Reports, Oil Conservation Commission, 1939–1942, NMRSA.

98. "Chairman Morgan Finds That New Tribal Enterprises Secured Will Be Great Help to Navajos," *Farmington Times Hustler*, January 12, 1940.

99. C. E. Dobbin, Senior Geologist, to John D. Northrop, U.S. Geological Survey, March 2, 1932, and accompanying report, received from Carl Yost, Bureau of Land Management, Farmington, New Mexico.

100. American Petroleum Institute, "Facts About Oil," New York: API, March 1969, in "Oil History File," Aztec, New Mexico, Museum.

101. Joseph A. Kornfeld, "A Half Century of Exploration in the Southwest," *Oil and Gas Journal* 50 (May 31, 1951): 209.

102. "San Juan Oil Development Program Hotter'n a Firecracker this Spring," *Farmington Times Hustler*, February 21, 1947.

103. Kornfeld, 213.

104. "Gas Strike May Mean War Industry Here," *Farmington Times Hustler*, July 24, 1942.

105. Secretary of the Interior to Jonathan M. Steere (President, Indian Rights Association), March 19, 1944, RG 75, Box 467, CCF 322–5816–44, NA.

106. "Government Lets Contract for Helium Plant . . . ," *Farmington Times Hustler*, March 19, 1943; "Secretary Ickes Names New Gas Project at Shiprock 'Navajo Helium Plant'," *Farmington Times Hustler*, September 3, 1943.

107. Harold Ickes to Jonathan M. Steere, March 18, 1944, RG 75, Box 467, CCF 322–5816–44, NA.

108. News article, *Aztec Independent*, June 20, 1947.

109. "Oil News," *Aztec Independent*, June 20, 1947; "Bureau of Mines Reactivates Helium Plant," *Aztec Independent*, August 22, 1952.

110. "Secretary Ickes Names New Gas Project at Shiprock Navajo Helium Plant," *Farmington Times Hustler*, September 3, 1943.

111. Marion Clawson (Director, Bureau of Land Management) to Commissioner of Indian Affairs (CIA), February 15, 1949, RG 75, Box 470, CCF 322–31555–47, NA.

112. Director of the U.S. Geological Survey to William Zimmerman, RG 75, Box 471, CCF 322.1–10671–47, NA.

113. See Richard White, *The Roots of Dependency: Subsistence, Environment, and Social Change Among the Choctaws, Pawnees and Navajos* (Lincoln: University of Nebraska Press, 1983).

114. Roessel, *Stock Reduction*, 70.

115. "J. C.," interview with author, November 2, 1997, Albuquerque, New Mexico.

116. Ruth Roessel, *Women in Navajo Society* (Rough Rock, Navajo Nation, Ariz.: Navajo Resource Center, Rough Rock Demonstration School, 1981), 106–107, 173.

117. Brian W. Dippie, *The Vanishing American: White Attitudes and U.S. Indian Policy* (Lawrence: University Press of Kansas, 1982), 321.

Chapter Six

1. Monroe E. Price, *Law and the American Indian: Readings, Notes and Cases* (Indianapolis: Bobbs-Merrill, 1973), 671.

2. Laura Thompson, *Personality and Government: Findings and Recommendations of the Indian Administration for Research*, forward by John Collier, Mexico, D.F.: Grafica Panamericana, 1951, John Collier Collection (JC), Microfilm, Reel 54, Center for Southwest Research, University of New Mexico (CSWR).

3. George Bowra, "Rips and Tears," *Aztec Independent*, June 4, 1948.

4. Max Drefkoff, "An Industrial Program for the Navajo Indian Reservation, 1948," Robert Young Personal Collection (RYC).

5. Randolph Downes and Elizabeth Clark, "Navajo Report," August 1, 1946, RYC, 46.

6. Angie Debo, *A History of the Indians of the United States* (Norman: University of Oklahoma Press, 1970), 350.

7. William Zimmerman, Jr., "The Role of the Bureau of Indian Affairs Since 1933," *Annals of the American Academy of Political and Social Science* 311 (May 1957): 35.

8. "Annual Report of the Commissioner of Indian Affairs," *Annual Report of the Secretary of the Interior* (Washington: GPO, 1952), 391.

9. Virginia Hoffman and Broderick H. Johnson, *Navajo Biographies* (Rough Rock, Ariz.: Diné and Board of Education, Rough Rock Demonstration School, 1970), 223.

10. Robert W. Young, *A Political History of the Navajo Nation*, (Tsaile, Ariz.: Navajo Community College Press, 1978), 122.

11. Alice B. Kehoe, *North American Indians: A Comprehensive Account*, 2d ed. (Upper Saddle River, N.J.: Prentice Hall, 1992), 420.

12. "Minutes of the Navajo Tribal Council," December 18–20, 1945, Resolution 1, JC, Reel 54; *Aztec Independent*, January 2, 1948.

13. Resolution of October 14, 1949, Navajo Tribal Council, *Navajo Tribal Council Resolutions, 1922–1951* (Window Rock, Ariz.: Navajo Nation, n.d.), 372.

14. Sam Ahkeah and Zhealy Tso, "The Navajos' Problem . . . As They See It," *Farmington Times Hustler*, March 4, 1949.

15. "Resolution of July 9, 1947," Navajo Tribal Council, *Navajo Tribal Council Resolutions 1922–1951* (Window Rock: Navajo Tribal Council, n.d.), 249.

16. Peter Iverson, "Legal Counsel and the Navajo Nation Since 1945," *American Indian Quarterly* 3 (Spring 1997): 2.

17. Ibid., 4; Robert Young interview with author, August 20, 1997, Albuquerque, New Mexico.

18. William Zimmerman to Sam Ahkeah, April 29, 1952, William Zimmerman Papers (WZ), Box 1, Folder 8, CSWR.

19. "Abridged Transcript of Proceedings, Hearings, before the Secretary of the Inte-

rior on Proposed Regulations to Govern Indian Tribal Attorney Contracts," January 3–4, 1952, Washington, D.C., JC, Reel 43.

20. "Facts About Oil," New York: American Petroleum Institute, March 1969, 5, Aztec Museum, Oil Display and Oil History File, Aztec, New Mexico (AM).

21. "San Juan Basin and Southwest to Experience Big Oil Exploration Program," *Aztec Independent*, February 6, 1948.

22. Robert W. Young, comp., *The Navajo Yearbook of Planning in Action for 1961* (Window Rock, Ariz.: Navajo Agency, 1961), 265.

23. George B. Bowra, "Farmington Changes from Quiet Cow Town to Oil Metropolis After Post-War Boom"; "Boyhood Dream a Reality for Tom Dugan as He Helps Stage Big Oil Celebration," *Western Oil Reporter* 28 (August 1971): 53, 19.

24. H. W. Dixon, "Navajo Resource Oil Prospecting Is Unabated," Vertical Files: Indians of North America, Navajos, Mineral Resources, Oil, Arizona Historical Society, Tucson, Arizona (AHS).

25. Emery C. Arnold, interview with author, August 20, 1996; "Resume of Oil and Gas Development, 1950–1962," from Arnold's personal collection.

26. Memorandum for Commissioner of Indian Affairs and "Summary of Royalty Prices for Calendar Years 1945 & 1946," Record Group (RG) 75, Box 471, Central Classified Files (CCF) 332-1–10671–47, National Archives (NA).

27. "Oil and Gas Lease Sale: Advertisement No. 33," August 30, 1951, RG 75, Box 468, CCF 322–5015–46, NA.

28. John A. Anderson (Roswell) to Area Director, BIA, September 22, 1952, Ibid.

29. Young, *Yearbook* (1961), 265.

30. Carl Yost, interview with author, Farmington, New Mexico, August 22, 1996.

31. Bill Richardson, interview with the author, Gallup, New Mexico, February 8, 1997.

32. Young interview.

33. Frank Toledo to Ray Yazzie, December 12, 1969, American Indian Oral History Collection (OHC), Box 11, Folder 275, CSWR.

34. "History of Basin Oil-Gas Development in 3 Parts; El Paso Hogs Post-1950 Era," *Western Oil Reporter* 28 (August 1971): 36.

35. Arnold, "Resume"; Arnold, second interview with author, August 21, 1996.

36. Regional Oil and Gas Supervisor to Area Director, BIA, May 28, 1953, RG 75, Box 468, CCF 322–5015–46, NA.

37. New Mexico School of Mines Bulletin 36, Sallie Wagner Collection, Navajo Files, New Mexico State Records and Archives, Santa Fe, New Mexico (NMSRA).

38. Donald L. Baars, *Navajo Country: A Geology and Natural History of the Four Corners Region* (Albuquerque: University of New Mexico Press, 1995), 152.

39. "Paradox Hits Twice," *Oil and Gas Journal* 54 (May 7, 1956): 99.

40. John Riddick, "$8 Million Bid for 4 Sections," (n.p.), May 29, 1957, Vertical File, AHS.

41. James R. Quinn, "Carter Wildcat Hits on Navajo Tract," *Denver Post*, November 7, 1956.

42. "Report of Commissioner, 1958," 225.

43. Ed McGhee, "Are You Planning to Drill In the Aneth Area?" *Oil and Gas Journal* 55 (June 24, 1957): 152.

44. W. W. Mize, "Drilling Problems Are Rugged in the San Juan Basin," *Oil and Gas Journal* 54 (May 16, 1955): 176.

45. Zimmerman, "The Role," 36.

46. Debo, 353.

47. Young, *Yearbook* (1958), 86.

48. "Glenn Emmons Has Definite Views on How to Solve Indian 'Problem,'" *Albuquerque Tribune* (n.d.), Gallup Public Library Files (GPL), Folder: Glenn Emmons, Gallup, New Mexico.

49. Glenn Emmons to Clair E. Gurley, April 7, 1954, Glenn Emmons Collection (GE), Box 4, Folder 3, CSWR.

50. "An Outline of a Proposal to Organize," (n.d.), GE, Box 5, Folder 1.

51. "Report of the American Indian Research Fund," December 7, 1955, Ibid.

52. *Albuquerque Tribune*, August 3, 1954, GE, Box 5, Folder 18.

53. "Navajo Council Gives Emmons Fresh Support," clipping, GE, Box 5, Folder 21; Young, *Yearbook*, 1958, 84.

54. "New Warehouse for Baby-Line Furniture," *Navajo Times*, June 7, 1961, 7; "Report of Commissioner, 1956," 209.

55. Howard Gorman, "Resources Development," paper from New Mexico Conference on Social Welfare, University of New Mexico, 10 June 1954, Herbert J. Hagerman Collection (HJH), Reel 8, Item 3, CSWR.

56. Hoffman and Johnson, 270.

57. Resolution of the Navajo Tribal Council, "United States Scholarship for Indian Students," April 7, 1955, HJH, Reel 8, Item 3.

58. Ibid.

59. Hoffman & Johnson, 200.

60. Clair E. Gurley to Emmons, February 24, 1954, GE, Box 4, Folder 3.

61. Emmons to General Superintendent, Navajo Agency, August 8, 1958, GE, Box 3, Folder 19.

62. "Resolutions of the Navajo Tribal Council," October 5, 1955, and October 16, 1955, RG 75, Box 468, CCF 322–5015–46, NA.

63. Harold F. Larkin, "General Memorandum," January 30, 1957, RG 75, Box 39, CCF 322 no number, NA.

64. "Navajos Seek to Gamble on Income from Oil," *Rocky Mountain News*, December 20, 1956, Western History Collection Clipping File, Denver Public Library (WHC), Folder: Navajo Petroleum.

65. "Tribe Pushes Deal," *Oil and Gas Journal* 54 (August 20, 1956): 106.

66. G. Warren Spaulding to Emmons, March 8, 1956; "Resolution of the Navajo Tribal Council," March 19, 1956, RG 75, Box 47, CCF 320–3669–56, NA.

67. National Congress of American Indians, Legislative Report Number 13, 85th Cong., 1st Sess., August 6, 1957, HJH, Reel 8, Item 6.

68. "Tribe Wants More," *Oil and Gas Journal* 56 (March 10, 1958): 96.

69. NCAI, "Resolutions," 16th Annual Convention, December 7–11, 1959, HJH, Reel 8, Item 6.

70. Press release, Bureau of Indian Affairs, April 5, 1957, RG 75, Box 39, CCF 322–3385–56, NA.

71. *Dallas Times-Herald*, July 30, 1958, GE, Box 5, Folder 20.

72. "Tribal Council," February 13, 1958, HJH, Reel 8, Item 3, 14.

73. Ibid., 16.

74. Robert W. Young, "The Rise of the Navajo Tribe," in *Plural Society in the Southwest*, Edward H. Spicer and Raymond H. Thompson, eds. (New York: Interbook, 1972), 224.

75. "Slow Market Conditions May Delay Leasing of Navajo Tribe Oil Lands," December 10, 1959, AHS; Sally Noe, interview with author, February 8, 1997, Gallup, New Mexico.

76. Arthur R. Gomez, *Quest for the Golden Circle: The Four Corners and the Metropolitan West, 1945–1970* (Albuquerque: University of New Mexico Press, 1994), 113.

77. Peter Iverson, *The Navajo Nation* (Westport, Conn.: Greenwood Press, 1981), 57.

78. Navajo Tribal Council Minutes, 1957, RG 75, Box 196, CCF 054–00–1957, p. 445, NA.

79. Bill Brenneman, "Navajos Spend Oil Royalties Prudently," *Rocky Mountain News*, November 10, 1956, WHC.

80. Journal of the Navajo Tribal Council, October 9, 1958, and August 6, 1959, HJH, Reel 8, Item 3.

81. Hoffman and Johnson, 260.

82. Iverson, "Legal Counsel," 5.

83. Ibid., 6.

84. Iverson, *Navajo Nation*, 86.

85. Gil Hinshaw, "Nakai Backers Protest Charges of Opponents," *Albuquerque Journal*, April 25, 1963, Province of St. John the Baptist, Records of the St. Michaels Mission, Arizona (St.M), Box 44, Folder 12, UA.

86. Paul R. Wieck, "Littell Files Court Action Against Udall in Contract Dispute," *Albuquerque Journal*, November 16, 1963, St.M, Ibid.

87. "Judge Signs Order Reinstating Littell," *Arizona Republic*, November 30, 1963.

88. Press release, February 4, 1967, St.M., Box 44, Folder 12; "Navajo Public Relations Office Claims Council Is Getting Tired of Littell," *Gallup Independent*, February 4, 1967.

89. St.M., Box 44, Folder 12.

90. "Navajo Vets Protest Inquiry," *Aztec Independent*, January 16, 1953.

91. L. M., interview with author, December 30, 1996, Albuquerque, New Mexico.

92. Young interview.

93. Joe T. Dickerson, Address at the 4th Conference on Industrial Development, University of Arizona, March 7, 1958, RG 75, Box 39, CCF 322–3385–56, NA.

94. "Reservation 'Mess' Blasted by Ahkeah," November 3, 1953, GE, Box 5, Folder 17.

95. "Statement of Paul Jones," April 21, 1959, Ibid.

96. H. C. Holdridge to Fred A. Seaton, November 16, 1959, GE, Box 5, Folder 10.

97. H. C. Holdridge to Christian Herter, May 11, 1959; Holdridge to President of the Gallup Chamber of Commerce, n.d., GE, Box 5, Folder 8.

98. Peter H. Eichstaedt, *If You Poison Us: Uranium and Native Americans* (Santa Fe: Red Crane, 1994), 11.

99. Ibid., 33.

100. Ibid., 42–43.

101. Philip Reno, *Navajo Resources and Economic Development* (Albuquerque: University of New Mexico Press, 1981), 134.

102. Young, *Yearbook* (1961), 268–69.

103. Ibid., 228–29.

104. Reno, *Navajo Resources*, 142.

105. Ibid., 116.

106. See Brian Jackson Morton, "Coal Leasing in the Fourth World: Hopi and Navajo Coal Leasing, 1954–1977," Ph.D. diss., University of California at Berkeley, 1985, for a full discussion of this topic. For a detailed account of John S. Boyden and his firm as well as Peabody Coal, see Charles Wilkinson, *Fire on the Plateau: Conflict and Endurance in the American Southwest* (Washington: Island Press, 1999), 169–171.

107. "Report of Commissioner, 1959," 255.

108. Robert O. Anderson, *Fundamentals of the Petroleum Industry* (Norman: University of Oklahoma Press, 1984), 132.

109. "Tribal Council," August 3, 1959, HJH, Reel 8, Item 3.

Chapter Seven

1. Al Henderson, "The Aneth Community: Oil Crisis in Navajoland," *The Indian Historian* 12 (Winter 1979): 33–34.

2. David A. Shaller, *Policy Studies Journal* (1978), in New Mexico Committee to the United States Commission on Civil Rights, *Energy Development in Northwestern New Mexico: A Civil Rights Perspective* (Washington: GPO, 1982), 47.

3. *Tucson Daily Citizen*, May 30, 1957, Vertical Files (VF), Arizona Historical Society, Tucson, Arizona (AH).

4. U.S. House of Representatives, "Inaugural Address of Raymond Nakai, April 13, 1963," *Congressional Record*, May 1, 1963, in Franciscans, Province of St. John the Baptist, Records of the St. Michaels Mission (St.M.), Arizona, Box 44, Folder 11, University of Arizona Special Collections (UA).

5. Clyde Benally, et al., *Dinéjí Nakee' Naahane': A Utah Navajo History* (Monticello, Utah: San Juan School District, n.d.), 98.

6. Garrick Bailey and Roberta Glenn Bailey, *A History of the Navajos: The Reservation Years* (Santa Fe: School of American Research Press, 1986), 204.

7. "Aneth Group Protests Use of Oil Money," *Navajo Times*, September 19, 1963.

8. Herbert J. Hagerman, "Report of H. J. Hagerman: Navajo Indian Reservation," Senate Document No. 64, 72d Cong., 1st Sess., Feb. 24, 1932.

9. U.S. Congress, Senate, Subcommittee on Indian Affairs of the Committee on In-

terior and Insular Affairs, "To Amend the Act of March 1, 1933," Unpublished Hearings, August 11, 1966 (hereafter cited as "Unpublished Hearings.")

10. Harry Anderson to Senator Jackson, "Unpublished Hearings."

11. U.S. Congress, Senate, Senate Bill 391, "To Amend 47 Stat. 1418," 90th Cong., 1st Sess., January 17, 1967.

12. "Aneth Group Protests," *Navajo Times*, op. cit.

13. Assistant Secretary of the Interior to Senator Jackson, March 22, 1967, exhibit, in "Unpublished Hearings."

14. Testimony of Harold Drake, Curley John, and Evans Holly, in "Unpublished Hearings."

15. Testimony of Milton A. Oman, Ibid.

16. Statements of Harry C. Rogers and Thomas Billie, Ibid.

17. Thomas Billie and Herbert Clay, "Letter to the Editor," *Navajo Times*, January 30, 1964.

18. "Unpublished Hearings."

19. Joe R. Nevarez, "Superior Oil Drilling Crew Runs Into Hopi Roadblock in Arizona," and Claiborne Nockolus, "U.S. Court Authorizes Road-Barring," *Navajo Times*, June 25, 1964.

20. Robert W. Young, *A Political History of the Navajo Tribe* (Tsaile, Ariz.: Navajo Community College Press, 1978), 126.

21. John Aloysius Farrell, "U.S. Fails to Stop Exploitation of Indians by Big Energy Firms," *Denver Post*, November 22, 1983, 9A.

22. New Mexico Committee, *Energy Development*, 91. The Office of Surface Mining (OSM) monitored coal production.

23. Marjane Ambler, *Breaking the Iron Bonds: Indian Control of Energy Development* (Lawrence: University Press of Kansas, 1990), 122–24.

24. Ibid., 139.

25. Robert W. Young, interview with author, August 20, 1997.

26. Richard Nafziger, "Transnational Energy Corporations and American Indian Development," in *American Indian Energy Resources and Development*, Roxanne Dunbar Ortiz, ed., no. 2 (Albuquerque: Institute for Native American Development, Native American Studies, University of New Mexico, 1980), 23.

27. Ambler, *Iron Bonds*, 79.

28. Donald L. Fixico, *The Invasion of Indian Country in the Twentieth Century: American Capitalism and Tribal Natural Resources* (Niwot: University Press of Colorado, 1998), 161.

29. Jeff Gillenkirk and Mark Dowie, "The Great Indian Power Grab," *Mother Jones*, Vertical File: Peter MacDonald 2, Gallup Public Library, Gallup, New Mexico (GPL), 24.

30. Joseph G. Jorgensen, "The Political Economy of the Native American Energy Business," in *Native Americans and Energy Development II*, Joseph G. Jorgensen and Sally Swenson, eds. (Boston: Anthropology Resource Center and Seventh Generation Fund, 1984), 13–15.

31. Daniel Peaches, "MacDonald Deserves Respect," *Gallup Independent*, February 16, 1989, GPL.

32. Peter MacDonald, *The Last Warrior, Peter MacDonald and the Navajo Nation*, Herman J. Viola, ed. (New York: Orion Books, 1993), 136.

33. Tacheeni Scott et al., "MacDonald, Himself, Brought in Feds," MacDonald 1, GPL.

34. Fixico, 160–62.

35. Peter Wiley and Robert Gottlieb, *Empires in the Sun: The Rise of the New American West* (Tucson: University of Arizona Press, 1982), 242.

36. Marjane Ambler, "Uncertainty in CERT," in *Native Americans and Energy Development II*, op. cit., 77.

37. Ambler, *Iron Bonds*, 101.

38. Fixico, 165.

39. Ambler, "Uncertainty," 71–72.

40. Gillenkirk and Dowie, 47–48.

41. Nafziger, 32.

42. Ambler, *Iron Bonds*, 155.

43. Ibid., 170.

44. C. Matthew Snipp, ed., *Public Policy Impacts on American Indian Development*, no. 4 (Albuquerque: Native American Studies, Institute for Native American Development, 1988), 16.

45. Lynn A. Robbins, "Energy Developments and the Navajo Nation: An Update," in *Native Americans and Energy Development II*, op. cit., 137.

46. Farrell, "U.S. Fails," 10A.

47. Lorraine Turner Ruffing, "Navajo Mineral Development," *American Indian Journal* 4 (September 1978): 8.

48. "Indians Criticize Carter Energy Moves," *Navajo Times*, August 2, 1979.

49. William R. Ritz, "Indians: We'll Help on Energy," *Navajo Times*, August 12, 1979.

50. Ambler, *Iron Bonds*, 77.

51. "Chapters May Control Their Own Destiny, Says Chairman," *Navajo Times*, November 29, 1979; Robbins, "Energy," 127–28.

52. Young interview.

53. Bailey and Bailey, 244.

54. Division of Economic Development, "The Navajo Nation Overall Economic Development Program: 1980, Annual Progress Report" (Window Rock, Ariz.: Navajo Tribe, October 1980), 37.

55. U.S. Congress, Senate, *Congressional Record* (S.R. 1894), 97th Congress, 2d Sess., August 17, 1982, vol. 128, Pt. 16, 21332.

56. Ibid., 21333.

57. U.S. Congress, Senate, "Hearings Before the Select Committee on Indian Affairs (on S.R. 1894)," 97th Cong., 2d Sess, February 12, 1982 (Washington: GPO, 1982), 142–43.

58. DNA (People's Legal Services, Inc.), *The Navajo Nation and Taxation* (Window Rock, Ariz.: Navajo Nation, 1976), 9.

59. Ambler, *Iron Bonds*, 89.

60. Ibid., 24.

61. John Riddick, "Oil Money Poses Problem for Navajo Council," *Tucson Daily Citizen*, May 30, 1957, Vertical File: Navajo Oil, Arizona Historical Society, Tucson, Arizona (AHS).

62. Ruffing, 8.

63. DNA, *Taxation*, 4.

64. Ambler, *Iron Bonds*, 197.

65. *Merrion v. Jicarilla Apache Tribe*, 455 U.S. 130 (1982), in *Indian Country Environmental Law: Cases and Materials* (South Royalton, Vt. and Grand Forks, N. Dak.: Vermont Law School and University of North Dakota School of Law, May 1999), 122; *Cotton Petroleum Corp. v. New Mexico*, 490 U.S. 163 (1989) dealt with New Mexico's ability to impose severance taxes on some production, Ibid., 122–27.

66. *Navajo Times*, October 5, 1978.

67. Ibid.

68. Scott et al., "MacDonald, Himself," GPL.

69. Peaches, "MacDonald," GPL.

70. Scott et al., "MacDonald, Himself," GPL.

71. U.S. Commission on Civil Rights, *The Navajo Nation, An American Colony* (Washington, D.C.: GPO, 1975), 21.

72. New Mexico Committee, *Energy Development*, 135.

73. "Oil Means a Job to Him," n.d., Vertical File: Indians of North America, Navajos, Mineral Resources, AHS.

74. Peter H. Eichstaedt, *If You Poison Us: Uranium and Native Americans*, (Santa Fe: Red Crane Books, 1994), 37.

75. Farrell, "U.S. Fails," A1.

76. Ibid., A8.

77. L. M., interview with author, December 30, 1996; Young interview.

78. New Mexico Committee, *Energy Development*, 51.

79. Ibid., 47.

80. Klara Bonsack Kelley and Harris Francis, *Navajo Sacred Places* (Bloomington: Indiana University Press, 1994), 163.

81. Ibid., 168.

82. Gillenkirk and Dowie, 52.

83. New Mexico Committee, *Energy Development*, 51.

84. David Rich Lewis, "Native Americans and the Environment: A Survey of Twentieth-Century Issues," *American Indian Quarterly* 19 (Summer 1995): 431.

85. Ambler, *Iron Bonds*, 77.

86. "UNDC Audit Is Positive, Officials Say," *Navajo Times*, January 26, 1978. According to the *Times*, UNDC was previously the San Juan Resource Development Council, in existence by 1966.

87. "Utah Agencies Under Fire," *Navajo Times*, January 12, 1978.

88. Ibid.

89. Ibid.

90. "Tribal officials Accepted Gratuities, Claims Report," *Navajo Times*, January 12, 1978.

91. A Concerned Diné, "Why Not Tell the Truth About UNDC" (Letter to the Editor), *Navajo Times*, February 16, 1978.

92. "Senator Hears Views on Energy," *Navajo Times*, January 12, 1978, 8.

93. "Texaco Agrees to Examine Complaints," *Navajo Times*, April 6, 1978, 10.

94. "Navajos Protest Pollution," *Santa Fe New Mexican*, April 4, 1978, A3; "Texaco Agrees . . . " *Navajo Times*, April 6, 1978.

95. "Indians, Oilmen Resume Talks," *Santa Fe New Mexican*, April 6, 1978, A4.

96. Tom Barry, "Aneth People Tired of Exploitation," *Navajo Times*, April 13, 1978, 2.

97. Ibid.

98. *Navajo Times*, nearly all issues in April 1978, but especially Tom Barry, "Aneth People Tired of Exploitation," April 13, 1978; "Situation in Aneth Is Worsening," August 10, 1978.

99. Barry, "Aneth People."

100. "MacDonald Closes Utah Reservation Area," *Navajo Times*, April 13, 1978, 4.

101. Ibid.

102. "Texaco Corporation Ends; Agreements Reached," *Navajo Times*, April 20, 1978, 6.

103. "Situation in Aneth Is Worsening; tribal officials afraid to visit," *Navajo Times*, August 10, 1978, 10.

104. Ibid.; also see Iverson, *Navajo Nation*, 187–88, for an overview.

105. "Reasons for the Montezuma Creek Walk," *Navajo Times*, November 30, 1978, A18.

106. Ibid.

107. Carol Sisco, "Navajos Go Thirsty for Spoils of Oil," *Salt Lake Tribune*, June 23, 1991.

108. Jerry Spangler, "Navajos Have Reservations About Oil Revenues," *Deseret News*, January 14, 1990.

109. "Trust Fund Belonging to Navajos Has Been Bled Dry," *High Country News*, December 16, 1991, 4.

110. Richard White, *The Roots of Dependency: Subsistence, Environment, and Social Change Among the Choctaws, Pawnees, and Navajos* (Lincoln: University of Nebraska Press, 1983), 222.

111. Russel Lawrence Barsh, "Indian Resources and the National Economy: Business Cycles," *Native Americans and Public Policy*, eds. Fremont J. Lyden and Lyman H. Letgers (Pittsburgh: University of Pittsburgh Press, 1992), 211; Barsh, "Progressive-Era Bureaucrats and the Unity of Twentieth-Century Indian Policy," *American Indian Quarterly* 15 (Winter 1991): 1–17.

112. Ruffing, "Mineral Development," 5.

113. U.S. Commission on Civil Rights, *Navajo Nation*, 11.

114. Duane Champagne, "Organizational Change and Conflict: A Case Study of the Bureau of Indian Affairs," *Native Americans and Public Policy*, op. cit., 40.

115. Peter MacDonald, "Navajo Nation Must Plan for the Future," *Navajo Times*, April 28, 1977, 14.

116. Nafziger, 16, 32.

117. Emery Arnold, "Review of the Early History of Oil and Gas Exploration, Drilling and Production in the San Juan Basin," *San Juan County Historical Society Newsletter* 7 (July 1996); also Emery Arnold, interview with author, August 21, 1996, in Aztec, New Mexico. In most instances, it seems that small, independent companies were not the ones who profited most in the development of oil on Navajo land.

118. White, 321.

119. "Oil Money Poses Problem for Navajo Council," *Tucson Daily Citizen*, May 30, 1957, Vertical File: Indians of North America, Navajos, Mineral Resources, AHS.

120. Ruth Roessel, *Women in Navajo Society* (Rough Rock, Navajo Nation: Navajo Resource Center, Rough Rock Demonstration School, 1981), 174.

121. Luci Tapahonso, "It Has Always Been This Way," *Saanii Dahataal: The Women Are Singing* (Tucson: University of Arizona Press, 1993), 17–18.

BIBLIOGRAPHY

PRIMARY SOURCES

COLLECTIONS

American Indian Oral History Collection. Center for Southwest Research. University of New Mexico. Albuquerque, New Mexico.

Arizona State Historical Society Library. Vertical Files: Indians of North America, Navajo, Mineral Resources. Tucson, Arizona.

Arizona, University of. Vertical Files: Navajo-Hopi Land Tenure, File 1. Library. Special Collections. Tucson, Arizona.

Chavez, Dennis. Center for Southwest Research. University of New Mexico.

Collier, John. Microfilm. Center for Southwest Research. University of New Mexico.

Emmons, Glenn L. Center for Southwest Research. University of New Mexico.

Fall, Albert B. Center for Southwest Research. University of New Mexico.

Fergusson, Erna. Scrapbooks. Center for Southwest Research. University of New Mexico.

Franciscans. Province of St. John the Baptist. Records of the St. Michaels Mission, Arizona, 1868–1978. Special Collections. University of Arizona Library.

Greenway, Isabella Collection. Arizona State Historical Society Library.

Hagerman, Herbert J. Microfilm. Center for Southwest Research. University of New Mexico.

Haile, Berard. Special Collections. University of Arizona Library.

Hannett, Arthur T. Correspondence Files. Mineral Leasing on Indian Lands, 1925–1926. Governor Papers. New Mexico State Records and Archives. Santa Fe, New Mexico.

Hinkle, James F. Correspondence Files. Letters Received and Sent: Department of the Interior, Indian Affairs, 1923–1924. Governor Papers. New Mexico State Records and Archives.

Hockenhull, Arthur. Navajo Files. Oil Problems: 1933–1934. Governor Papers. New Mexico State Records and Archives.

Hubbell Trading Post Collection. Special Collections. University of Arizona Library.

Johnson, Charlotte. Oral History Collection. Center for Southwest Research. University of New Mexico.

Mechem, Merritt. Indian Affairs. Governor Papers. New Mexico State Records and Archives.

Miles, John. Special Issues. Indian Matters, 1939–1942. Governor Papers. New Mexico State Records and Archives.

Navajo Files. Gallup Public Library. Special Collections. Gallup, New Mexico.

Oil History Collection. Aztec Museum. Aztec, New Mexico.

Oral History Collection. Farmington Museum. Farmington, New Mexico.

Seligman, Arthur. Special Issues. Indian Matters: 1931–1932. Governor Papers. New Mexico State Records and Archives.

Stacher Family Papers. Center for Southwest Research. University of New Mexico.

Territorial Archives of New Mexico. Microfilm. New Mexico State Records and Archives.

Tingley, Clyde. Indian Matters: 1935–1936. Governor Papers. New Mexico State Records and Archives.

Van Valkenberg, Richard. Subgroup 1: Papers from 1880–1946. Arizona State Historical Society Library.

Wagner, Sallie. Navajo Files. New Mexico State Records and Archives.

Western History Collection. Newspaper Clipping Files: Navajo Petroleum. Denver Public Library. Denver, Colorado.

Wilson, Francis C. New Mexico State Records and Archives.

Work, Hubert. Clipping Files. Denver Public Library. Western History Collection.

Works Progress Administration Files. McKinley and San Juan Counties. New Mexico State Records and Archives.

Young, Robert W. Personal Paper Collection. Albuquerque, New Mexico.

Zimmerman, William, Jr. Papers, 1933–1965. Center for Southwest Research, University of New Mexico.

GOVERNMENT DOCUMENTS (NAVAJO)

Armstrong, W. D. "A Report on Mineral Revenues and the Navajo Economy: Navajo Minerals Development, 1966–1985." Window Rock, Ariz.: The Navajo Tribe, Office of Minerals Development, 1976.

Benson, Michael. *The Navajo Nation and Taxation.* Window Rock, Ariz.: DNA, Peoples' Legal Services, 1976.

Everson, David. *Population and Personal Income in Shiprock, New Mexico.* Prepared for the Navajo Tribal Council by Stanford Research Institute, October 1956. Research Project No. 1–1824.

Littell, Norman M., and Charles J. Alexander, comp. *Navajo Tribal Resolutions.* Supplement. 1956.

MacDonald, Peter. Annual Report of the Navajo Nation. Window Rock, Ariz.: Navajo Tribal Council, 1972–1976.

Navajo Nation. Division of Economic Development. "The Navajo Nation Overall Economic Development Program: 1980 Annual Progress Report." Window Rock, Ariz.: Navajo Tribe, October 1980.

Navajo Tribal Council. Navajo Tribal Council Resolutions, 1922–1951. N.d., 1952.

——. "Proceedings of the Delegation of the Navajo Tribal Council in Washington, D.C." May 13–25, 1946.

Schoepfle, G. Mark, et al. *A Study of Navajo Perceptions of the Impact of Environmental Changes Relating to Energy Resource Development*. Final Report. Shiprock, N. Mex.: Navajo Community College, 1979.

Young, Robert W., comp. *The Navajo Yearbook of Planning in Action*. 1954 through 1961. Window Rock: Navajo Agency, 1955.

GOVERNMENT DOCUMENTS (U.S.)

Aberle, David F. "A Plan for Navajo Economic Development." *Toward Economic Development for Native American Communities: Volume 1, Part 1: Development Prospects and Problems*. Compendium of papers submitted to the Subcommittee on Economy in Government of the Joint Economic Committee, U.S. Congress, 91st Cong., 1st Sess., Washington, D.C.: GPO, 1969.

Bliss, James D. *Stratigraphic, Structural, and Tectonic References: Index for the Navajo Indian Reservation, Arizona, New Mexico, and Utah*. U.S. Geological Survey: Open-File Report 82–731, March 1982.

Cohen, Felix. *Handbook of Federal Indian Law*. Washington: GPO, 1942.

Federal Trade Commission. Bureau of Competition. "Report to the Federal Trade Commission on Mineral Leasing on Indian Lands." Staff report by James Dick, October 1975. Not adopted.

National Archives Administration. Washington, D.C.
    Record Group #75
    Record Group #98
    Record Group/Special Collections #200
Navajo Tribal Council Meeting Minutes 1938–1958

U.S. Board of Indian Commissioners. Annual Reports of the Board of Indian Commissioners. Vol. 53–62. Washington, D.C.: GPO, 1922–1931.

U.S. Commission on Civil Rights. *The Navajo Nation, An American Colony*. Washington, D.C.: GPO, 1975.

U.S. Congress. House. Hearing before the Committee on Indian Affairs. "Leasing Unallotted Navajo Lands [H.R. 11687]." 67th Cong. 22d Sess. June 5, 1922. Washington, D.C.: 1922.

——. Hearings on H.R. 3476, Navajo and Hopi Rehabilitation. 81st Cong. 1st Sess. April 18, 19, 22, May 16–18, 1949.

U.S. Congress. Senate. *Congressional Record*. 64th Cong. 1st Sess. Vol. 1–3. February 7, 1916.

——. *Congressional Record*. 67th Cong. 2d Sess. Vol. 62. April 29, 1922.

——. *Congressional Record*. 69th Cong. 2d Sess. Vol. 68. Part 2. January 11, 1927.

——. *Congressional Record*. 97th Cong. 2d Sess. Vol. 128. Part 16. August 17, 1982.

——. *Condition of the Indian Tribes*. Report of the Joint Special Committee Appointed Under Joint Resolution of March 3, 1865. 39th Cong. 2d Sess. No. 156.

——. Hearings before the Select Committee on Indian Affairs on S.R. 1894. 97th Cong. 2d Sess. February 12, 1982, March 16, 1982.

——. Hearings before a Subcommittee of the Committee on Appropriations: Appropriations Bill for 1936. 74th Cong. 1st Sess. April 4–5, 1935.

————. Hearings before a Subcommittee of the Committee on Appropriations: Appropriations Bill for 1940. 76th Cong. 1st Sess. March 28, April 7, 1939.

————. Hearings on S.R. 1407, Navajo and Hopi Rehabilitation. 81st Cong. 1st Sess. April 20, 1949.

————. Hearing before the Committee on Public Lands. S.R. 1315. Unpublished hearing. May 26, 1947.

————. Hearings before a Subcommittee of the Committee on Indian Affairs. *Survey of Conditions of the Indians in the United States.* Senate Resolution 79, 308. 71st Cong. 3d Sess. Part 18. April 27-May 20, 1931.

————. Subcommittee of the Committee on Indian Affairs. *Survey of Conditions of the Indians in the United States.* 71st Cong. 3d Sess. January 30–31, February 3, 5, 1931.

————. Subcommittee of the Committee on Indian Affairs. *Survey of Conditions of the Indians in the United States.* Part 34. 75th Cong. 1st Sess. March 18–25, August 17–30, 1936.

————. Subcommittee of a Committee on Indian Affairs. 75th Cong. 1st Sess. Part 34: Navajo Boundary and Pueblos in New Mexico, 1937. May 14–14, August 17–30, 1936.

————. Subcommittee of the Committee on Interior and Insular Affairs. "To Amend the Act of March 1, 1933." Unpublished Hearings. 73d Cong. 1st Sess. August 11, 1966.

U.S. Department of the Interior. *Annual Report of the Secretary of the Interior.* Washington, D.C.: GPO, 1922–1961.

U.S. Department of the Interior. Bureau of Indian Affairs. *Annual Report of the Commissioner of Indian Affairs.* Washington, D.C.: GPO, 1923–1960.

U.S. Department of the Interior. General Land Office. Circulars and Regulations of the General Land Office. Washington, D.C.: GPO, 1930.

U.S. Department of the Interior. Office of Indian Affairs. "Regulations Relating to the Navajo Tribe of Indians." Washington, D.C.: GPO, January 27, 1923.

GOVERNMENT DOCUMENTS (NEW MEXICO)

New Mexico Commission on Indian Affairs. "Indian News, 1961–1962." Santa Fe: New Mexico Commission on Indian Affairs, 1962.

New Mexico Committee to the United States Commission on Civil Rights. *Energy Development in Northwestern New Mexico: A Civil Rights Perspective.* Washington: GPO, 1982.

GOVERNMENT DOCUMENTS (MCKINLEY COUNTY, NEW MEXICO)

McKinley County and Ramah Indian Reservation Development Committee. *McKinley County Ramah Reservation Redevelopment Areas: Overall Economic Development Plans.* Gallup, N. Mex.: 1963.

EDITED GOVERNMENT DOCUMENTS

Indian Country Environmental Law: Cases and Materials. *South Royalton, Vt. and Grand Forks, N. Dak.: Vermont Law School and University of North Dakota School of Law. May 1999.*

Kelly, Lawrence C., comp. *Navajo Roundup: Selected Correspondence of Kit Carson's Expedition Against the Navajo, 1863–1865.* Boulder, Colo.: Pruett, 1970.

NEWSPAPERS

Albuquerque Herald.
Albuquerque Journal.
Aztec Independent.
Colorado Springs Gazette.
Denver Post.
Deseret News.
Farmington Republican.
Farmington Times Hustler.
Gallup Herald.
Gallup Independent.
High Country News (Colorado).
Navajo Times.
New York Times.
Rocky Mountain News (Colorado).
Salt Lake [City] *Tribune*
San Juan Review (Farmington).
Santa Fe New Mexican.

INTERVIEWS

Arnold, Emery. Interview with author. August 19, August 21, 1996.
Chavez, Tom. Telephone interview with author. May 28, 1996.
Dugan, Tom. Interview with author. August 22, 1996.
Holm, Wayne. Interview with author. May 22, 1995.
J. C. Interview with author. December 30, 1996.
L. M. Interview with author. September 14, 1997.
Midgette, Sally. Interview with author. May 15, 1995.
Noe, Sally. Interview with author. February 7, 1997.
Richardson, Bill. Interview with author. February 7, 1997.
Young, Robert. Interview with author. August 20, 1997.
Yost, Carl. Interview with author. August 22, 1996.
Zaman, Akhtar. Telephone interview with author. May 28, 1996.

NAVAJO LANGUAGE SOURCES

Austin, Martha, and Regina Lynch. *Saad Ahąąh Sinil: Dual Language, A Navajo-English Dictionary.* Rev. ed. Chinle, Ariz.: Rough Rock Press, 1990.
Diné Bizaad Bóhoo'aah II: A Conversational Navajo Text for Secondary Schools, Colleges, and Adults. 1986; Farmington, N. Mex.: Navajo Preparatory School, 1994.
Wall, Leon, and William Morgan. *Navajo-English Dictionary.* Washington: Bureau of Indian Affairs, 1958; New York: Hippocrene Books, 1994.

Wilson, Garth A. *Conversational Navajo Dictionary: English to Navajo.* Blanding, Utah: Conversational Navajo Publications, 1989.

Young, Robert W., and William Morgan. *The Navajo Language: A Grammar and Colloquial Dictionary.* Albuquerque: University of New Mexico Press, 1980.

SELECTED SECONDARY SOURCES

BOOKS

Aberle, David F. *Matrilineal Kinship,* edited by David M. Schneider and Kathleen Gough. Berkeley: University of California Press, 1961.

———. "Navajo Exogamic Rules and Preferred Marriages." In *The Versatility of Kinship,* edited by Linda S. Cordell and Stephen Beckerman, 105–163. New York: Academic Press, 1980.

———. *The Peyote Religion Among the Navaho.* New York: Wenner-Gren Foundation for Anthropological Research, 1966.

Adams, William Y. *Shonto: A Study of the Role of the Trader in a Modern Navajo Community.* Bureau of American Ethnology Bulletin 188. Washington, D.C.: Smithsonian Institution, 1963.

Ahmad, Aijaz. "Imperialism and Progress." In *Theories of Development: Mode of Production or Dependency?,* edited by Ronald H. Chilcote and Dale L. Johnson, 33–73. Vol. 2. Beverly Hills, Calif.: Sage, 1983.

Alexander, Charles C. *Holding the Line: the Eisenhower Era, 1952–1961.* Bloomington: Indiana University Press, 1976.

Allen, Frederick Lewis. *Only Yesterday: An Informal History of the 1920s.* New York: Harper and Row, 1931, 1964.

Ambler, Marjane. *Breaking the Iron Bonds: Indian Control of Energy Development.* Lawrence: University Press of Kansas, 1990.

———. "Uncertainty in CERT." In *Native Americans and Energy Development, Vol. 2,* edited by Joseph G. Jorgensen. Boston: Anthropology Resource Center and Seventh Generation Fund, 1984.

American Petroleum Institute. *The Future of American Oil: The Experts Testify,* compiled by Hastings Wyman, Jr., and edited by Patricia Maloney Markin. Washington, D.C.: API, 1976.

Anderson, Robert O. *Fundamentals of the Petroleum Industry.* Norman: University of Oklahoma Press, 1984.

Baars, Donald L. *Navajo Country: A Geological and Natural History of the Four Corners Region.* Albuquerque: University of New Mexico Press, 1995.

———. "Rattlesnake Pennsylvania BCD (oil)." In *Oil and Gas Fields of the Four Corners Region,* edited by James E. Fassett, 1008–10. Vol. III. N.p.: Four Corners Geological Society, 1983.

Bailey, Garrick, and Roberta Glenn Bailey. *A History of the Navajos: The Reservation Years.* Santa Fe: School of American Research Press, 1986.

Bailey, Lynn R. *The Long Walk: A History of the Navajo Wars 1846–68.* Los Angeles: Westernlore, 1964.

Barsh, Russel Lawrence. "Indian Resources and the National Economy: Business Cycles and Policy Cycles." In *Native Americans and Public Policy*, edited by Fremont J. Lyden and Lyman H. Letgers, 193–221. Pittsburgh: University of Pittsburgh Press, 1992.

Bates, J. Leonard. *The Origins of Teapot Dome, Progressives, Parties and Petroleum, 1909–1921.* Urbana: University of Illinois Press, 1963.

———. *The United States, 1898–1928: Progressivism and a Society in Transition.* New York: McGraw-Hill, 1976.

Begay, Keats. *Navajos and World War II.* Tsaile, Ariz.: Navajo Community College, 1977.

Benally, Clyde, et al. *Dinéji Nakee' Naahane: A Utah Navajo History.* Monticello, Utah: San Juan School District, n.d.

Benavides, Alonso de. *Memorial of 1630*, edited by Cyprian J. Lynch and translated by Peter P. Forrestral. Washington, D.C.: Academy of American Franciscan History, 1954.

Benedek, Emily. *Beyond the Four Corners of the World: A Navajo Woman's Journey.* New York: Alfred A. Knopf, 1995.

Berkhofer, Robert F., Jr. "The Political Context of a New Indian History." In *The American Indian: Essays from Pacific Historical Review*, edited by Norris Hundley, 101–26. Santa Barbara, Calif.: CLIO, 1974.

———. *The White Man's Indian: Images of the American Indian from Columbus to the Present.* New York: Random House, 1979.

Berman, William C. *The Politics of Civil Rights in the Truman Administration.* Columbus: Ohio State University Press, 1970.

Bernstein, Alison R. *American Indians and World War II: Toward a New Era in Indian Affairs.* Norman: University of Oklahoma Press, 1991.

Bierhorst, John. *The Mythology of North America.* New York: William Morrow, 1985.

Blair, John M. *The Control of Oil.* New York: Pantheon, 1976.

Bliss, James D. *Stratigraphic, Structural, and Tectonic References: Index for the Navajo Indian Reservation, Arizona, New Mexico, and Utah.* Washington: U.S. Geological Survey, 1982.

Bodley, John H. *Victims of Progress.* 2d ed. Palo Alto, Calif.: Mayfield, 1982.

Boyce, George A. *When Navajos Had Too Many Sheep: The 1940s.* San Francisco: Indian Historian Press, 1974.

Braeman, John, Robert H. Bremner, and David Brody. *The New Deal: The State and Local Levels.* Columbus: Ohio State University Press, 1975.

Bruchac, Joseph. *Native American Stories.* Golden, Colo.: Fulcrum, 1991.

Brugge, David M. *A History of the Chaco Navajos.* Reports of the Chaco Center 4. Albuquerque: Department of the Interior, National Park Service, 1980.

———. "Henry Chee Dodge: From the Long Walk to Self-Determination." In *Indian Lives: Essays on Nineteenth- and Twentieth-Century Native American Leaders*, edited by L. G. Moses and Raymond Wilson, 91–110. Albuquerque: University of New Mexico Press, 1985, 1993.

———. "Navajo Land Use: A Study in Progressive Diversification. In *Indian and Span-*

ish Adjustments to Arid and Semi-Arid Environments, edited by Clark S. Knowlton, 16–25. Lubbock: Texas Technological College, 1964.

———. *Navajo Pottery and Ethnohistory.* Navajolands Publications Series 2. Window Rock, Ariz.: Navajo Tribal Museum, 1963.

———. *Navajos in the Catholic Church Records of New Mexico, 1694–1875.* Research Reports No. 1. Window Rock, Ariz.: Research Section, Parks and Recreation Department, Navajo Tribe, 1968.

———. *Tsegai: An Archeological Ethnohistory of the Chaco Region.* Washington, D.C.: U.S. Department of the Interior, National Park Service, 1968.

Bryant, Keith L., Jr. "Oklahoma and the New Deal." In *The New Deal: The State and Local Levels,* edited by John Braeman, et al., 166–97. Columbus: Ohio State University Press, 1975.

Burge, Morris. *The Navajos and the Land: The Government, the Tribe, and the Future.* New York: National Association on Indian Affairs and American Indian Defense Association, 1937.

Burke, Robert E., and Richard Lowitt. *The New Era and the New Deal, 1920–1940.* Arlington Heights, Ill.: Harlan Davidson, 1981.

Burns, James MacGregor. *The Workshop of Democracy.* New York: Alfred A. Knopf, 1985.

Burt, Larry W. *Tribalism in Crisis: Federal Indian Policy, 1953–61.* Albuquerque: University of New Mexico Press, 1982.

Calloway, Colin G., ed. *New Directions in American Indian History.* Norman: University of Oklahoma Press, 1988.

Castile, George Pierre. "Indian Sign: Hegemony and Symbolism in Federal Indian Policy." In *State and Reservation: New Perspectives on Federal Indian Policy,* edited by George P. Castile and Robert L. Bee, 165–86. Tucson: University of Arizona Press, 1992.

———. and G. Kushern, eds. *Persistent Peoples: Cultural Enclaves in Perspectives.* Tucson: University of Arizona Press, 1981.

Champagne, Duane. "Organizational Change and Conflict: A Case Study of the Bureau of Indian Affairs." In *Native Americans and Public Policy,* edited by Fremont J. Lyden and Lyman H. Letgers, 33–61. Pittsburgh: University of Pittsburgh Press, 1992.

Chilcote, Ronald H., and Dale L. Johnson. *Theories of Development: Mode of Production or Dependency?* Vol. 2. Beverly Hills, Calif.: Sage, 1983.

Christiansen, Paige W. *The Story of Oil in New Mexico.* Socorro, N. Mex.: Bureau of Mines and Mineral Resources, 1989.

Clifford, James, and George E. Marcus, eds. *Writing Culture: The Poetics and Politics of Ethnography.* Berkeley: University of California Press, 1986.

Cline, Dorothy I. *New Mexico's 1910 Constitution: A 19th Century Product.* Santa Fe: Lightning Tree, 1985.

Collier, John. *On the Gleaming Way: Navajos, Eastern Pueblos, Zunis, Hopis, Apaches and Their Land, and Their Meanings to the World.* Denver: Sage, 1949, 1962.

Coolidge, Dane, and Mary Roberts Coolidge. *The Navajo Indians.* Boston: Houghton Mifflin, 1930.

Crane, Leo. *Indians of the Enchanted Desert: An Account of the Navajo and Hopi Indians and the Keams Canon Agency.* 2d ed. Glorieta, N. Mex.: Rio Grande Press, 1972.

Curry, George. *George Curry, 1861–1947, An Autobiography,* edited by H. B. Hening. Albuquerque: University of New Mexico Press, 1958.

Davis, Ellis Arthur, ed. *The Historical Encyclopedia of New Mexico.* Albuquerque: New Mexico Historical Association, n.d.

Debo, Angie. *A History of the Indians of the United States.* Norman: University of Oklahoma Press, 1970.

——. *And Still the Waters Run.* New York: Gordian Press, 1966.

DeNovo, John A. *American Interests and Policies in the Middle East, 1900–1939.* Minneapolis: University of Minnesota Press, 1963.

Dippie, Brian W. *The Vanishing American: White Attitudes and U.S. Indian Policy.* Lawrence: University Press of Kansas, 1982.

Donnelly, Thomas Claude. *Rocky Mountain Politics.* Albuquerque: University of New Mexico Press, 1940.

Downs, James F. *Animal Husbandry in Navajo Society and Culture.* Berkeley: University of California Press, 1964.

——. *The Navajo.* Prospect Heights, Ill.: Waveland, 1984.

Dutton, Bertha P. *Navahos and Apaches: The Athabascan Peoples.* Englewood Cliffs, N.J.: Prentice-Hall, 1975.

Dyk, Walter, ed. *Son of Old Man Hat: A Navajo Autobiography.* Lincoln: University of Nebraska Press, 1938.

Ellis, Florence Hawley. "An Anthropological Study of the Navajo Indians." In *Navajo Indians I,* edited by David A. Horr. New York: Garland, 1974.

Ellis, Richard N., ed. *New Mexico Past and Present, A Historical Reader.* Albuquerque: University of New Mexico Press, 1971.

Emenhiser, JeDon, ed. *Rocky Mountain Urban Politics.* Logan: Utah State University Press, 1971.

Erickson, Edward W. "The Energy Crisis and the Oil Industry." In *Future of American Oil,* 27–38.

Etulain, Richard W., et al., eds. *The American West in the Twentieth Century.* Norman: University of Oklahoma Press, 1994.

Fall, Albert Bacon. *The Memoirs of Albert B. Fall,* edited by David H. Stratton. Southwestern Studies Series, Vol. 4. El Paso: Texas Western Press, 1960.

Fassett, James E., ed. *Oil and Gas Fields of the Four Corners Area.* Vol. 3. N.p.: Four Corners Geological Society, 1983.

Feinman, Ronald L. *Twilight of Progressivism: The Western Republican Senators and the New Deal.* Baltimore: Johns Hopkins University Press, 1981.

Fergusson, T. J., et al. "Twentieth Century Zuni Political and Economic Development in Relationship to Federal Indian Policy." In *Public Policy Impacts on American In-*

dian *Economic Development,* edited by C. Matthew Snipp. Albuquerque: Institute for Native American Development, 1988.

Fey, Harold E. *Indian Rights and American Justice.* Chicago: Christian Century Foundation, 1955.

Fixico, Donald L. *The Invasion of Indian Country in the Twentieth Century: American Capitalism and Tribal Natural Resources.* Niwot: University of Colorado Press, 1998.

———. *Termination and Relocation: Federal Indian Policy, 1945–1960.* Albuquerque: University of New Mexico Press, 1986.

Forbes, Jack D. *Apache, Navajo and Spaniard.* Norman: University of Oklahoma Press, 1960.

Foreman, Grant, ed. *A Pathfinder in the Southwest, The Itinerary of Lieutenant A. W. Whipple During his Explorations for a Railway Route from Fort Smith to Los Angeles in the Years 1853 and 1854.* Norman: University of Oklahoma Press, 1941.

Francisco, Nia. *Blue Horses for Navajo Women.* Greenfield Center, N.Y.: Greenfield Review Press, 1988.

Frank, Andre Gunder. *Capitalism and Underdevelopment in Latin America: Historical Studies of Chile and Brazil.* New York: Monthly Review Press, 1967.

Frederick, Richard G., comp. *Warren G. Harding, A Bibliography.* Westport, Conn.: Greenwood Press, 1992.

Galbraith, John Kenneth. *The New Industrial State.* 4th ed. Boston: Houghton Mifflin, 1985.

Geisler, Charles C., et al. *Indian SIA: The Social Impact Assessment of Rapid Resource Development on Native Peoples.* Ann Arbor: University of Michigan, Natural Resources Sociology Research Lab, 1982.

Gibson, Arrell Morgan. *Between Two Worlds: The Survival of Twentieth Century Indians.* Oklahoma City: Oklahoma Historical Society, 1986.

Giddens, Paul H. *Early Days of Oil, A Pictorial History of the Beginnings of the Industry in Pennsylvania.* Princeton: Princeton University Press, 1948.

Giebelhaus, August W. *Business and Government in the Oil Industry: A Case Study of Sun Oil, 1876–1945.* Greenwich, Conn.: JAI, 1980.

Gilbreath, Kent. *Red Capitalism: An Analysis of the Navajo Economy.* Norman: University of Oklahoma Press, 1973.

Glasscock, Carl B. *Then Came Oil: The Story of the Last Frontier.* New York: Grosset and Dunlap, 1938.

Goetzmann, William H. *Army Exploration in the American West, 1803–1863.* New Haven, Conn.: Yale University Press, 1959.

Gomez, Arthur R. *Quest for the Golden Circle: The Four Corners and the Metropolitan West, 1945–1970.* Albuquerque: University of New Mexico Press, 1994.

Goodman, James M. *The Navajo Atlas: Environments, Resources, People, and History of the Diné Bikéyah.* Norman: University of Oklahoma Press, 1982.

Goralski, Robert, and Russell W. Freeburg. *Oil and War: How the Deadly Struggle for Fuel in World War II Meant Victory or Defeat.* New York: William Morrow, 1987.

Gordon, Milton M. *Assimilation in American Life: the Role of Race, Religion, and Natural Origins.* New York: Oxford University Press, 1964.

Gregory, Herbert E. *The Navajo Country, A Geographic and Hydrographic Reconnaissance of Parts of Arizona, New Mexico, and Utah.* Paper 380. Washington, D. C.: GPO, 1916.

——. *Geology of the Navajo Country.* Professional Paper 93. Washington, D.C.: Government Printing Office, 1917.

Grinde, Donald A., and Bruce E. Johansen. *Ecocide of Native America: Environmental Destruction of Indian Lands and Peoples.* Santa Fe: Clear Light, 1995.

Grossman, George S. "Indians and the Law." In *New Directions in American Indian History,* edited by Colin G. Calloway, 97–126. Norman: University of Oklahoma Press, 1988.

Hagerman, Herbert J. *Letters of a Young Diplomat.* Santa Fe: Rydal, 1937.

Hall, Edward T. *West of the Thirties: Discoveries Among the Navajo and Hopi.* New York: Doubleday, 1994.

Hall, Linda B. *Oil, Banks, and Politics: The United States and Postrevolutionary Mexico, 1917–1924.* Austin: University of Texas Press, 1995.

Hall, Thomas D. *Social Change in the Southwest, 1350–1880.* Lawrence: University of Kansas Press, 1988.

——. "Patterns of Native American Incorporation into State Societies." In *Public Policy Impacts on American Indian Economic Development,* edited by C. Matthew Snipp. Albuquerque: Institute for Native American Development, 1988.

Hammond, George P., and Agapito Rey, eds. and trans. *The Re-discovery of New Mexico, 1580–1594.* Coronado Cuatro Centennial Publications 3. Albuquerque: University of New Mexico Press, 1966.

Harmon, Robert B. *Government and Politics in New Mexico: An Information Source Survey.* Monticello, Ill.: Vance Bibliographies, 1979.

Hart, E. Richard, ed. *Zuni and the Courts, A Struggle for Sovereign Land Rights.* Lawrence: University Press of Kansas, 1995.

Hawley, Ellis W. "Herbert Hoover as Economic Stabilizer, 1921–1922." In *Herbert Hoover as Secretary of Commerce: Studies in New Era Thought and Practice,* edited by Ellis W. Hawley, 43–79. Iowa City: University of Iowa Press, 1981.

Hayes, Samuel P. *Conservation and the Gospel of Efficiency: The Progressive Conservation Movement, 1890–1920.* Cambridge, Mass.: Harvard University Press, 1959.

Hecht, Robert A. *Oliver La Farge and the American Indian.* Metuchen, N.J.: Scarecrow Press, 1991.

Hechter, Michael. *Internal Colonialism.* Berkeley: University of California Press, 1975.

Henderson, Al. "Tribal Enterprises: Will They Survive?" In *Economic Development in American Indian Reservations,* compiled by Roxanne Dunbar Ortiz, 114–18. Albuquerque: University of New Mexico, Native American Studies Center, 1979.

Hester, James J. *Navajo Migrations and Acculturation in the Southwest.* Santa Fe: Museum of New Mexico, 1962.

Hicks, John D. *Normalcy and Reaction, 1921–1933*. No. 32. Washington, D.C.: American Historical Association, 1960.

——. *Republican Ascendancy, 1921–1922*. New York: Harper, 1960.

Hoffman, Virginia, and Broderick H. Johnson. *Navajo Biographies*. Rough Rock, Ariz.: Diné, Inc., and Board of Education, Rough Rock Demonstration School, 1970.

Holmes, Jack E. *Politics in New Mexico*. Albuquerque: University of New Mexico Press, 1967.

Hughes, J. Donald. *North American Indian Ecology*. 1983. El Paso: Texas Western Press, 1996.

Iverson, Peter. *The Navajo Nation*. Westport, Conn.: Greenwood Press, 1981.

——. "Speaking Their Language: Robert W. Young and the Navajos." In *Between Indian and White Worlds: The Cultural Broker*, edited by Margaret Connell Szasz, 155–72. Norman: University of Oklahoma Press, 1994.

Jacoby, Neil H. *Multinational Oil: A Study in Industrial Dynamics*. New York: Macmillan, 1974.

Johnson, Arthur M. *Petroleum Pipelines and Public Policy, 1906–1959*. Cambridge, Mass.: Harvard University Press, 1967.

Jorgenson, Joseph G., et al. *Native Americans and Energy Development*. Cambridge, Mass.: Anthropology Resource Center, 1978.

——, and Sally Swenson. *Native Americans and Energy Development II*. Boston: Anthropology Resource Center and Seventh Generation Fund, 1984.

Kammer, Jerry. *The Second Long Walk: The Navajo-Hopi Land Dispute*. Albuquerque: University of New Mexico Press, 1980.

Kehoe, Alice B. *North American Indians: A Comprehensive Account*. 2d ed. Upper Saddle River, N.J.: Prentice Hall, 1992.

Keleher, William A. *Memoirs: 1892–1969, A New Mexico Item*. Santa Fe: Rydal, 1969.

Kelley, Klara B. *The Chaco Canyon Ranch: Ethnohistory and Ethnoarchaeology*. Navajo Nation Papers in Anthropology 8. Window Rock, Ariz.: Navajo Nation Cultural Resource Management Program, 1982.

——. "Federal Indian Land Policy and Economic Development in the United States." In *Economic Development in American Indian Reservations*, comp. by Roxanne Dunbar Ortiz, 30–42. Albuquerque: University of New Mexico, Native American Studies Center, 1979.

——. *Navajo Land Use: an Ethnoarchaeological Study*. Orlando, Fla.: Academic Press, 1986.

——. "Navajo Political Economy Before Fort Sumner." In *The Versatility of Kinship*, edited by Linda S. Cordell and Stephen Beckerman, 307–32. New York: Academic Press, 1980.

——. and Harris Francis. *Navajo Sacred Places*. Bloomington: University of Indiana Press, 1994.

——. and Peter M. Whiteley. *Navajoland: Family and Settlement and Land Use*. Tsaile, Ariz.: Navajo Community College Press, 1989.

Kelly, Lawrence C. *The Assault on Assimilation: John Collier and the Origins of Indian Policy Reform*. Albuquerque: University of New Mexico Press, 1983.

———. "Charles Henry Burke, 1921–29." In *The Commissioners of Indian Affairs, 1824–1977*, edited by Robert M. Kvasnicka and Herman J. Viola, 251–61. Lincoln: University of Nebraska Press, 1979.

———. "Charles James Rhoads, 1929–33." In *The Commissioners of Indian Affairs, 1824–1977*, edited by Robert M. Kvasnicka and Herman J. Viola, 262–71. Lincoln: University of Nebraska Press, 1979.

———. *The Navajo Indians and Federal Indian Policy, 1900–1935*. Tucson: University of Arizona Press, 1968.

Kim, Uichol, and John W. Berry, ed. *Indigenous Psychologies: Research and Experience in Cultural Context*. Vol. 17. Cross-Cultural Research and Methodology Series. Newbury Park, Calif.: Sage, 1993.

Kluckhohn, Clyde, and Dorothea Leighton. *The Navajo*. Revised edition. Cambridge, Mass.: Harvard University Press, 1962.

Klyza, Christopher McGrory. *Who Controls Public Lands? Mining, Forestry, and Grazing Policies, 1870–1990*. Chapel Hill: University of North Carolina Press, 1996.

Kneale, Albert H. *Indian Agent*. Caldwell, Idaho: Caxton, 1950.

Knowles, Ruth S. *The Greatest Gamblers: the Epic of American Oil Exploration*. 2d ed. Norman: University of Oklahoma Press, 1984.

Koogler, C. V., and Virginia Koogler Whitney. *Aztec: A Story of Old Aztec from the Anasazi to Statehood*. Fort Worth, Texas: American Reference, 1972.

Kuhn, Paul J., ed. *Oil and Gas in the Four Corners*. Amarillo: National Petroleum Bibliography, 1958.

Kutz, Jack. *Grassroots New Mexico: A History of Citizen Activism*. Albuquerque: Inter-Hemispheric Education Resource Center, 1989.

Kvasnicka, Robert M., and Herman J. Viola. *The Commissioners of Indian Affairs, 1824–1977*. Lincoln: University of Nebraska Press, 1979.

La Botz, Dan. *Edward L. Doheny: Petroleum, Power, and Politics in the United States and Mexico*. New York: Praeger, 1991.

La Duke, Winona. "The Council of Energy Resource Tribes." In *Native Americans and Energy Development, Vol. 2*, edited by Joseph G. Jorgensen. Boston: Anthropology Resource Center and Seventh Generation Fund, 1984.

Lamar, Howard R. *The Far Southwest 1846–1912, A Territorial History*. New Haven, Conn., and London, Engl.: Yale University Press, 1966.

Lamphere, Louise. *To Run After Them: Cultural and Social Basis of Cooperation in a Navajo Community*. Tucson: University of Arizona Press, 1977.

Langley, Lester D. *Mexico and the United States: The Fragile Relationship*. Boston: Twayne, 1991.

Leighton, Alexander H., and Dorothea C. Leighton. *The Navajo Door, An Introduction to Navajo Life*. Cambridge, Mass.: Harvard University Press, 1944.

Leubben, Thomas E. *American Indian Natural Resources: Oil and Gas*. Washington, D.C.: Institute for the Development of Indian Law, 1980.

Leupp, Francis E. "The Indian and His Problem." In *Poverty, U.S.A., the Historical Record*, edited by David J. Rothman. Reprint. New York: Charles Scribner's Sons, 1910; New York: Arno and the *New York Times*, 1971.

Levitan, Sar A., and Barbara Hetrick. *Big Brother's Indian Programs—with Reservations*. New York: McGraw-Hill, 1971.

——, and William B. Johnston. *Indian Giving: Federal Programs for Native Americans*. Baltimore, Md.: Johns Hopkins University Press, 1975.

Littlefield, Alice, and Martha C. Knack, eds. *Native Americans and Wage Labor: Ethnohistorical Perspectives*. Norman: University of Oklahoma Press, 1996.

Lloyd, Christopher. *The Structures of History*. Oxford, Engl.: Blackwell, 1993.

Locke, Raymond Friday. *The Book of the Navajo*. Los Angeles: Holloway House, 1976, 1986.

Lord, Russell. *The Wallaces of Iowa*. Boston: Houghton Mifflin, 1947.

Lowitt, Richard. *Bronson M. Cutting: Progressive Politician*. Albuquerque: University of New Mexico Press, 1992.

Lyden, Fremont J., and Lyman H. Letgers, eds. *Native Americans and Public Policy*. Pittsburgh: University of Pittsburgh Press, 1992.

MacDonald, Eleanor D., and John B. Arrington. *The San Juan Basin: My Kingdom Was a County*. Denver: Green Mountain Press, 1970.

MacDonald, Peter. *The Last Warrior, Peter MacDonald and the Navajo Nation*, edited by Herman J. Viola. New York: Orion Books, 1993.

McAuliff, Dennis, Jr. *The Deaths of Sybil Bolton: An American History*. New York: Times Books, 1994.

McNitt, Frank. *The Indian Traders*. Norman: University of Oklahoma Press, 1962.

——. *Navajo Wars*. Albuquerque: University of New Mexico Press, 1972.

McPherson, Robert S. *The Northern Navajo Frontier, 1860–1900: Expansion Through Adversity*. Albuquerque: University of New Mexico Press, 1988.

Martin, F. David. *Overview of Crude Oil Production—New Mexico and Prospects for Enhanced Recovery*. Socorro: New Mexico Petroleum Recovery Research Center, New Mexico Institute of Mining and Technology, May 1986.

Miller, J. R. *Skyscrapers Hide the Heavens: A History of Indian-White Relations in Canada*. 1991. Reprint. Toronto: University of Toronto Press, 1994.

Miner, H. Craig. *The Corporation and the Indian: Tribal Sovereignty and Industrial Civilization in Indian Territory, 1865–1907*. Columbia: University of Missouri Press, 1976.

Moore, John H. *The Political Economy of North American Indians*. Norman: University of Oklahoma Press, 1993.

Moran, Philip R. *Calvin Coolidge 1872–1933: Chronology, Documents, Bibliographical Aids*. Dobbs Ferry, N.Y.: Oceana Publications, 1970.

Moses, L. G., and Raymond Wilson. *Indian Lives: Essays on Nineteenth- and Twentieth-Century Native American Leaders*. Albuquerque: University of New Mexico Press, 1985, 1993.

Murray, Robert K. *The Harding Era: Warren G. Harding and His Administration*. Minneapolis: University of Minnesota Press, 1969.

——. *The Politics of Normalcy: Government Theory and Practice in the Harding-Coolidge Era.* New York: W. W. Norton, 1973.

Nafziger, Richard. "Transnational Energy Corporations and American Indian Development." In *American Indian Energy Resources and Development,* edited by Roxanne Dunbar Ortiz. No. 2. Albuquerque: Institute for Native American Development, Native American Studies, University of New Mexico, 1980.

Nash, Gerald D. *United States Oil Policy 1890–1964.* Pittsburgh: University of Pittsburgh Press, 1968.

Nash, Lee, ed. *Understanding Herbert Hoover, Ten Perspectives.* Stanford, Calif.: Hoover Institution Press, 1987.

Newcomb, Franc Johnson. *Hosteen Klah: Navajo Medicine Man and Sand Painter.* Norman: University of Oklahoma Press, 1964.

——. *Navaho Neighbors.* Norman: University of Oklahoma Press, 1966.

Noggle, Burl. "Oil and Politics." In *Change and Continuity in Twentieth Century America: The 1920s,* edited by John Braeman, Robert Bremner, and David Brody, 33–65. Columbus: The Ohio State University Press, 1968.

——. *Teapot Dome: Oil and Politics in the 1920s.* Baton Rouge: Louisiana State University Press, 1962.

Nordhauser, Norman E. *The Quest for Stability: Domestic Oil Regulation, 1917–1935.* New York: Garland, 1979.

Noreng, Oystein. *Oil Politics in the 1980s: Patterns of International Cooperation.* New York: McGraw-Hill, 1978.

O'Connor, Richard. *The Oil Barons: Men of Greed and Grandeur.* Boston: Little, Brown, 1971.

Olien, Roger M., and Diana Davids Olien. *Easy Money: Oil Promoters and Investors in the Jazz Age.* Chapel Hill: University of North Carolina Press, 1990.

——. *Wildcatters, Texas Independent Oilmen.* Austin: Texas Monthly Press, 1984.

Olson, Paul A., ed. *The Struggle for the Land, Indigenous Insight and Industrial Empire in the Semiarid World.* Lincoln: University of Nebraska Press, 1990.

Ortiz, Roxanne Dunbar, ed. *American Indian Energy Resources and Development.* No. 2. Albuquerque: Native American Studies, University of New Mexico, 1980.

Painter, David S. *Oil and the American Century: the Political Economy of U.S. Foreign Oil Policy, 1941–1954.* Baltimore, Md.: Johns Hopkins University Press, 1986.

Parman, Donald Lee. *The Navajos and the New Deal.* New Haven, Conn.: Yale University Press, 1976.

Patterson, James T. *America in the Twentieth Century: A History.* New York: Harcourt Brace, 1976, 1994.

Peterson, Charles S. *Take Up Your Mission: Mormon Colonizing Along the Little Colorado River, 1870–1900.* Tucson: University of Arizona Press, 1973.

Philp, Kenneth R. *Indian Self Rule: First-hand Accounts of Indian-White Relations from Roosevelt to Reagan.* Logan: Utah State University Press, 1995.

——. *John Collier's Crusade for Indian Reform, 1920–1954.* Tucson: University of Arizona Press, 1977.

Pickens, William. "The New Deal in New Mexico." In *The New Deal: The State and*

Bibliography ✳ 161

Local Levels, edited by John Braeman, et al., 311–54. Columbus: The Ohio State University, 1975.

Price, Monroe E. *Law and the American Indian: Readings, Notes and Cases.* Indianapolis, Ind.: Bobbs-Merrill, 1973.

Ray, Dixy Lee. "Oil Companies in the Uranium Industry." In *The Future of American Oil: The Experts Testify,* compiled by Hastings Wyman, Jr., and edited by Patricia Maloney Markun, 257–67. Washington, D.C.: API, 1976.

Reichard, Gladys A. *Dezba, A Woman of the Desert.* New York: J. J. Augustin, 1939.

———. *Social Life of the Navajo Indians.* New York: Columbia University Press, 1928.

Reno, Philip. *Navajo Resources and Economic Development.* Albuquerque: University of New Mexico Press, 1981.

———. *Mother Earth, Father Sky, and Economic Development: Navajo Resources and their Use.* Albuquerque: University of New Mexico Press, 1981.

Richardson, Gladwell. *Navajo Trader.* Edited by Philip Reed Rulon, 1986. Reprint. Tucson: University of Arizona Press, 1991.

Rock Point School. *Between Sacred Mountains: Stories and Lessons from the Land.* Chinle, Ariz.: Rock Point Community School, 1982.

Roessel, Ruth. *Women in Navajo Society.* Rough Rock, Navajo Nation, Ariz.: Navajo Resource Center, Rough Rock Demonstration School, 1981.

———, ed. *Navajo Stories of the Long Walk Period.* Tsaile, Navajo Nation, Arizona: Navajo Community College Press, 1973.

———, and Broderick H. Johnson. *Navajo Livestock Reduction: A National Disgrace.* Chinle, Ariz.: Navajo Community College Press, 1974.

Rostow, W. W. *The Stages of Economic Growth.* Cambridge: Cambridge University Press, 1960.

Ruffing, Lorraine Turner. "The Role of Policy in American Indian Mineral Development." In *American Indian Energy Resources and Development,* edited by Roxanne Dunbar Ortiz. No. 2. Albuquerque: Institute for Native American Development, Native American Studies, University of New Mexico, 1980.

Rundell, Walter. *Oil in West Texas and New Mexico: A Pictorial History of the Permian Basin.* College Station, Tex.: Permian Basin Petroleum Museum Library, 1982.

Russell, Francis. *The Shadow of Blooming Grove: Warren G. Harding in His Times.* New York: McGraw-Hill, 1968.

Salmerón, Zaraté. *Relaciones,* translated by Alicia Ronstadt Milich. Albuquerque: Horn & Wallace, 1966.

Sampson, Anthony. *The Seven Sisters: the Great Oil Companies and the World They Made.* New York: Viking, 1975.

Sasaki, Tom. *Fruitland, New Mexico: A Navajo Community in Transition.* Ithaca, N.Y.: Cornell University Press, 1960.

Shepardson, Mary. *Navajo Ways in Government: A Study in Political Process.* Memoir 96. Volume 65, Part 2. Menasha, Wisc.: American Anthropological Association, June 1963.

Shepardson, Mary, and Blodwen Hammond. *The Navajo Mountain Community.* Berkeley: University of California Press, 1970.

Simpson, James H. (Lt.). *Navajo Expedition: Journal of a Military Reconnaissance from Santa Fe, New Mexico, to the Navajo Country Made in 1849*, edited by Frank McNitt. Norman: University of Oklahoma Press, 1964.

Smith, Gene. *The Shattered Dream: Herbert Hoover and the Great Depression*. New York: Morrow, 1970.

Snipp, C. Matthew, ed. *Public Policy Impacts on American Indian Economic Development*. No. 4. Albuquerque, N. Mex.: Native American Studies, Institute for Native American Development, 1988.

Stanley, Sam, ed. *American Indian Economic Development*. The Hague, Neth.: Mouton, 1978.

Stoiber, Susanne A., ed. *Legislative Politics in the Rocky Mountain West: Colorado, New Mexico, Utah, and Wyoming*. Boulder, Colo.: Bureau of Governmental Research and Service, University of Colorado, 1967.

Stratton, David H. *Tempest Over Teapot Dome: The Story of Albert B. Fall*. Norman: University of Oklahoma Press, 1998.

Szasz, Margaret Connell, ed. *Between Indian and White Worlds: The Cultural Broker*. Norman: University of Oklahoma Press, 1994.

Tapahonso, Luci. *Sáanii Dahataal#: The Women Are Singing, Poems and Stories*. Tucson: University of Arizona Press, 1993.

Taylor, Graham D. *The New Deal and American Indian Tribalism: The Administration of the Indian Reorganization Act, 1934–1935*. Lincoln: University of Nebraska Press, 1980.

Taylor, Theodore W. *The Bureau of Indian Affairs*. Boulder, Colo.: Westview, 1984.

Thomas, Clive S., ed. *Politics and Public Policy in the Contemporary American West*. Albuquerque: University of New Mexico Press, 1991.

Thompson, Laura. *Personality and Government: Findings and Recommendations of the Indian Administration for Research*. Foreword by John Collier. Mexico, D.F.: Grafica Panamericana, 1951.

Tinsley, Jim Bob. *The Hash Knife Brand*. Gainesville: University Press of Florida, 1993.

Trafzer, Clifford E. *The Kit Carson Campaign: The Last Great Navajo War*. Norman: University of Oklahoma Press, 1982.

Trosper, Ronald L. "That Other Discipline: Economics and American Indian History." In *New Directions in American Indian History*, edited by Colin G. Calloway, 199–222. Norman: University of Oklahoma Press, 1988.

Twenty-Two Navajo Men and Women. *Stories of Traditional Life and Culture*. Tsaile, Ariz.: Navajo Community College Press, 1977.

Tygiel, Jules. *The Great Los Angeles Swindle: Oil, Stocks, and Scandal During the Roaring Twenties*. New York: Oxford University Press, 1994.

Underhill, Ruth M. *The Navajos*. Norman: University of Oklahoma Press, 1956, 1958.

Van Valkenburgh, Richard F. "A Short History of the Navajo People." In *Navajo Indians III*, edited by David A. Horr, 201–67. New York: Garland, 1974.

Vigil, Maurilio E., Michael Olsen, and Roy Lujan. *New Mexico Government and Politics*. Lanham, Md.: University Press of America, 1990.

Walker, Captain J. G., and Major O. L. Shepherd. *The Navajo Reconnaissance: A*

Military Exploration of the Navajo Country in 1859, edited by Lynn R. Bailey. Los Angeles: Westernlore, 1964.

Wall, Bennett H. *Growth in a Changing Environment: A History of Standard Oil Company (New Jersey, Exxon Corporation)*. New York: McGraw Hill, 1988.

Ward, Elizabeth. *No Dudes, Few Women: Life with a Navajo Range Rider*. Albuquerque: University of New Mexico Press, 1951.

Warshaw, Shirley Anne. *Reexamining the Eisenhower Presidency*. Westport, Conn.: Greenwood Press, 1993.

Watkins, Mel, ed. *Dene Nation: The Colony Within*. Toronto: University of Toronto Press, 1977.

White, Richard. *"It's Your Misfortune and None of My Own": A New History of the American West*. Norman: University of Oklahoma Press, 1991.

——. *The Roots of Dependency: Subsistence, Environment and Social Change Among the Choctaws, Pawnees and Navajos*. Lincoln: University of Nebraska Press, 1983.

Wilbur, Ray L. *The Hoover Policies*. New York: Scribner, 1937.

Wiley, Peter, and Robert Gottlieb. *Empires in the Sun: The Rise of the New American West*. Tucson: University of Arizona Press, 1982.

Wilkins, David E. *Diné Bibeehaz: A Handbook of Navajo Government*. Tsaile, Ariz.: Navajo Community College Press, 1987.

Wilkinson, Charles. *Fire on the Plateau: Conflict and Endurance in the American Southwest*. Washington: Island Press, 1999.

Wilkinson, Richard G. *Poverty and Progress, an Economic Perspective on Economic Development*. New York: Praeger, 1973.

Williams, Aubrey W. *Navajo Political Process*. Washington, D.C.: Smithsonian Institution Press, 1970.

Willink, Roseann Sandoval, and Paul G. Zolbrod. *Weaving a World: Textiles and the Navajo Way of Seeing*. Santa Fe: Museum of New Mexico Press, 1996.

Wilson, John P. *Military Campaigns in the Navaho Country, Northwestern New Mexico, 1800–1846*. Santa Fe: Museum of New Mexico, 1967.

Wilson, Terry P. *The Underground Reservation: Osage Oil*. Lincoln: University of Nebraska Press, 1985.

Winter, Joseph C. *Navajo Country=Diné Bikéyah*. Albuquerque: Office of Contract Archaeology and Maxwell Museum of Anthropology, University of New Mexico, 1993.

Wyman, Leland C. *Blessingway*, translated by Father Berard Haile. Tucson: University of Arizona Press, 1975.

Yazzie, Ethelou, ed. *Navajo History*. Vol. 1. Many Farms, Ariz.: Navajo Community College Press, 1971.

Young, Robert W. *A Political History of the Navajo Tribe*. Tsaile, Ariz.: Navajo Community College Press, 1978.

——. "The Rise of the Navajo Tribe." In *Plural Society in the Southwest*, edited by Edward H. Spicer and Raymond H. Thompson. New York: Interbook, 1972.

——. *The Role of the Navajo in the Southwestern Drama*. Gallup, N. Mex.: Gallup Independent and the author, 1968.

———, and William Morgan, eds. *The Trouble at Round Rock*. Washington, D.C.: U.S. Department of the Interior, Bureau of Indian Affairs, 1952.

Zolbrod, Paul G. *Diné Bahane: The Navajo Creation Story*. Albuquerque: University of New Mexico Press, 1984.

JOURNAL ARTICLES

Anders, Gary. "The Reduction of a Self-Sufficient People to Poverty and Welfare Dependence: an Analysis of the Courses of Cherokee Indian Underdevelopment." *American Journal of Economics and Sociology* 40 (1981): 225–37.

Andrews, Tracy J. "Ecological and Historical Perspectives on Navajo Land Use and Settlement Patterns in Canyons de Chelly and Del Muerto." *Journal of Anthropological Research* 47 (Spring 1991): 39–67.

Arnold, Oren. "The Navajo Wind That Speaks." *American Mercury* (December 1956): 132–36.

Arrington, Leonard J. "The New Deal in the West: A Preliminary Statistical Inquiry." *Pacific Historical Review* 38 (August 1969): 311–16.

Barsh, Russel Lawrence. "Are We Stuck in the Slime of History?" *American Indian Quarterly* 15 (Winter 1991): 59–64.

———. "Progressive-Era Bureaucrats and the Unity of Twentieth-Century Indian Policy." *American Indian Quarterly* 15 (Winter 1991): 1–17.

Bee, Robert, and Ronald Gingrich. "Colonialism, Causes, and Ethnic Identity: Native Americans and the National Political Economy." *Studies in Comparative International Development* 12 (1977): 70–93.

Blanchard, Frances A. "The Deplorable State of Our Indians." *Current History* 18 (July 1923): 630–36.

Blauner, Robert. "Internal Colonialism and Ghetto Revolt." *Social Problems* 16 (1969): 393–408.

Blumfeld, Arthur A. "Oil and Gas, Three-Letter Words for Progress in New Mexico's San Juan Basin." *New Mexico Business* 10 (September 1957): 2–7.

Bonacich, Edna. "A Theory of Ethnic Antagonism: The Split Labor Market." *American Sociological Review* 37 (1972): 547–59.

Boxberger, Daniel L. "Individualism or Tribalism?: The Dialectic of Indian Policy." *American Indian Quarterly* 15 (Winter 1991): 29–31.

Bunker, Stephen G. "Modes of Extraction, Unequal Exchange." *American Journal of Sociology* 89 (1984): 1017–64.

Chirot, Daniel, and Thomas D. Hall. "World System Theory." *Annual Review of Sociology* 8 (1982): 81–106.

Collier, John. "The Indian Bureau's Record." *Nation* 135 (October 5, 1932): 303–5.

Creel, George. "What Do These Senators Want?" *Colliers* 71 (March 10, 1923): 9–10.

Deloria, Vine, Jr. "Federal Policy and the Perennial Question." *American Indian Quarterly* 15 (Winter 1991): 19–28.

Downes, Randolph C. "A Crusade for Indian Reform, 1922–1934." *Mississippi Valley Historical Review* 32 (December 1945): 331–54.

"For Whose Benefit?" *Nation* 122 (March 10, 1926): 248.

Giddens, Paul H. "The Naval Oil Reserve, Teapot Dome, and the Continental Trading Company." *Annals of Wyoming* 53 (Spring 1981): 14–27.

Glad, Paul W. "Progressives and the Business Culture of the 1920s." *Journal of American History* 53 (June 1966): 75–89.

Goulet, Denis. "Development as Liberation: Policy Lessons from Case Studies." *World Development* 7 (June 1979): 555–66.

Gurian, Jay. "The Importance of Dependency in Native American-White Contact." *American Indian Quarterly* 3 (Spring 1977): 16–36.

Hall, Linda B., and Don M. Coerver. "Oil and the Mexican Revolution: The Southwestern Connection." *The Americas* 41 (October 1984): 229–44.

Harding, Warren G. "Less Government in Business and More Business in Government." *World's Work* 41 (November 1920): 25–27.

Henderson, Al. "The Aneth Community: Oil Crisis in Navajoland." *Indian Historian* 12 (Winter 1979): 33–36.

Henderson, Eric. "Navajo Livestock Wealth and the Effects of the Stock Reduction Program of the 1930s." *Journal of Anthropological Research* 45 (Winter 1989): 379–403.

Hill, W. W. "Some Aspects of Navajo Political Structure." *Plateau* 13 (October 1, 1940): 23–28.

Hinson, H. H. "Reservoir Characteristics of Rattlesnake Oil and Gas Field, San Juan County, New Mexico." *Bulletin of the American Association of Petroleum Geologists* 31 (April 1947): 731–71.

"History of Basin Oil-Gas Development in Three Parts: El Paso Hogs Post-1950 Era." *Western Oil Reporter* 28 (August 1971): 36.

Hoy, James F. "The Indian Through the Eyes of The Cattleman." *Indian Historian* 12 (Summer 1979): 41–62.

Hurley, Edward N. "Uncle Sam — General Manager?" *Colliers* 68 (July 2, 1921): 5–6, 29–30.

"Indians Might Do Better with Less Protection." *Saturday Evening Post* 223 (July 29, 1950): 10, 12.

Iverson, Peter. "Building Toward Self-Determination: Plains and Southwestern Indians in the 1940s and 1950s." *Western Historical Quarterly* 16 (April 1985): 163–73.

———. "Legal Counsel and the Navajo Nation Since 1945." *American Indian Quarterly* 3 (Spring 1977): 1–15.

Jacobson, Cardell K. "Internal Colonialism and Native American Indian Labor. . . ." *Social Science Quarterly* 16 (1984): 158–71.

Jorgenson, Joseph G. "A Century of Political Economic Effects on American Indian Society, 1880–1980." *Journal of Ethnic Studies* 6 (1978): 1–82.

Kelly, Lawrence C. "Anthropology and Anthropologists in the Indian New Deal." *Journal of the History of the Behavioral Sciences* 16 (January 1980): 6–24.

———. "The Indian Reorganization Act: The Dream and the Reality." *Pacific Historical Review* 44 (August 1975): 291–312.

———. "John Collier and the Pueblo Lands Board Act." *New Mexico Historical Review* 58 (January 1983): 5–34.

Kornfeld, Joseph A. "A Half Century of Exploitation in the Southwest." *Oil and Gas Journal* 50 (May 31, 1951): 186–214.

Lewis, David Rich. "Native Americans and the Environment: A Survey of Twentieth-Century Issues." *American Indian Quarterly* 19 (Summer 1995): 423–50.

Lyon, William H. "Gladys Reichard at the Frontiers of Navajo Culture." *American Indian Quarterly* 13 (Spring 1989): 137–63.

McGhee, Ed. "Are You Planning to Drill in the Aneth Area?" *Oil and Gas Journal* 55 (June 24, 1957): 150–52.

McPherson, Robert S. "Boundaries, Bonanzas, and Bickering: Consolidation of the Northern Navajo Frontier, 1870–1905." *New Mexico Historical Review* 62 (April 1987):169–90.

———. "Canyons, Cows, and Conflict: A Native American History of Montezuma Canyon, 1874–1933." *Utah Historical Quarterly* 60 (Summer 1992): 238–58.

———. "Naalyehe Ba Hooghan: House of Merchandise, The Navajo Trading Post as an Institution of Cultural Change, 1900–1930." *American Indian Cultural and Research Journal* 16 (January 1992): 23–43.

Miller, Michael. "The Professional Papers of Francis C. Wilson: Santa Fe Attorney and Oil Industry Pioneer, 1876–1952." *Southwest Heritage* 13 (Spring 1983).

Mize, W. W. "Drilling Problems Are Rugged in the San Juan Basin." *Oil and Gas Journal* 54 (March 16, 1955): 176–77.

Noggle, Burl. "The Origins of the Teapot Dome Investigation." *Mississippi Valley Historical Review* 44 (September 1957): 237–66.

Nowels, K. B. "Oil Production in Rattlesnake Field." *Oil and Gas Journal* 27 (June 7, 1928): 106–107, 43–44.

"Paradox Hits Twice." *Oil and Gas Journal* 54 (May 7, 1957): 99–100.

Parman, Donald L. "J. C. Morgan: Navajo Apostle of Assimilation." *Prologue* 12 (Summer 1972): 83–98.

Philp, Kenneth C. "Albert B. Fall and the Protest from the Pueblos, 1921–1923." *Arizona and the West* 12 (Autumn 1970): 237–54.

———. "Herbert Hoover's New Era: A False Dawn for the American Indian." *Rocky Mountain Social Science Journal* 9 (April 1972): 53–60.

"Politics in the West." *Journal of the West* 13 (October 1974). Special topic issue.

Ruffing, Lorraine Turner. "Navajo Mineral Development." *American Indian Journal* 4 (September 1978): 2–16.

———. "The Navajo Nation: A History of Dependence and Underdevelopment." *Review of Radical Political Economics* 11 (Summer 1979): 25–43.

Snipp, C. Matthew. "American Indians and Natural Resource Development: Indigenous Peoples' Land, Now Sought After, Has Produced New Indian-White Problems." *American Journal of Economics and Sociology* 45 (October 1986): 457–74.

———. "The Changing Political and Economic Status of the American Indians: From Captive Nations to Internal Colonies." *American Journal of Economics and Sociology* 45 (April 1986): 145–57.

Stratton, David Hodges. "New Mexico Machiavellian: The Story of Albert B. Fall." *Montana, the Magazine of Western History* 7 (October 1957): 2–14.

———. "Teapot Dome Protagonists: Thomas J. Walsh and Albert B. Fall." *Record* 35 (1974): 58–71.

Szasz, Margaret Garretson. "Indian Reform in a Decade of Prosperity." *Montana, the Magazine of Western History* 20 (January 1970): 16–27.

"Tribe Wants More." *Oil and Gas Journal* 56 (March 10, 1958): 96.

Triplett, Grady. "How Long Will Our Oil Last?" *Oil Weekly* 40 (January 5, 1926): 50, 147.

Van Valkenburg, Richard. "The Government of the Navajos." *Arizona Quarterly* 1 (Winter 1945): 63–73.

"Wilber Outlines Government Policy." *Oil Weekly* 55 (December 26, 1929): 41.

Yinger, J. Milton, and George Eaton Simpson. "The Integration of Americans of Indian Descent." *Annals of the American Academy of Political and Social Science* 436 (1978): 137–51.

Zimmerman, William, Jr. "The Role of the Bureau of Indian Affairs Since 1933." *Annals of the American Academy of Political and Social Science* 311 (May 1957): 31–40.

UNPUBLISHED SECONDARY SOURCES

Cummings, James D. "The Administration and Resignation of Governor Herbert J. Hagerman, 1906–1907." M.A. thesis, New Mexico State University, 1979.

Ellis, Michael G. "The Navajo: A Comparative Systems Study of Economic Conflict." Ph.D. diss., University of California at Riverside, 1975.

Fanale, Rosalie A. "Navajo Land and Land Management: A Century of Change." Ph.D. diss., Catholic University of America, 1982.

Hagerman, Herbert J. "A Statement in Regard to Certain Matters Concerning the Governorship and Political Affairs in New Mexico in 1906–1907." Report. 1909.

Henderson, Al. "The Navajo Nation Energy Policy: A Means to Economic Prosperity for the Navajo Nation." M.A. thesis, University of New Mexico, 1982.

Kessell, John L. "The Navajo Tribal Council in the 1920s." Unpublished court report, presented June 24, 1981, Albuquerque, New Mexico.

Lemley, Doris Jean. "An Analysis of the Growth of Gallup, New Mexico, from 1865 to 1935." M.A. thesis, Adams State College, 1968.

Morton, Brian Jackson. "Coal Leasing in the Fourth World: Hopi and Navajo Coal Leasing, 1954–1977." Ph.D. diss., University of California, Berkeley, 1985.

Praisner, Edward Michael. "A Political Study of James F. Hinkle and his Governorship, 1923–1925." M.A. thesis, University of New Mexico, 1950.

Roberts, Susan Ann. "The New Mexico Supreme Court, 1910–1970: Politics and the Legal Community." Ph.D. diss., University of New Mexico, 1974.

Rollings, Willard. "The Congressional Career of Andrieus Aristieus Jones, 1917–1927." M.A. thesis, New Mexico State University, 1975.

Stratton, David H. "Albert B. Fall and the Teapot Dome Affair." Ph.D. diss., University of Colorado, 1955.

Thompson, Robert G. "The Administration of Governor Arthur T. Hannett, A Study in New Mexico Politics, 1925–1927." M.A. thesis, 1949.

Weiss, Lawrence David. "The Development of Capitalism in Navajo Nation." Ph.D. diss., State University of New York at Binghamton, 1979.
Williams, Aubrey Willis, Jr. "The Function of the Chapter House System in Contemporary Navajo Political Structure." Ph.D. diss., University of Arizona, 1964.
Young, Robert Allan. "Regional Development and Rural Poverty in the Navajo Indian Area." Ph.D. diss., University of Wisconsin, 1976.

MISCELLANEOUS

Minugh, Carol J., Glenn T. Morris, and Rudolph C. Ryser. "Indian Self-Governance: Perspectives on the Political Status of Indian Nations in the United States of America." Papers from a symposium on Indian self-governance, Evergreen State College, Olympia, Washington, October 1988.
Ritts-Benally, Karen. "I Was Born at Oak Spring Canyon: Life Family, and Land Use Histories Along the Transwestern Pipeline Corridor." *Papers from the Third, Fourth, Sixth Navajo Studies Conference.* Window Rock: Navajo Nation Preservation Department, October 1993.

INDEX

Farmington Times Hustler, 15, 66, 87
Field, Neill B., 44–45, 60, 127n.69
First Navajo National Bank, 91, 102
Fort Defiance, 6, 11, 25, 36
Fort Defiance Agency, Arizona, 11, 14–15,
    22, 24, 26, 28, 36–37, 43, 66, 72, 75,
    77. Also Called Southern Navajo
    Agency.
Fort Sumner, 6. See Also Bosque
    Redondo.
Fort Wingate, 11
Foutz, Joseph Lehi, 9
Foutz, Junius, 9, 24, 122n.45
Frazier, Lynn J., 58–59
Fryer, E. Reeseman, 66, 74–75, 77,
    79–81

Gallup (Na'nízhoozhí), New Mexico,
    10–11, 23, 25, 40, 70, 78, 82, 90–91,
    93
General Leasing Act of 1920, 20
Gorman, Howard, 51, 63, 71, 75, 79–80,
    93–94
Graves, Julius K., 6–7
Gregory, Herbert E., 32
Gulf Oil Company 95; "Electronic
    Bird," 82

Hagerman, Herbert J., 24–25, 27–33, 35,
    37, 39–50, 52–57, 70, 72, 81, 100,
    127n.69, 129n.27; Described, 27, 44,
    59, 62–63; As Governor of New
    Mexico, 27, 45, 62, 131n.78; And
    Pueblo Indians, 40, 58, 60; And
    Hearings of 1931, 51, 53, 57–65
Haile, Berard (Father), 14, 26, 77
Harding, Warren G., 17
Harrison, E. M., 20–21, 41, 121n.20
Hatathly, Bill, 95
Hayden, Carl, 19, 40–41, 59, 70
Hayzlett, G. W., 15
Helium, 65, 82, 85; Navajo Helium
    Plant, 82–83, H
Hinkle, James, 56

Hinojos, Blas de, 4
Hogback (Oil Site), ix, 17, 21, 23, 25, 30,
    32, 34–35, 46, 51–54, 60–61, 68–69,
    114, C
Holdridge, Herbert C., 95–96
Hoover, Herbert H., 50–51, 68
Hopi Tribal Council, 97, 101–2, 100
Huff, George Franklin, 15–16
Hunter, John G., 75–76

Ickes, Harold L., 68–69, 72
Inca Oil Company, 31
Indian Mineral Development Act, 107–8
Indian Office. See Bureau of Indian
    Affairs.
Indian Mineral Leasing Act of 1891, 13,
    15, 19–20, 34, 41, 121n.20
Indian Oil Act of 1927, 41, 63
Indian Oil Leasing Act of 1924, 34, 37, 41
Indian Reorganization Act (Wheeler-
    Howard Act), 70, 74–77, 81, 83–84,
    86; And Navajo Constitution, 77.
    See Also New Deal Programs.
Indian Rights Association, 39, 51
Indian Tribal Government Tax Status
    Act, 107
Interstate Oil Compact, 69

Johnson, Lyndon B., 103
Jones, Andrieus A., 41, 56
Jones, Paul, 91–96, 99, 114, D

Keams Canyon Agency (Hopi), 14, 28,
    37
Kearny, Stephen Watts, 5
Kerr-McGee Corporation, 104; Kerr-
    McGee Corporation v Navajo Tribe,
    108
King, William H., 55
Kinney Oil and Gas Company, 21, 23–
    25, 31
Kneale, Albert H., 36
Kooros, Ahmed, 104–5
Krug, Julius, 85

Rattlesnake (Oil Site), 17, 31–32, 44–48, 51–54, 60–61, 65, 68–69, 82, 85, 114, C, G

Rattlesnake, Town of, 48–49. *See Also Rattlesnake Oil Site.*

Reagan, Ronald, 106

Refineries, 46–47, 52–53, 89

Returned Students Organization, 51, 65–66, 71, 76

Rhoads, Charles J., 51–52, 55, 58, 61, 64, 72

Rio Arriba County (New Mexico), 10, 56, 89

Roads 39, 45, 52, 87–88, 90; Arizona Highway Commission, 93; Atomic Energy Commission, 93; Route 666, ix, 45, 55, 93

Roosevelt, Franklin D., 65–66, 68–69, 72, 75

Royalties, 19, 40–44, 52–53, 57, 63, 83–85, 88, 92–93, 97–103, 112–14; Debate Over, 53–55; Resolutions Involving, 36, 65; Allotments, 36, 55, 88–89, 96, 105, 114

St. Michaels Mission, 26, 78

Salmeron, Geronimo de Zarate, 3

San Juan Agency, 14–15, 17, 21–26, 30, 36–37, 52, 77, 86, 110; Agencies Dismantled, 78. *Also Shiprock Agency.*

San Juan Basin Livestock & Grazing Association, 70

San Juan County (New Mexico), 10, 52, 70

San Juan County (Utah), 96, 99, 101, 110

San Juan River, 1, 9–10, 12, 38, 88

Santa Fe Company, 32, 40, 44–45, 47, 53–54, 82. *See Also S.F. Muñoz.*

Santa Fe New Mexican, 39, 57

Scattergood, Joseph H., 52, 58, 61, 64

Seaton, Fred A., 92

Seismographic Testing, 81–82

Shash Bitoo, 5, 10

Shell Oil Company, 13, 95

Shell Pipe Line Company, 95–96

Shelton, William T., 7

Shii Shi Keyah Project, 105

Shiprock (Naa'táanii Nez), New Mexico, 9, 77, 93, B

Sioux, 16, 87

Sniffen, Matthew K., 39

Standard Oil Company, 13, 19, 26, 28–29, 46–47, 81, 95. *See Also Midwest Company; See Also The Ohio Company.*

Stanton, Edwin M., 7

Stacher, S.F., 11, 56–57

Stanolind, 81

Stewart James M., 70, D

Stock Reduction. *See Livestock Reduction.*

Stockton, Ike & Port, 9–10

Stone, Harlan, 20–21, 41

Sumner, Edwin V., 5

Sun Oil Company, 13, 89

Superior Oil Company, 89, 95, 101–2, 108, 112. *See Also Kerr McGee Corporation.*

Table Mesa (Oil Site), 17, 31–32, 51, 60, 68–69, 82, 114, C

Taliman, Henry, 81, 93–94

Tappan, Samuel, 7

Taxation, Navajos, 107–8, 114n.65; Jicarilla Apaches, 105, 108

Teapot Dome Scandal, 17, 28, 50, 61. *See Also Albert B. Fall.*

Termination (*PL 280*), 86, 90–92; And Relocation, 86, 90

Texaco Oil, xi, 13, 89, 99, 111–13; As Texas Oil Company, 89

Tingley, Clyde, 70, 78

Toadlena, New Mexico, 10, 29, B

Tocito (Oil Site), 17, 25–26, 32, 60, C

Traders, Roles of, 11, 26, 49, 78

Treaty of 1868, 5, 7, 13, 119n.45. *Also Naaltsoos Saani.*

Tribal Enterprises. *See Employment.*

True, Clara, 59, 61
Truman, Harry S, 86, 88, 90
Tso, Andrew, 110
Tuba City Agency, 14, 37–38, 43. *Also Western Navajo Agency.*

U.S. Bureau of Mines, 17, 27, 52, 54, 61, 82
U.S. Commission on Civil Rights, 109, 113
U.S. Department of Agriculture, 18, 73; Soil Conservation Service, 73–74
U.S. Department of Energy (DOE), 104–5
U.S. Department of the Interior, xi, 7, 18, 21, 23, 25, 27, 31, 44, 54–56, 65, 69, 72, 75, 82, 92, 94, 104–10, 113–14. *See Also Separate Bureau and Agency Listings.*
U.S. District Court, 94; Salt Lake City, 21, 101, 110
U.S. Environmental Protection Agency (EPA), 106, 112
U.S. Federal Energy Administration, 103–4
U.S. Forest Service, 18
U.S. General Accounting Office, 103
U.S. General Land Office, 20, 121n.20
U.S. Geological Survey, 32, 82, 102–3
U.S. Senate Committee on Indian Affairs, 41, 52, 59; Subcommittees of (1931), 51–52, 58–65, (1936), 71–72
U.S. Senate Committee on Interior and Insular Affairs, 101
U.S. v Standard Oil of New Jersey, 13
Udall, Stewart L., 91, 93–96, 107

Uranium, 12, 89, 96–97, 104, 114; And Environment, 96–97, 102
Utah Indian Affairs Commission, 100–101, 109–10
Utah Navajo Development Council, 110–12, 144n.86; Utah Navajo Industries, 110
Utes, 3–4, 21, 23, 97, 100, 105; Reservation, B

Vizcarra, Jose Antonio, 4
Vlassis, George, 103

Washington, James Macrae, 5
Wauneka, Annie, 93–94, 97–98
Wetherill, John, 12, 96
Wheeler, Burton K., 58, 61, 64
Whipple, Amiel Weeks, 6
White, Richard, 83, 113
Wilbur, Ray Lyman, 58, 67–68, 70, 83, 131n.79
Willeto, Frank Chee, 111
Williams, E.T., Company, 21, 23–25
Window Rock, Arizona, 11, 74, 78–80, 91, 95, 98–102, 112, B
Women (Navajo), xi–xii, 83, 115
Work, Hubert, 21, 28, 30–33, 39, 58, 129n.27
Wyant, L.D. (Report of), 54–55

Yakamas, 25
Young, Robert W., 35, 77, 87, 89

Zah, Peterson, 105–6
Zeh, William H., 65
Zimmerman, William, 87